To Can the Kaiser

To Can the Kaiser
Arkansas and the Great War

Edited by Michael D. Polston and Guy Lancaster

BUTLER
CENTER
BOOKS

www.butlercenter.org

The Butler Center for Arkansas Studies
Central Arkansas Library System
100 Rock Street
Little Rock, Arkansas 72201

BUTLER
CENTER
BOOKS

www.butlercenter.org

First edition: May 2015

ISBN 978-1-935106-80-7
ISBN 978-1-935106-81-4(e-book)

Manager: Rod Lorenzen
Book & cover design: Mike Keckhaver
Copyeditor/proofreader: Ali Welky

Library of Congress Cataloging-in-Publication Data

To Can the Kaiser : Arkansas and the Great War / edited by Michael D. Polston and Guy Lancaster.
     pages cm
  Includes bibliographical references and index.
  ISBN 978-1-935106-80-7 (pbk. : alk. paper) -- ISBN 978-1-935106-81-4 (e-book)
1. World War, 1914-1918--Arkansas. 2. World War, 1914-1918--Social aspects--Arkansas. 3. World War, 1914-1918--Public opinion. 4. War and society--Arkansas--History--20th century. 5. Arkansas--History, Military--20th century. 6. Public opinion--Arkansas. I. Polston, Mike, editor II. Lancaster, Guy, 1976-, editor III. Title: Arkansas and the Great War.

  D570.85.A8T62 2015
  940.3'767--dc23

2015008933

Butler Center Books, the publishing division of the Butler Center for Arkansas Studies, was made possible by the generosity of Dora Johnson Ragsdale and John G. Ragsdale Jr.

Printed in the United States of America

This book is printed on archival-quality paper that meets requirements of the American National Standard for Information Sciences, Permanence of Paper, Printed Library Materials, ANSI Z39.48-1984.

Contents

Introduction

By Guy Lancaster

World War I exerted some profound changes upon Arkansas. The most obvious of these were the establishment of military facilities in the state, an economic boost for agricultural and industrial enterprises, and an influenza pandemic that killed thousands and was accelerated by soldiers returning home. There were some more-subtle changes, too, including a wartime shift in public attitudes that promoted patriotism and enforced conformity in such a way that resulted in violent conflicts with more independent-minded Arkansans. For instance, the open celebration of German culture died out as immigrants and their descendants strove to prove themselves true Americans. Also, the experience of seeing the world revealed to many Arkansas soldiers possibilities they had never before dreamed of. For black Arkansans, in particular, this meant a world in which they could be treated with the same respect they had been shown by French citizens. Back in Arkansas, though, this dream too often died at the end of a noose or the barrel of a gun.

Though the Great War changed Arkansas dramatically, there has not yet been published a single-volume work focusing upon those war years, something perhaps analogous to C. Calvin Smith's book on World War II, *War and Wartime Changes: The Transformation of Arkansas, 1940–1945*, published by the University of Arkansas Press in 1986. So the centennial commemoration of the Great War seems a propitious time to put forward such a volume. Michael D. Polston, co-editor of this book, has long been researching the lives of World War I soldiers, having conducted oral histories with many veterans in Arkansas years back, as well as collecting letters sent home, especially those published in various local newspapers across the state. That expertise is reflected in his chapters of this book. Aside from the experience of the soldiers, this book covers early propaganda efforts to build support for the war, as well as resistance to the new regime of enforced patriotism; the building of military bases and the economic effects upon the state as industries (cotton, mineral extraction, timber) adapted to war production; intolerance on the homefront, with a focus upon the experience of African Americans and those of German descent; the role of women in their support of the war effort; how Arkansas's congressional delegation voted on major war-related legislation; the impact of the worldwide influenza epidemic upon the state; and how the war has been commemorated on the landscape in various monuments and buildings.

Aside from providing a single-volume study of the Great War in Arkansas, this book also exists at the nexus of several important resources here at the Butler Center for Arkansas Studies. In 2013, the Butler Center launched the *Arkansas and the Great War* website (http://

www.butlercenter.org/arkansas-and-the-great-war/), a digital portal to the center's many letters, manuscript collections, and oral histories that pertain to World War I. In addition, the Encyclopedia of Arkansas History & Culture website (http://www.encyclopediaofarkansas.net/) offers entries on many of the noteworthy soldiers of the Great War as well as military installations such as Eberts Field (and also coverage of the more obscure wartime structures, such as Little Rock Aviation Supply Depot), as well as entries on industries and groups affected by wartime changes. Finally, the Butler Center partners with the Pulaski County Historical Society to produce the award-winning journal the *Pulaski County Historical Review*, which published some noteworthy articles on World War I at the start of the centennial commemoration.

No book is the product of a single mind alone, and that holds especially true with an edited volume such as this one. Aside from the contributors, we must also acknowledge the hard work of Rod Lorenzen, the manager of the Butler Center's publishing division, in bringing this book to print. Our colleague Nathania Sawyer helped us navigate the Butler Center's photograph collection, while Ali Welky and Michael Keckhaver exhibited the same professionalism they have brought to bear on other book projects in copyediting and design, respectively. Finally, Bob Razer, the Archie House Fellow at the Butler Center, made a significant monetary donation in support of this book, which we greatly appreciate, and we hope that this volume meets his expectations.

Chapter 1

Arming Arkansas: Putting the State on a War Footing

By Steven Teske

When the Great War began in Europe in the summer of 1914, citizens of Arkansas felt secure that they were unlikely to become involved. A cartoon appeared in the *Arkansas Gazette* on July 31, 1914, showing Uncle Sam sitting calmly with his back turned to the cloud of turmoil rising over Europe. The cartoon's caption read, "Uncle Sam has the chance of his life / to sit tight, keep his hands in his pockets and his mouth shut."[1] The United States had fought a war against Spain less than twenty years earlier, but even that had been fought mainly in the Caribbean Sea and the Pacific Ocean. The foreign policy of the United States generally held to the position that European politics were not the business of the American government and that the politics of the western hemisphere were not the business of any European government.

As a result, the U.S. government was far more interested in the ongoing civil war in Mexico than it was in the new European war. American troops were sent to Veracruz, a port city in Mexico, in 1914 to protect American interests, and American soldiers—including the Arkansas National Guard—guarded the border between Mexico and New Mexico in 1916.[2] Although the Arkansas soldiers did not see action, their presence was meant to deter Mexican warlord Pancho Villa from raiding American property to capture supplies for his troops. Other American forces did enter Mexico in 1916 and early 1917, pursuing Villa and his soldiers, but they failed to capture Villa. By the beginning of 1917, the fighting in Mexico had subsided enough that American troops were not needed to protect the border.[3]

During his 1916 presidential campaign, President Woodrow Wilson sought reelection with the boast that he had kept America out of war. After the election, though, Wilson worked to persuade the United States to enter the Great War. By this time, American lives and property were being lost in the Atlantic Ocean as a result of the war. Great Britain was attempting to blockade Germany, trying to keep war supplies—and even food and clothing—from reaching the German people. Germany responded to the blockade with submarine warfare. German U-boats were effective in their attacks on surface ships, but the U-boat crews could not always distinguish American vessels from British vessels. The U.S. government protested every loss of an American ship, as well as American lives lost on ships of other nations such as Great Britain, but German leaders did not change their wartime activities. In fact, early in 1917, German authorities renounced an earlier treaty they had signed with the U.S. government in which Germany had promised to try to avoid attacking American ships.[4]

This affront alone was considered by some Americans sufficient reason for the United States to declare war upon Germany.

Another factor in Wilson's thinking about the war was the revolution in Russia. Russia had been allied with Great Britain and France in their fight against Germany and Austria, but unrest turned to revolution early in 1917. In March, Tsar Nicholas II abdicated, and Russia became a republic—one which swiftly left the war.[5] As a result, Wilson could portray the Great War as a war to preserve democracy, given that both Great Britain and France were, after all, democracies, while Germany and Austria were led by emperors.[6] Wilson further dreamed that American involvement in the Great War would change the institution of war itself. None of the European governments that entered into war in 1914 had expected fighting to last more than a few months. For nearly a century— since the Napoleonic wars had ended—confrontations between European countries had been limited to battles of only a few weeks. The continued warfare that dragged on month to month and year to year fostered a growing sense that the horrors of war could no longer be tolerated. Even though the governments in Europe seemed unable to stop the Great War, politicians there and around the world were already speaking of it as the Last War, and even as the War to End All Wars.

Propaganda

President Wilson asked the U.S. Congress to declare war upon Germany, which Congress did on April 6, 1917.[7] Immediately, the country had to place itself on a war footing. Soldiers had to be recruited and trained, supplies for the soldiers needed to be gathered, money had to be raised to pay for the war effort, and patriotic support for the war needed to be encouraged. Communication was very limited in 1917; there were no television broadcasts and no Internet. Arkansas did not yet even have a radio station.[8] Newspapers were the primary source of information for most citizens. Meetings and visual advertisements such as posters were also very important both for communicating facts about the war effort and for encouraging patriotic support for American involvement in the war.

Advertising posters were very common in Arkansas cities and towns in the early years of the twentieth century, so the production of posters supporting the war effort surprised no one. Some posters called for volunteers to join the army and fight "the Hun."[9] Others called upon citizens to purchase Liberty Bonds, to support the American Red Cross, and to conserve resources. The Poster Advertising Association assisted the American government by donating designs, producing posters, and even offering free space for the display of posters.[10] Through these posters, Arkansans received frequent and powerful reminders that their country was at war and that their support was needed to win the war.

Matching the persistence of the visual campaign was a speaking campaign of "Four Minute Talks." Speakers made use of every public gathering to speak to audiences about the war. School assemblies and

programs, church services, public concerts, movies, and lodge meetings
were all preceded (or sometimes followed) by a four-minute message
encouraging support for the war effort.[11] The earliest-known four-
minute talks in Arkansas were scheduled in motion-picture theaters and
vaudeville houses beginning on June 11, 1917.[12] By July, the "Arkansas
Branch of Four Minute Men" was being organized. Community leaders
and celebrities were enlisted to conduct these brief talks. Betty Brooks
received front-page attention in Little Rock when, based on her career in
opera and musical comedy in New York and Chicago, she sang her four-
minute message at the Royal Theater.[13]

Of course, the newspapers in the state remained one of the most effective
ways to focus attention of Arkansans on the Great War and their role in it.
Roughly 300 newspapers were being published in Arkansas—some once a
week, some twice a week, and at least two dozen daily. In addition to news
reports about the war in Europe and the war effort at home, newspapers
published editorials encouraging patriotism and participation, and they
printed advertisements—often full-page—with the same message. The
Arkansas Gazette, like other newspapers in the state, reported news of
the war each day, ran cartoons and editorials favoring the war effort, and
warned against any talk or activity that would undermine the work of the
United States to defeat German aggression.

Newspaper writers and editors were not required to create their
own material to support the war effort, as information and rhetoric were
supplied to them in great quantities. The source of this material was
the Arkansas Council of Defense, a civilian group linked to the National
Council of Defense. Congress had created the national council in August
1916, but Arkansas's council met for the first time only a few hours after
the United States declared war on Germany.[14] Initially consisting of
twelve men appointed by Governor Charles Hillman Brough, the council
eventually grew to thirty-two men and one woman. Most of them were
business leaders, although the council also included Dr. John C. Futrall
(president of the University of Arkansas in Fayetteville), former Arkansas
governor Junius Marion Futrell, Judge Jacob Trieber, and J. L. Bond,
who was state superintendent of education.[15] Clio Harper, a newspaper
writer from Little Rock and a member of the council, estimated that the
state's newspapers used only ten percent of the material sent to them
by the council, so copious was its output.[16] The Four Minute Talks were
also coordinated by the council, which met in Little Rock every Monday
afternoon during and after the war. County councils of defense were
created in each of Arkansas's seventy-five counties, and nearly 5,000
community councils served Arkansas's cities, towns, and unincorporated
communities.[17]

Recruitment
The messages distributed by these councils via posters, public talks,
and newspapers were not limited to information about the war and calls for

patriotic support of the war effort. The councils also targeted very specific groups for certain messages. Probably the highest priority was to call young men to register for service in the U.S. armed forces, urging them to volunteer for service prior to being drafted. The federal government then called for all men between the ages of twenty-one and thirty to register on or before June 5, 1917.[18] In 1918, the draft age was extended to forty-five.[19] According to official records, 199,857 men registered in Arkansas in obedience of the law.[20] Over the years, the registration cards have become a valuable resource for historians and genealogists, providing information about a large segment of the population: name, age, address, family status, occupation, and appearance. Of course, the government used this information simply to conscript soldiers. From Arkansas, 51,858 men were inducted[21] (not including volunteers and those already in the service), more than one quarter of the eligible population.

Not every man of eligible age was enrolled at this time. A few broke the law to avoid the draft, but others did not enroll because they were already serving. For example, the Second Arkansas Infantry, fresh from their time at the border with Mexico, included 110 officers and 6,317 enlisted men ready for service.[22] They were re-designated the 142nd Field Artillery of the U.S. Army and began training for their new role at Fort Logan H. Roots in North Little Rock.

When volunteers reported for duty, or when draftees were enrolled, some were declined for military service. Physical examinations were conducted for every potential soldier, and some men were rejected due to physical disabilities, including being underweight. Others were rejected because of illnesses, including venereal diseases. Some men were granted deferments because of family members who depended upon their income in Arkansas. At first, in 1917, all married men were exempt from military service; as the need for fighting men grew, regulations were changed. For instance, men who had been deferred due to illness were reexamined several months later. Others were deferred because their jobs were considered vital to the war effort at home; this group included farmers and some industrial workers. By the summer of 1918, men employed in essential fields were required to be working six days a week.[23] Local councils of defense enforced rules against loafing on Saturdays or working irregular hours.

The Saline County Defense Council was typical of all the local councils that served under the state's Defense Council during the war. The *Benton Courier* regularly carried its announcements, including news about the responsibility of young men to register for the draft. On May 14, 1917, the council sponsored a movie, *Life and Training in the U.S. Navy*, shown at the Imperial Theater in Benton. This prompted three local men to enlist at the Benton post office the next morning. A patriotic meeting was held on the courthouse lawn in Benton on May 24, with several patriotic speakers, including General John Rison Gibbons, a former Confederate colonel. Registration Day was declared a holiday; the post office was closed that day, as were banks, stores, and manufacturing firms. A total of 1,525 men registered at their various townships in Saline County. At an afternoon celebration in Benton, those present were given a red-white-and-blue ribbon during a ceremony that featured music and speeches, as well as the raising of a large flag to the top of a sixty-foot flagpole.[24]

As part of the program to encourage enlistment, or at least registration for the draft, the councils in their various communications characterized men unwilling to enlist or register as "slackers." The label of slacker was generally treated as the equivalent of "traitor." Sometimes, the term was applied to those who objected to the war, or at least those who preferred not to participate in the war effort. Often, it was extended to all who were unemployed, and even to those who found time to relax outside of their jobs. Council minutes record statements against "those wretched creatures of feeble brain and feeble spine, those cowards we call slackers."[25] Frank Pace, complaining in March 1918 that the state's vagrancy statute was weak, called for legislation against people "generally known in the community in which they live as consumers and not as producers," suggesting that such people should "go to work, go to war, or go to jail."[26] Acting under orders from various local councils, communities in Arkansas closed down pool halls, which were described as "a menace to the morals of the young men and productive of habits of idleness."[27]

In some cases, authorities arrested men who had refused to register for the draft. Some of these were "slackers" in the sense that they failed to register largely out of laziness and inertia. Other men were genuinely opposed to the war, or at least firmly opposed to their own participation in it. On June 10, 1918, Sheriff Cox of Saline County, with four deputies and four U.S. marshals, arrested four men from western Saline County who were described as leaders of the draft resistance movement. As a result of this arrest, six more resisters voluntarily registered with the draft board in Benton the following week.[28] The most famous confrontation between draft resisters and the state's authorities happened in the Heber Springs area in July 1918. Eight Russellites (later known as Jehovah's Witnesses), who by their faith were opposed to military service under any national government, were pursued by a force that eventually included more than 200 residents of Cleburne County, accompanied by thirty soldiers from Camp Pike. The confrontation, which began with an armed conflict at the home of Russellite Tom Adkisson, ended a week later with the surrender of the resisters, who had spent most of the week hiding in the countryside.[29] Other armed conflicts took place at Hatton's Gap in Polk County, in Grannis, and in Mena. (See chapters 4 and 5 for more on resistance to the war in Arkansas.)

Locating slackers, and also finding deserters, was foremost in the minds of members of the Arkansas Council of Defense. Community councils were asked to report to the state council any men who had enlisted or been drafted and then had returned home. Any unfamiliar man in uniform was to be stopped and questioned. Surprise raids, with the cooperation of Justice Department officers, required local men to display their cards to prove that they had registered. A community council could win a fifty-dollar prize for capturing a slacker or a deserter.[30] Camp Pike gave the names of deserters to the state council, and the army also provided the council with names of deserters from other camps.[31]

Merely speaking against the war effort, or some aspect of it, could get an Arkansan into hot water. The day after the U.S. Congress declared war on Germany, a Helena resident was jailed for having "uttered sentiments disloyal to the United States."[32] A few days later, a German flag was displayed near Harrison, but it was immediately "riddled with bullets by the natives."[33] Near Magnolia, a man was charged with "attempting to incite negroes to seditious outbreaks and with spreading pro-German propaganda."[34] A man was arrested in March 1918 for making unpatriotic remarks in Newport, largely to the effect that people were supporting the war effort under duress and not out of genuine patriotism.[35] A Hot Springs resident was publicly assaulted for expressing doubts regarding war news that was broadcast on the radio.[36] A Baptist minister in Sheridan was arrested for espionage after preaching that congregation members were devoting too much of their time to the American Red Cross and the Young Men's Christian Association (YMCA).[37]

Arkansans were sometimes treated with suspicion merely because of German ancestry. Subiaco Abbey in Logan County was raided by local government officials, who sought to destroy the abbey's radio to prevent communication with German authorities.[38] Little Rock public schools ceased German language classes in April 1918, as did Stuttgart's schools and the Catholic Board of Education for Johnson County.[39] To avoid trouble, the residents of Germania in Saline County petitioned the U.S. Post Office for a change of name; with government permission, they renamed their community Vimy Ridge to honor a famous battle-scarred city in France.[40] Likewise, the German National Bank in Little Rock officially changed its name to the American National Bank. (See chapter 8 for more on the plight of ethnic Germans in the state.)

Fundraising, Supplying, and Rationing

As has already been suggested, war efforts included far more than enlisting soldiers. The U.S. government needed money to fight the war, and citizens were repeatedly urged to purchase bonds. One large advertisement, sponsored by the Union Trust Company, was printed in the *Arkansas Gazette* on October 16, 1917. Titled "On to Berlin, We're in to Win," it said in part:

If we are to win this war with a minimum loss of life and suffering and in the shortest length of time each and every American man, woman, and child MUST MAKE SACRIFICES. We should not expect the soldier boy at the front to bear the whole burden—You Must Do Your Part. *Our appeal to you in the matter of money.* Money will win the war: it would be lost without it. Stop! Think! See if you could not eliminate something from your daily list of expenditures, not merely luxuries or pleasures, but set aside a portion of your salary or income UNTIL IT HURTS.

The Union Trust Company was, of course, selling government bonds and was making them available to citizens who wanted to make several smaller payments over time because they could not afford the full cost of the bonds.[41]

Along with banks and credit companies, posters and public speakers also urged the purchase of war bonds. There were five money drives in Arkansas, four that were called "Liberty Loans" and a fifth called "Victory Loan." Each of the drives had a quota, set by the U.S. government and based on population. Although Arkansas fell short of its quota in the first Liberty Loan, due to poor organization,[42] overall it exceeded its combined quota for the five money drives—the federal government had asked the citizens of Arkansas for a total of $85,776,301 and received a total of $89,057,800.[43] Additional money drives were conducted by the American Red Cross, the YMCA, the Salvation Army, the Jewish Welfare Board, the National Catholic War Council, the Camp Community Service, and the American Library Association. In all, citizens of Arkansas provided nearly $110 million for the war effort.[44]

In addition to money, specific supplies were required for the troops. Contributions were provided in various ways, often through the American Red Cross or other charitable organizations. For example, in early February 1918, two large crates were shipped via the Red Cross from Benton to St. Louis, Missouri, containing 100 pajama sets, 100 bed shirts, thirty pairs of bed socks, one dozen linen handkerchiefs, five helmets, thirteen pairs of socks, and one muffler, all gifts from Saline County residents.[45] The government of Jefferson County prohibited the sale of wheat flour on April 1, 1918, placing 10,000 barrels of the commodity at the disposal of the government to provide for American soldiers in Europe.[46] In Little Rock, the Hotel and Restaurant Committee of the State Food Administration made all the hotels and restaurants "wheatless" as of April 14, 1918, also to provide for American soldiers.[47] Saline County residents contributed money to supply soldiers with packages provided by the American Tobacco Company; for each contribution of twenty-five cents, the company promised to give a soldier three packages of Bull Durham smoking tobacco, one tin of Tuxedo tobacco, one can of Lucky Strike smoking tobacco, and a corn-cob pipe.[48] In November 1918, Arkansas residents returned one-fourth of their sugar allotment to the government so that every American soldier in Europe might receive a box of candy at Christmas.[49] Governor Charles Brough traveled out of state making hundreds of speeches to support the war effort and to boast of Arkansas's contributions; he claimed that Arkansas led the nation in conservation of food and of fuel.[50] Pledge cards were given to families that agreed to observe meatless days and wheatless days each week for the duration of the war.

Even as men were taken for military training, the need to feed them and to feed the nation as well remained a high priority. Farmers were urged to remain at work on their farms and to treat their agricultural careers as a patriotic duty. A poem printed on the front page of the *Benton Courier* in March 1918 urged farmers,

> Nail the flag to the plow—
> The soldiers must eat
> While defending the trenches
> Or suffer defeat.
> You can help the brave soldier
> At this time of need
> By increasing your acres
> And planting more seed.[51]

Attention was frequently directed toward the need to keep the farms running at full efficiency. At the same time, all citizens were warned not to waste food. Being wasteful with food was equated with being a slacker. One poster proclaimed the slogan, "In her wheatless kitchen she's doing her part to win the war,"[52] and another called upon women to "Can Vegetables, Fruit, and the Kaiser too."[53]

The Means of War

Armies need weapons, and the raw materials for those weapons were available in Arkansas. The hardwoods of the Delta region were ideal for rifle stocks, and in 1914, a total of 25 million feet of walnut was processed in Helena and Bransfield, and then sent across the Mississippi River to Memphis, Tennessee, to be milled into gunstocks.

This interest in lumber was matched by a need for metals. Lead and zinc are mined in northern Arkansas, and the call for these metals brought about a surge in mining. Zinc was used in brass shell casings and as a lining in munition boxes to protect the ammunition from corrosive salt air. Before 1914, Arkansas zinc mines had produced between 474 and 994 short tons of concentrates. Zinc production doubled in 1915, as producers were receiving $100 a ton for the metal. By 1916, that number had grown to 6,815 short tons, refined from 203,600 short tons of crude ore.[54] That same year, lead production peaked, with 813 short tons of galena ore bringing $76,000 into the state economy.[55] Three zinc smelters operated in Arkansas, one in Van Buren and two in Fort Smith. Not only did these smelters provide jobs to Arkansas workers, but they also purchased natural gas from the two cities, with natural gas being another Arkansas product that was mined in various parts of the state.

Bauxite, an aluminum ore, was also needed for the war. Aluminum was needed for shell fuses and for motor parts, and Arkansas is one of the world's best suppliers of aluminum ore. The demand for aluminum created a fifty percent increase in bauxite production, giving jobs to more than 2,000 workers in central Arkansas.[56]

Probably the greatest need supplied by Arkansas was the call for cotton. Uniforms and bandages were made from cotton, and the war threatened shipment of cotton from Asia to Great Britain and France. As the demand for cotton exceeded the supply, farmers and land owners scrambled to increase production, even neglecting food crops. Buyers had paid only 15.1 cents per pound of cotton in 1910; by 1917, the price per pound had increased to 23.5 cents.[57] Even after the war ended, the price did not immediately drop; as late as 1920, buyers were paying 33.9 cents per pound of cotton.[58]

Much wartime production happened openly and was well-documented, but some wartime industry was more clandestine. The federal government built three factories—one in Little Rock, one in Georgia, and one in Michigan—to manufacture picric acid, a chemical used in explosives. By the time the Little Rock plant was operating, labor was already scarce in Arkansas, and the government brought in workers from Oklahoma and Texas. Eventually, Puerto Ricans were hired by the plant. Department of Labor documents indicate that 1,436 Puerto Ricans came to work in Little Rock, with the following description of their condition:

> These island workmen were barefoot, thinly clad, poorly fed, unable to speak or understand English; they reached the scene in the early fall, just ahead of the influenza epidemic. At first they were housed in tents with wooden floors, but later they were barracked at Liberty Hall, a temporary auditorium in Little Rock. The contractors bought them winter outfits, and their organizer testified that they were considerately treated. But they were unable to work effectively, homesickness seized them, and influenza, following, reaped a harvest of death among them. It was two months before a vessel could be had to return them to their native land, and when they embarked, they left 176 of their number in the graveyards of Little Rock.[59]

The plant was closed in December 1918 after the November 11 armistice.[60] (See chapter 11 for more on the influenza epidemic in Arkansas.)

Women and African Americans

In the farms and in the factories, women often stepped in to take the place of men. Although Rosie the Riveter is remembered more from World War II, she had many prototypes in the Great War. Ida Frauenthal of Conway led the Woman's Committee Arkansas Council of Defense for Arkansas from July 1917 until the end of 1918; members of the council aided draft registrations and Liberty Loan drives and knitted sweaters for soldiers.[61] Allie Shoppach of Benton organized knitting groups in Saline

County to knit sweaters, mittens, socks, and other garments for the Navy Comfort Committee.[62] Arkansas farmwomen made their own soap and experimented with cooperative laundries and community canneries. The Pulaski County Women's Council provided entertainment to the soldiers training at Camp Pike.[63] (See chapter 7 for more on the work of women in the war effort.)

The war effort also turned its attention to African American citizens in a way that was unprecedented in Arkansas and other southern states. A few leaders in the state feared that racial tensions could create a new war front in Arkansas, but most welcomed and encouraged African American participation in the war effort. The Colored Auxiliary State Council was appointed in September 1918, consisting of African American men described as "conservative in their views and good representative men with considerable influence among their people."[64]

Long before this council was established, black Arkansans were as active as their white neighbors in buying Liberty Loan bonds, registering for the draft, and cooperating with all the requirements of the war effort. Preachers urged the men in their congregations to register for the draft and even to volunteer for the army. Bishop J. M. Conner, who led the African Methodist Episcopal Church in Arkansas and Oklahoma, encouraged members of the church to go to war for their country, saying, "Side by side with white men we are going to fight for our country, yes, die for it....In this crisis in American history, we should forget our creeds, classes, colors, and conditions and stand out for Americanism—unsullied, untrammeled, and undismayed."[65] Bishop James R. Winchester concurred, promising black participation "as evidence of the patriotism of the colored people of Arkansas, who will unite with our patriotic white citizenship to place their bodies as living walls between their country and those who would destroy it."[66] Black women gathered in Pine Bluff, Little Rock, and Camden to participate in American Red Cross efforts to sew garments and prepare bandages for soldiers.

Military Installations and the Red Cross

Arkansas gave its young men, its money, and many of its resources to the war effort. It also gave land for war preparation. Fort Logan H. Roots in North Little Rock was a gathering place for enlistment of soldiers from Arkansas and neighboring states, but it was too small for training the large number of soldiers being gathered. The Little Rock Chamber of Commerce offered purchase and lease of lands to the federal government for a new military facility that would be known as Camp Pike. A sum of half a million dollars was raised in private donations to obtain the land for Camp Pike, near North Little Rock.[67] Construction began in June 1917 and was completed by November of the same year.

The Eighty-Seventh Division of the U.S. Army trained at Camp Pike, beginning with soldiers from Arkansas, Alabama, Louisiana, and Mississippi; they were later joined by 20,000 soldiers from New Jersey and New York. After the trainees departed in the summer of 1918, Camp Pike was used as a replacement training center until the fall of 1919.[68] The camp, now known as Camp Joseph T. Robinson, has continued to be used for military purposes, especially by the Arkansas National Guard, although a large part of it was returned to the citizens of Arkansas for other purposes, such as North Little Rock's large public park, Burns Park.

The citizens of Pulaski County also offered a site for an aviation school, but their offer was exceeded by that of Lonoke County, which furnished the federal government with a tract of 960 acres. The Lonoke Chamber of Commerce also built a railroad to connect the site with the Rock Island Railroad. The training school, Eberts Field, had an enlistment of about 1,000 cadets, with a total of 1,500 enlisted men and officers located at the school.[69] Their training was not completed before the Great War ended, and the field was abandoned after the war. (See chapter 2 for more information on the state's military installations.)

The American Red Cross had been founded by Clara Barton in Washington DC in 1881. Before the Great War began, the Red Cross had no chapters in Arkansas. A chapter of the Red Cross was founded in Garland County in 1917, followed by a chapter in northeastern Arkansas.[70] J. R. Vinson, a member of the Arkansas Council of Defense, was made state chairman of the Red Cross. The organization conducted two drives for money, raising more than a million dollars,[71] and also gathered people to sew garments and prepare bandages for soldiers. The work of the Red Cross was so highly regarded in Arkansas that in May 1918, a citizen of Saline County was publicly beaten for speaking against its efforts.[72]

The End of the War

At the end of the war, as soldiers were returning home to Arkansas, the Arkansas Council of Defense took the lead in helping these soldiers accommodate again to civilian life. Working through the Adjutant General's office, the council mailed 65,000 cards to former employers of soldiers, asking that they be accepted back into their former jobs upon their discharge from the armed forces. The council sent a further 40,000 cards to businesses, planters, contractors, and manufacturers asking them to hire veterans.[73] About the same number of cards were sent to returning soldiers and to their families, asking if they had employment, as well as asking the name of their last employers and the kind of work they were fit to do. In July 1919, R. B. Keating, the federal director for Arkansas of the United States Employment Service, claimed that "there is not an idle man in the state who really desires work" although he admitted that "a small percentage of those returned from over-sea service are idle of their own volition."[74]

The economic impact of the end of the war was, of course, felt in Arkansas. Lead, zinc, and bauxite were no longer in high demand, and the prices for metal dropped rapidly, leading to a decline in mining. Prices for cotton and for food dropped more gradually, but during the 1920s, farmers struggled to earn enough to pay their bills. The impact was particularly felt by tenant farmers, who did not always benefit from the increase in prices during the war but who were now forced to accept lower reimbursement when the prices dropped.

Efforts to unionize farm workers, which had been seen intermittently in Arkansas since the 1880s, increased in parts of the state, particularly in the cotton fields of eastern Arkansas. Land owners felt threatened by the demands of their workers, especially when the landowners were white and the workers were black. A shooting at one organizational meeting of the Progressive Farmers and Household Union in Hoop Spur near Elaine on September 30, 1919 (when cotton prices were still artificially high), led to a massacre in which dozens, perhaps hundreds, of African Americans were gunned down by vigilantes, some of them associated with the Phillips County sheriff's office. Troops from Camp Pike were needed to quell the disturbance. Hundreds of African Americans were rounded up and accused of rioting and other acts of violence, but no white rioters were arrested.[75]

Higher education was one Arkansas enterprise that benefited from the end of the war. In 1917, when the United States entered the war, enrollment in the state's public and private colleges dropped precipitously. Many schools enacted military programs or offered their campuses to the armed services as sites for training programs. The new college in Jonesboro, one of four agricultural colleges that had opened earlier in the decade, required male students to drill from 11:00 a.m. until noon every day, and female students signed up for courses in Red Cross nursing.[76] Dormitories exercised military discipline, and students invested in uniforms and guns. In 1918, a Student Army Training Corps unit was approved for the campus. Robert E. Lee Wilson, a member of the school's board of directors, donated $2,000 worth of lumber to build additional barracks on campus. The war ended before construction was completed, and the unit was mustered out on December 14.[77] After the armistice, enrollment boomed once again in all the state's colleges.

Long-term economic changes in Arkansas as a result of the war were not as dramatic as those noticed mid-century after World War II. The boom and bust cycle of wartime production and its aftermath was less noticeable than the effects of natural disasters, both flood and drought, in the following decade. Increased racial tension and the relocation of many farm workers—both black and white—to northern cities were noted in the 1920s, but the same situation might have occurred without the Great War. In the end, the impact of World War I was just part of the changing world in which the people of Arkansas found themselves during the first quarter of the twentieth century.

Patriotism in Arkansas did not end with the armistice of November 1918 or with the return of soldiers in the following months. Shortly after the war, monuments began to appear on courthouse lawns and other public places remembering the soldiers, especially those who had lost their lives on the battlefields of France. (The final chapter of this book covers efforts to memorialize the war in the state.) The surviving soldiers also were not forgotten. In February 1919, in Paris, France, a group of American soldiers met and organized a veterans' organization they called the American Legion. The first meeting of the legion in America was held in St. Louis, Missouri, in May 1919.[78] On May 12, Arkansas became the first state to incorporate the American Legion.[79] The first post established was Eberts Post on East Capitol Street in Little Rock. By the beginning of 1922, 150 American Legion posts had been established in Arkansas.[80] Among their reasons to meet were, "to foster and perpetuate a 100 per cent Americanism, to preserve the memories and incidents of our association in the great war...[and] to consecrate and sanctify our comradeship by our devotion to mutual helpfulness."[81]

1. *Arkansas Gazette* political cartoon, July 31, 1914, p. 6.

2. Jack F. Diggs, *The 142d Field Artillery, 1889–1976* (Fayetteville, AR: 1976), 22.

3. Ibid., 24.

4. William Kelleher Storey, *The First World War: A Concise Global History* (Lanham, MD: Rowman & Littlefield, 2009), 109–110.

5. Ibid., 117–19.

6. Ibid., 111.

7. Ibid.

8. Ray Poindexter, *Arkansas Airwaves* (North Little Rock, AR: 1974), 1.

9. Pearl James, *Picture This: World War I Posters and Visual Culture* (Lincoln: University of Nebraska Press, 2009), 61.

10. Ibid., 5.

11. Joseph Carruth, "World War I Propaganda and Its Effects in Arkansas," *Arkansas Historical Quarterly* 56 (Winter 1997): 388.

12. Ibid., 393.

13. Ibid.

14. Austin L. Venable, "The Arkansas Council of Defense in the First World War," *Arkansas Historical Quarterly* 2 (June 1943): 116.

15. Ibid., 117.

16. Ibid., 119.

17. Ibid., 118.

18. Dallas T. Herndon, *Centennial History of Arkansas* (Chicago: S. J. Clarke Publishing Company, 1922), 718.

19. Ibid.

20. Ibid.

21. Ibid.

22. Diggs, 27.

23. David O. Demuth, "An Arkansas County Mobilizes: Saline County, Arkansas, 1917–1918," *Arkansas Historical Quarterly* 36 (Autumn 1977): 230.

24. Ibid., 212–13.

25. Gerald Senn, "Molders of Thought, Directors of Action: The Arkansas Council of Defense, 1917–1918," *Arkansas Historical Quarterly* 36 (Autumn 1977): 284.

26. Ibid.

27. Ibid., 285.

28. Demuth, 228.

29. James F. Willis, "The Cleburne County Draft War," *Arkansas Historical Quarterly* 26 (Spring 1967): 24–39.

30. Senn, 285.

31. Ibid.

32. Carruth, 394.

33. Ibid.

34. Ibid.

35. Ibid.

36. Ibid., 295.

37. Ibid., 396–97.

38. James M. Woods, *Mission and Memory: A History of the Catholic Church in Arkansas* (Little Rock: August House, 1993), 177.

39. Carruth, 392.

40. Demuth, 229.

41. *Arkansas Gazette*, advertisement for the Union Trust Company, October 16, 1979, p. 7.

42. Herndon, 725.

43. Ibid.

44. Ibid., 725–26.

45. Demuth, 223.

46. Carruth, 391.

47. Ibid.

48. Demuth, 223.

49. Ralph W. Widener Jr., "Charles Hillman Brough," *Arkansas Historical Quarterly* 34 (Summer 1975): 114.

50. Ibid.

51. Demuth, 225.

52. James, 293.

53. Ibid.

54. Dwight Pitcaithley, "Zinc and Lead Mining along the Buffalo River," *Arkansas Historical Quarterly* 37 (Winter 1978): 302–3.

55. Ibid.

56. Carl H. Moneyhon, *Arkansas and the New South, 1874–1929* (Fayetteville: University of Arkansas Press, 1977), 100.

57. Ibid., 96.

58. Ibid.

59. Evin Demirel, "Arkansas Mystery: Marker Dedicated to Puerto Rican Immigrants Sparks a Historical Rediscovery," *Sync*, July 10, 2012; online at http://www.syncweekly.com/news/2012/jul/10/arkansas-mystery/ (accessed January 24, 2015).

60. Ibid.

61. Senn, 289.

62. Demuth, 219.

63. Senn, 290.

64. Ibid., 288.

65. Randy Finley, "Black Arkansans and World War I," *Arkansas Historical Quarterly* 49 (Autumn 1990): 259.

66. Ibid.

67. Tracy Nieser, "The History of Camp Pike, Arkansas," *Pulaski County Historical Review* 41 (Fall 1993): 65.

68. Herndon, 723.

69. Ibid.

70. "About the American Red Cross in Arkansas." Online at http://www.redcross.org/arkansas/about (accessed January 24, 2015).

71. Herndon, 725.

72. Demuth, 227–28.

73. Venable, 124.

74. Ibid., 125.

75. Grif Stockley, *Blood in Their Eyes: The Elaine Race Massacres of 1919* (Fayetteville: University of Arkansas Press, 2001), 89.

76. Lee A. Dew, *The ASU Story: A History of Arkansas State University, 1909–1967* (Jonesboro: Arkansas Sate University Press, 1968), 13.

77. Ibid., 14.

78. Hempstead, 726.

79. "A Brief Early History of the Department of Arkansas." Online at http://www.
arlegion.org/about_us.html (accessed January 24, 2015).

80. Hempstead, 726.

81. Ibid.

Chapter 2

World War I Training in Arkansas

By David Sesser

L ate arrivals to the conflict in Europe, citizens of the United States watched the progress of the war with interest after the outbreak of fighting in 1914. The federal government also viewed the events across the Atlantic with interest and began to make preparations for the country's entry into the conflict well before 1917. With the declaration of war on April 6, 1917, the United States officially entered the Great War as an associated partner of the allies.

In order to face the Central Powers on the battlefield, the United States' military needed a massive influx of new recruits. These troops joined the small regular army as well as already established National Guard units. Military facilities to support this increase in armed forces were planned and constructed across the country, including in Arkansas. The state received two major posts, and numerous smaller locations were established to provide military training during the war. These facilities would continue to have an impact on the state well after Armistice Day.

Camp Pike

Only one major military post existed in the state before the outbreak of war. Opened in 1897, Fort Logan H. Roots replaced the United States Arsenal formerly located in Little Rock. This post stood on Big Rock Mountain in North Little Rock, overlooking the Arkansas River. Over the next two decades, the fort expanded and served as a training location for troops moving to the U.S.–Mexico border to protect American interests during the Mexican Revolution. After the declaration of war by Congress in 1917, the Arkansas National Guard mobilized at Fort Roots. The War Department soon determined that Fort Roots and many other existing military installations could not support a large-scale mobilization effort and began to look for suitable replacement sites. By the end of the war, thirty-two new army camps had been established around the country.[1]

Local businessmen in Pulaski County, along with elected officials in both Little Rock and North Little Rock, knew that construction of a new military installation could be a potential economic boon for the area. A total of 13,000 acres of land north of North Little Rock was either purchased or leased by local citizens in an effort to entice the army to build there. Supplemented by funds totaling $500,000 from the state and area cities, the War Department chose the land on June 11, 1917. The U.S. Army pledged $3.5 million to construct the new post, officially named Camp Pike in honor of Brigadier General Zebulon Pike, the namesake of Pikes Peak in Colorado.[2]

Construction on the military post began almost immediately. The first building raised at the camp was completed on June 26. The workforce used to complete the camp fluctuated between 3,000 and 5,000, and the monthly payroll was estimated to be around $2.5 million. Arkansas could not supply enough skilled and unskilled laborers needed for the project, so workers from both Texas and Oklahoma joined men from Puerto Rico at the camp.

James Stewart & Company of St. Louis and New York was awarded the contract for the construction project. Major John Fordyce, a Little Rock businessman holding a reserve commission in the Engineer Corps, supervised the construction, in which union and non-union workers labored side by side. Using a firm hand with any labor disputes that surfaced during the construction, Fordyce quickly placed into the guardhouse any man accused of trying to circumvent the labor rules at the camp. The major claimed that he prevented any disagreements between unionized and non-unionized workers by preventing each side from retaliating against workers who were of the opposite persuasion. Fordyce claimed after the war that he never researched the legality of his decisions but rather determined that the good of the country relied on a smoothly running project.[3]

The first contingent of future troops arrived at the camp on September 5, 1917. By this point, the new post had barracks space for 35,000 troops and 800 officers. Additionally, the post could feed 12,000 men a day and provide thirty gallons of water for 20,000 individual soldiers. The men arriving at the post underwent a number of medical tests and received vaccinations for smallpox, typhoid, and paratyphoid. The soldiers at the camp were not the only beneficiaries of military medical treatment. With the establishment of Camp Pike and other military posts in central Arkansas, the U.S. Public Health Service took control of public health endeavors in both Pulaski and Lonoke counties. Using this power, the Health Service vaccinated more than 300,000 people for smallpox in the two counties and established a medical training facility for officers. These officers trained at both Camp Pike and in nearby towns before being posted across the country and overseas.[4]

The medical care of troops at Camp Pike remained both a priority and a problem for the remainder of the war. A higher-than-average rate of men serving at Camp Pike suffered from diseases such as pneumonia and measles, as well as venereal diseases. In January 1918, the camp had both the highest rate of venereal disease and the second-highest rate of other diseases of any post in the regular army. As more men moved onto the post, the rates of disease only increased. In a one-week period in December 1917, Camp Pike experienced a more than forty-percent increase in the number of cases of illness on the post. Part of this increase came from an outbreak of measles during this period.[5]

As the troops arrived at the post to begin their training, construction continued at a breakneck pace in order to complete the entire facility.

Only parts of the camp were available for military use until the summer of 1918, when construction projects were finally completed and the army moved into all of the newly constructed buildings. The initial large group of draftees to use the completed base arrived on June 1, 1918, numbering 10,000. These men joined the enlisted men posted at Camp Pike. This group was shortly followed by a second group of 17,000 on June 20, and the post quickly became a bustling city.[6]

Immediately placed into quarantine upon arrival at Camp Pike, new troops remained separated from other soldiers for ten days to allow any contagious diseases that the men might bring onto the post to run their natural courses and not infect any men already in service. After this initial period, the men were released from the barracks and issued clothing and equipment.[7] James Atkinson from Little Rock reported receiving "two good pair of shoes, two shirts, (woolen) two pr. trousers, 3 pr. socks, belt, hat, two suits underwear, comb, brush, two woolen blankets, 2 towels, toothbrush, soap, 1 pr. leggins [sic], mess kit, knife fork spoon, cup, bed sack."[8] These newly outfitted soldiers were then ready to embark on a rigorous training regimen.

The structures at Camp Pike were functional but not grandiose. The barracks consisted of long, wooden two-story buildings. The troops slept on the top floor, while a mess hall and squad room occupied the first floor. Approximately 100 men resided in each building; each man had a cot, a straw-filled mattress, and a single blanket. Other structures at the site included railroad tracks to move men and equipment, as well as numerous miles of roads constructed both on and nearby the post.[9]

Even with the massive amount of construction completed at the camp by the summer of 1918, the camp administration struggled to support the large number of men undergoing training. By July 3, more than 1,500 troops lived in tents, and more men arrived at the post every day.[10]

The great influx of enlisted men in the army required a corresponding number of trained officers. Along with four other posts, Camp Pike hosted a training camp for men interested in serving as officers. Open to both enlisted men and civilians alike, the course at Camp Pike consisted of four months of training. New classes began every month to ensure a constant stream of newly qualified officers. Ultimately, all of the officers trained at Camp Pike graduated after the end of the war in November 1918.[11]

Many of the troops at Camp Pike resided in Arkansas before the war, but other states also sent troops to train at the post. White men from Arizona, Iowa, Missouri, Nebraska, New Mexico, and Oklahoma trained at the camp. While the majority of troops training at the camp were white, African Americans also served at Camp Pike. The first, Lambert Hayes from Magee, Mississippi, arrived on September 7, 1917. Eventually, African Americans from Louisiana, Missouri, and Nebraska also trained at the post.[12]

While most of the soldiers' days at Camp Pike focused on training, commanders allowed some recreation time for the men. One popular diversion was both attending and playing in baseball games. On March 27, 1918, the Brooklyn Dodgers and the Boston Red Sox visited the post to play the first in a series of exhibition games. The Dodgers won the first game. They fell to the Red Sox in the second game on March 30 after a ninth-inning homerun by Babe Ruth. The soldiers at the camp also formed their own teams, with 122 men representing seventeen different regiments playing in the spring of 1918.[13]

While morale at the camp remained high during most of the war, some dissent about the United States' role in the war arose among a few troops. In April 1918, a soldier of the 345th Infantry Regiment faced a court-martial for expressing his desire that American transports would be sunk by German U-boats. Quickly convicted of sedition, the former resident of Chicago, Illinois, faced a sentence of ten years at the disciplinary barracks in Leavenworth, Kansas. Troops from the post also participated in a manhunt to find a party of draft dodgers west of Heber Springs. (See chapters 4 and 5 for more on resistance to the war in Arkansas.) After local law enforcement officials exchanged gunfire with the party, killing three, the army dispatched fifty soldiers from Camp Pike armed with machineguns to assist in the search.[14]

Hundreds of thousands of troops trained at the camp from September 1917, including the Eighty-Seventh Division, through the end of the war on November 11, 1918. This division became the only large unit trained at Camp Pike to enter service in Europe. Transferred to Camp Dix, New Jersey, the division arrived in France during the months of August and September 1918. The division never saw combat, although it did serve at the front in November 1918, immediately before the armistice.[15]

Even with the end of hostilities, training continued at Camp Pike, albeit at a much reduced pace. The last class of reserve officers graduated on February 14, 1919. While it no longer trained troops for active combat, the post continued to be useful, as it served as both a discharge center for troops within a 350-mile radius of the camp and as a rehabilitation center for wounded troops.

While most of the troops stationed at the camp prepared to reenter civilian life, some were deployed to eastern Arkansas during racial unrest shortly after the end of the war. During the Elaine Massacre in October 1919, approximately 500 troops moved from the camp to eastern Arkansas to assist local authorities in responding to the events in Phillips County. (Chapter 8 covers the African American postwar experience in greater detail.) Additional troops from the camp traveled to Desha County in 1920 after a prisoner escape. While many of the troops stationed at the post continued to perform regular military duties, others underwent specialized training. Some of the troops at the camp trained as pharmacists at a school of chemistry constructed in 1920.[16]

In the face of a major drawdown in military funding after the end of the war, the War Department moved to close most of the new facilities that had been constructed during the mobilization effort. Camp Pike, along with six other posts across the country, closed as a federal military post. The Third Division, then stationed at Camp Pike, transferred to Camp Lewis in Washington State. The last regular military units stationed at the camp ceased to operate in 1921, but the facility continued to serve the state, first as a citizen military training camp and later as a National Guard training area. Renamed in 1937 in honor of Senator Joseph T. Robinson, Camp Robinson served as a training facility in World War II and continues to operate as part of the Arkansas Army National Guard with a portion of the post retaining the Camp Pike name.[17]

Eberts Training Field

While Camp Pike served as the largest and most well-known military base in Arkansas during the war, other smaller facilities also played important roles in the war effort. Located in Lonoke County, Eberts Field served as a training center for army aviators both during and immediately after the war. The need for trained air crews in the armed forces quickly grew during the expansion of the military after the United States' entrance into the war. Extensive use of aircraft in the skies above the battlefields of Europe proved to both the military leadership and the American public that airplanes were an integral part of the war effort. The U.S. Army had small numbers of aircraft before the outbreak of hostilities but lacked sufficient numbers to operate effectively above the Western Front.

At least twenty-nine fields across the country entered service under the command of the Aviation Section of the Signal Corps. Located mainly in the South, the airfields took advantage of better-than-average year-round flying weather. Most fields were named in memory of army or civilian aviators who lost their lives in plane crashes. Eberts Field's namesake was Melchior Eberts, a Little Rock native. Eberts, a graduate of the U.S. Military Academy, trained as a pilot and received the rank of junior military aviator on March 3, 1917. He was killed during a routine flight on May 15, 1917.[18]

Lonoke County competed with Pulaski County to obtain the airfield. Local businessmen and the county government in Lonoke County worked together to create an attractive offer for the government. With an offer of 960 free acres and a nearby rail spur that connected with the Rock Island Railroad, the army selected the location near Lonoke on November 19, 1917. The army contracted with the county to pay a rental fee of $1 per year for use of the land. Construction on the new facility began on December 19 and continued for several months. The first troops to arrive at the field resided at the local high school gymnasium, as their barracks were still under construction. The officers boarded in town, most notably at the Frank Barton House, which still stands in Lonoke. Eventually, more than fifty buildings were constructed at the site to support both flight operations and to provide housing and other necessary support services to troops. By the end of the war, the War Department had spent almost $2 million on construction at the site.[19]

The airfield consisted of a large area where all takeoffs and landings took place. This area measured approximately one mile in length and almost one-half mile in width. Eberts Field served as a primary flying school, focusing on training in basic flight skills. The eight weeks of instruction soldiers received at primary flight school were followed by advanced training at another airfield. Using the Curtiss JN-4 "Jenny" for instruction, students took regular flights with instructor pilots before soloing. While a total of 1,000 men received instruction at the field during the war, classes were limited to only 300 students per session.[20]

During their service in Arkansas, the pilots at Eberts Field remained aware of the dangerous nature of their training. As the field was located directly across the road from the local cemetery, the flying men saw the burial ground as a constant reminder of the possibility they might not return from their next flight. Unfortunately for the students, accidents occurred with some regularity. One noteworthy accident took place after the end of the war in which a chaplain stationed at Camp Pike and a pilot were killed in July 1919 when their plane collided midair with another Eberts Field plane.[21]

It was not uncommon for civilians in Little Rock and other central Arkansas towns to see several hundred planes overhead, just some of the thousands of planes that saw use at the field. The soldiers training at the field anxiously awaited their chance to test their flying skills over the battlefields of Europe, but this never occurred. The armistice, signed on November 11, 1918, came shortly before the first class graduated. Most of the troops undergoing training at this time completed their rotations at Eberts Field, but none saw active flight service in World War I.[22]

Eberts Field remained an active military post immediately after the cessation of hostilities. An army flight exhibition team visiting Little Rock used the field for a base of operations in November 1919. Named the Flying Carnival, it attracted more than 3,000 people who watched the team fly under the bridges over the Arkansas River in Little Rock. Several thousand more watched the team perform the next day in Lonoke.[23]

The field continued to be used for a variety of purposes after the end of the war. The first newspapers ever delivered in the state by air arrived at the field from Little Rock on June 18, 1919. Flown by Lieutenant C. E. Johnson, these 300 copies of the *Arkansas Gazette* demonstrated the quickly growing communication possibilities utilizing aviation.[24]

With the end of the war, the War Department quickly reduced the number of military facilities across the country. Eberts Field was among those locations closed, and the last military units there departed at the end of 1919. Local citizens purchased and moved the remaining structures at the field, and little remains today of the military post. A few concrete foundations are visible, as well as a low dirt mound once used for target practice.[25]

Little Rock Aviation Supply Depot

Located south of 12th Street in Little Rock near the present-day Bill and Hillary Clinton National Airport, the Little Rock Aviation Supply Depot became a major storage facility during World War I. One of only six aviation supply depots in the country during the war, the post covered approximately fifty-five acres. Consisting of a main warehouse based on the aviation supply depot in Dayton, Ohio, the post also had assorted other buildings to support and house the 500 officers and enlisted men assigned to the depot.[26]

Built in 1918 and designated as a major supply point for the southern United States, the depot ultimately served Arkansas, Texas, Tennessee, Louisiana, and Oklahoma. While the majority of the supplies housed at the depot supported the operations in those states, supplies from the depot were sometimes shipped from Little Rock to other airfields across the country. For example, forty-eight aircraft engines from the Little Rock depot were transferred to Fairfield, Ohio, when that facility ran low on necessary equipment. The depot held more than 13,000 engines at the peak of the war, as it served as the principal engine facility for the entire army.[27]

With the signing of the armistice, the depot became less important to the long-term goals of the army, and eventually it closed, just as Eberts Field had. The depot did operate into the early 1920s, but the closure of fields to the east necessitated the movement of important parts to a new depot in Texas, where western fields could be better supported.[28]

Little Rock Airport

Today, the Bill and Hillary Clinton National Airport is a modern facility that connects Arkansas with the rest of the world. However, it first opened as an army airfield in 1917. Called the Little Rock Intermediate Air Depot, the field served as a stopping point between other military airfields across the country. With the end of the war, the forty-acre field became the responsibility of the Arkansas National Guard.[29]

Student Army Training Corps

While the military bases created across the state had a major impact on both the physical landscape and the economy of Arkansas, another group of army-related buildings had a much longer-lasting impact on the educational system. The Student Army Training Corps (SATC) served as both an avenue for the military to gain educated recruits and as a way for many male students to attend an institution of higher education regardless of their economic background. At least six colleges and universities across the state hosted SATC units during the war.

Part of the Selective Service Act of 1917, the establishment of the SATC served two major purposes during the war. First, the expansion of the military required large numbers of trained officers. Making officers out of men with at least some college education was deemed to be preferable

to promoting enlisted men. Second, many colleges and universities
suffered from greatly reduced enrollments, as male students enlisted in
large numbers. Men who enrolled in the program received thirty dollars a
month from the army, along with uniforms, room and board, and necessary
supplies. The colleges and universities provided college-level course work,
supplemented by technical and vocational training offered by the military.
Offering students a way to start or continue their education during the
war while at the same time ensuring that many colleges and universities
continued to operate, the SATC provided valuable service to the war
effort.[30]

The largest institution of higher education in the state, the University
of Arkansas in Fayetteville, hosted a unit of SATC students for the
duration of the war. President John Futrall and the university registrar
attended a meeting at Fort Sheridan, Illinois, in August 1918, where they
successfully obtained the unit for the university. The university already
hosted a Reserve Officer Training Corps (ROTC) unit, which was replaced
by the SATC unit for the duration of the war. Major George Martin served
as the officer in charge of ROTC on campus and took command of the
SATC unit when it activated, taking the title University of Arkansas
Commandant. Thus, the university became a military post with authority
split between President Futrall and Major Martin.[31]

Female students continued to take classes and lived on campus in
Carnall Hall, while male students not in the SATC were also allowed to
continue to take classes but had to live off campus. The male students
residing off campus received passes signed by Major Martin and were
limited to entering and exiting the campus at the east gate located on
Arkansas Avenue. Approximately fifty civilian male students attended
the university during this period. These students were almost exclusively
freshmen too young to actively serve in the military.[32]

At the scheduled start of classes in September, 500 SATC troops were
on campus. Unprepared for this sudden influx of students, the university
postponed the start of classes to the first day of October and also changed
to a quarter system to allow students to complete coursework in shorter
periods. While waiting for the college-level classes to begin, the SATC
students learned military skills and drilled, while also making several
physical improvements to the campus. The trainees built sidewalks
stretching from Old Main to the southeastern corner of campus as part
of an engineering exercise. The troops lived in five wooden barracks
constructed exclusively for their use and used university maintenance
shops and another wooden building that later served as the band hall for
military classes. Among the classes offered were radio communication and
a section titled "War Aims," which explored the reasons why the United
States entered the conflict.[33]

The 1918 influenza epidemic pushed the already postponed start of
the fall term back even more. (Chapter 11 has more information on the
epidemic.) By October 9, the university had 235 cases of flu on campus,

while the entire town of Fayetteville was placed under quarantine. Before the epidemic subsided on campus, six students had died. The fall term finally opened on October 28, followed by the signing of the armistice on November 11. Many of the SATC students ceased attending classes with the end of the war and pushed for discharges. By December 21, all of the students who desired a discharge had received one, although a handful of SATC students remained on campus through the end of the term to complete their coursework. The entire SATC experience on the University of Arkansas campus lasted only four months.[34]

The First District Agricultural School (now Arkansas State University) in Jonesboro also hosted an SATC unit in 1918. Desiring a unit on campus to keep the school open during the war, the board of trustees dispatched two of its members to Washington DC to request a detachment. When informed by the War Department that only schools offering collegiate coursework were allowed to support SATC units, the administration agreed to move from a high-school-only curriculum to one that also offered junior college courses. The high school classes continued to be taught, but the majority of courses offered after 1917 were of the collegiate level. The school reorganized to offer two-year coursework in agriculture, home economics, and teaching.[35]

Troops arrived on campus to begin classes in September, but the barracks to house them were not yet completed. The SATC students lived in the campus gymnasium while waiting on the housing to be constructed. Trustee Robert E. Lee Wilson donated lumber for the construction of the new buildings, but the war ended before construction could begin. Immediately after the armistice, the school received word that the program would continue, but that decision was rescinded several days later. The last troops received their discharges on December 14, and the detachment closed. While short lived, the SATC unit in Jonesboro had a long-lasting impact on the institution, eventually leading to the establishment of a four-year undergraduate curriculum.[36]

Other, much smaller schools also hosted units. Arkansas College (now Lyon College) in Batesville received a unit of fifty men. The SATC program required institutions to have 100 or more male students, while Arkansas College had only around twenty-five men attending classes at the time. Through the personal lobbying of President William Lacy and a local insurance agent, the War Department gave the small college a unit in August 1918. Like most of the colleges in the state, Arkansas College had existed in a precarious financial position for most of its history. President Lacy knew that the existence of an SATC unit on campus could provide a financial windfall for the college. For every student enrolled in the unit, the War Department paid the college $100 per month. The War Department also gave the college an instructor, Captain W. L. Barry. As at other colleges in the state with SATC units, most of the instruction given to the cadets was delivered by regular faculty.[37]

Construction of a new wooden barracks building began almost

immediately, replacing a dormitory that burned in December 1917. The local Chamber of Commerce raised most of the money needed for the building.[38]

The SATC unit at Arkansas College disbanded on December 20, 1918, after the armistice. Of the fifty men serving in the unit, only a few returned to the college for the spring semester. Eventually, four of the men from the unit received degrees from Arkansas College.[39]

Hendrix College in Conway hosted another SATC unit during the war. Awarded to the college for the 1918–19 academic year, the SATC unit followed a volunteer organization that drilled on campus the previous year. The Hendrix administration moved quickly to prepare for the influx of students and, over the summer, constructed a total of six wooden structures, including three barracks, a hospital, and a bathhouse. After ending the previous year with an enrollment of 225, Hendrix opened the fall semester on October 3 with more than 400 students, including more than 200 SATC members. Almost immediately, the campus closed in the face of the growing influenza epidemic, and classes did not resume for almost three weeks. Two SATC members died from the illness before classes met again on October 29.[40]

Wartime changes to the Hendrix curriculum moved away from the traditional liberal arts areas and included the addition of classes in science, modern languages, and business, as well as domestic science. The SATC troops drilled regularly and guarded the campus as they prepared to move overseas. With the end of the war, the unit quickly disbanded, and life returned to normal on campus. The buildings constructed to support the SATC unit remained in use on the campus, and the names of the two men who died in the influenza epidemic were included on a memorial constructed on campus to honor Hendrix men who lost their lives in the war.[41]

The small town of Arkadelphia hosted one SATC unit split between two colleges during the war. Henderson-Brown College (now Henderson State University) and its cross-ravine rival, Ouachita Baptist College (now Ouachita Baptist University), supported a combined company which trained together. Henderson-Brown previously supported a volunteer unit for students interested in military drill. In 1916, an ROTC unit began operations on campus with an enrollment of fifty men. Commanded by Captain F. R. Sessions, the students enrolled in the course each received both a khaki uniform and a monthly salary of nine dollars in exchange for regular drill. In response to the Selective Service Act, the ROTC unit was soon replaced by an SATC company.

Enrolling men into two sections, one at each college, the SATC unit began service during the fall 1918 semester. New students entered one of two tracks. The two sections employed in Arkadelphia were split into collegiate and vocational tracks. Students interested in pursuing an undergraduate degree entered the collegiate track, while other students— some as young as nine years old—followed the vocational track.[42]

The sudden influx of young men serving in the unit necessitated the construction of new wooden barracks on each campus. Ouachita built two new buildings, while Henderson-Brown constructed one. Around 250 men served in the SATC units at both colleges, with about 100 at Henderson-Brown and the remainder at Ouachita. Commanded by Captain A. A. Roe and three lieutenants, the units trained Tuesday through Saturday with a mixture of military and classroom work. The members of the unit operated under military discipline, and passes were required of any member who wished to leave either campus.[43]

The entire unit officially joined the U.S. Army on October 1, 1918. In a ceremony attended by most of the population of Arkadelphia and the surrounding area, the entire unit marched through the town before arriving at Ouachita's football field. Accompanied by the entire student bodies of both colleges and Arkadelphia High School on their march, the assembled men took their places on the field in front of the crowd. There, they recited their oath of allegiance to the army, followed by speeches from the presidents of both colleges.[44]

The sudden conclusion of the war brought an end to the SATC unit in Arkadelphia, as it did at campuses across the state. The company stationed at Henderson continued to operate as the men awaited orders, eventually learning that they would receive their discharges on December 13. The night before the cadets departed, campus was filled with hijinks. The young men who had felt stifled under military discipline for the past several months played pranks on the regular students on campus. Leaving the next morning with both their new winter uniforms and an extra month's pay in their pockets, the cadets were well remembered by some of their fellow students and most of the local community.[45]

After the closure of the SATC program, both Henderson-Brown and Ouachita worked to gain postwar ROTC programs. Ouachita succeeded immediately after the war, while military training returned to Henderson in 1936, several years after the institution moved to state control. The two barracks built on the Ouachita campus were moved to the Henderson-Brown campus in 1920 and connected to the existing single barracks building. After the exterior was bricked, the new dormitory opened as the first on-campus housing for male students.[46]

The troops that were trained in the SATC units across the state never saw combat in World War I, but the exposure to higher education had a long-lasting impact on many cadets. While few actually completed degrees at the schools where they were stationed, most of the men in the program would have never had the chance to attend classes on a college campus if not for the military service.

One notable SATC student who did graduate eventually became White House chief of staff for President Harry Truman. The son of lower-middle-class cotton farmers in Calhoun County, John Steelman attended college at Henderson-Brown, obtaining admission through the SATC program and rising to the rank of corporal. Graduating in 1922 from Henderson-

Brown, Steelman earned graduate degrees at Vanderbilt University and
the University of North Carolina before taking the post of assistant to the
president in 1946.[47]

Conclusion
While the United States participated in World War I for just eighteen
months, the impact of the conflict on Arkansas continues to be felt today.
The establishment of the largest airport in the state, the construction of
a major military base, and an expansion of higher-education institutions
across Arkansas are just some of the changes that the war brought to the
state. Although its history is often overshadowed by that of World War II,
this conflict had a deep impact on the citizens and physical landscape of
Arkansas.

1. Rachel Silva, "Fort Logan H. Roots Military Post Historic District," *Pulaski County
Historical Quarterly* 58 (Spring 2010): 30, 34; Tracy Nieser, "The History of Camp Pike,
Arkansas," *Pulaski County Historical Quarterly* 41 (Fall 1993): 64.

2. Nieser, 64–65.

3. Ibid.

4. Ibid., 67–68.

5. "Health Conditions at Camps Still Bad," *New York Times*, December 20, 1917, p. 3.

6. Nieser, 68–69.

7. Michael Polston, "'Time Does Not Count Here:' Letters of an American Doughboy
Stationed at Camp Pike," *Pulaski County Historical Quarterly* 33 (Winter 1985): 77.

8. Ibid.

9. Ibid.; Nieser, 65–66.

10. Nieser, 68, 69–70.

11. "Open Five Training Camps," *New York Times*, July 6, 1918, p. 15.

12. "130,201 More Men Called in Draft," *New York Times*, August 9, 1918, p. 6;
"New Draft Drawing Set for Tomorrow," *New York Times*, June 26, 1918, p. 5; "Crowder
Summons 181,838 More Men," *New York Times*, September 17, 1918, p. 5; Nieser, 68,
69–70.

13. "122 Nines Formed at Camp Pike," *New York Times*, March 17, p. 30; "Dodgers
Show New Life," *New York Times*, March 28, 1918, p. 12; "Ruth Robs Dodgers Again," *New
York Times*, March 31, 1918, p. 21.

14. "Seditious Soldier Gets Ten Years," *New York Times*, April 11, 1918, p. 24; "3
Killed in Battles with Draft Evaders," *New York Times*, July 8, 1918, p. 8; James F. Willis,
"The Cleburne County Draft War," *Arkansas Historical Quarterly* 26 (Spring 1967): 24–39.

15. *Brief Histories of Division of the U.S. Army, 1917–1918*, Historical Branch, War
Plans Division, General Staff, June 1921.

16. "Six More are Killed in Arkansas Riots," *New York Times*, October 3, 1919, p. 6;
"Avert Arkansas Race Riot," *New York Times*, January 23, 1920, p. 5; "Nearly 3,000 Men
Join Army Weekly," *New York Times*, April 18, 1920, p. E6; Nieser, 70; Grif Stockley, *Blood
in Their Eyes: The Elaine Race Massacres of 1919* (Fayetteville: University of Arkansas
Press, 2001).

17. "Army to Abandon Seven Big Camps," *New York Times*, July 27, 1921, p. 6; Nieser,
70–71.

18. Some confusion exists about the details of Eberts's service. He is variously listed
as both a lieutenant and a captain, and his place of death appears both as Columbus, New
Mexico, and Columbus, Ohio. "Army Aviator is Killed," *New York Times*, May 16, 1917,
p. 8; "Army-Navy Notes," *New York Times*, June 2, 1918, p. 54; "Location of U.S. Aviation
Fields," *New York Times*, July 21, 1918, p. 42; "Eberts Field," *New York Times*, August 11,

1918, p. 32.

19. Johnnie Singleton Bransford, "Lonoke's Vanished Airport," *Newsletter of the Lonoke County Historical Society* 2 (Winter 1983): 1; Johnnie Carolyn Bransford, "Eberts Training Field," *Encyclopedia of Arkansas History & Culture*, http://www.encyclopediaofarkansas.net/encyclopedia/entry-detail.aspx?entryID=1184 (accessed February 23, 2015).

20. Arthur Sweetser, *The American Air Service: A Record of Its Problems, Its Difficulties, Its Failures, and Its Final Achievements* (New York: D. Appleton, 1919), 348; Bransford, "Lonoke's Vanished Airport," 1.

21. Bransford, "Eberts Training Field"; "Air Collision Kills Two," *New York Times*, July 13, 1919, p. 2.

22. Bransford, "Lonoke's Vanished Airport," 1, 2.

23. Bransford, "Eberts Training Field."

24. Bransford, "Lonoke's Vanished Airport," 2.

25. Ibid., 1.

26. William McAlexander, "Little Rock Aviation Supply Depot," *Encyclopedia of Arkansas History & Culture*, http://www.encyclopediaofarkansas.net/encyclopedia/entry-detail.aspx?entryID=4234 (accessed February 23, 2015).

27. Ibid.

28. Ibid.

29. C. Fred Williams, *Historic Little Rock: An Illustrated History* (San Antonio, TX: Historical Publishing Network, 2008), 114.

30. James Lester, *Hendrix College: A Centennial History* (Conway, AR: Hendrix College Centennial Committee, 1984), 92.

31. Robert LeFlar, *The First 100 Years: Centennial History of the University of Arkansas* (Fayetteville: University of Arkansas Foundation, 1972), 291.

32. Ibid., 131, 291.

33. Harrison Hale, *University of Arkansas, 1871–1948* (Fayetteville: University of Arkansas Alumni Association, 1948), 214; LeFlar, 291–92.

34. Ibid.

35. Lee Dew, *The A.S.U. Story: A History of Arkansas State University, 1909–1967* (Jonesboro: Arkansas State University Press, 1968), 13.

36. Ibid., 13–14.

37. Brooks Blevins, *Lyon College: 1871–2002* (Fayetteville: University of Arkansas Press, 2003), 82–83.

38. Ibid.

39. Ibid.,84.

40. Lester, 92.

41. Ibid., 92–93.

42. Bennie Gene Bledsoe, *Henderson State University: Education since 1890* (Houston, TX: D. Armstrong, 1986), 266–67; John Gladden Hall, *Henderson State College: The Methodist Years* (Arkadelphia, AR: Henderson State College Alumni Association, 1974), 139.

43. Bledsoe, *Henderson State University*, 267; Hall, *Henderson State College*, 141.

44. Bledsoe, *Henderson State University*, 267.

45. Ibid. 268–69.

46. Trennis Henderson, ed. *Ouachita Voices: Celebrating 125 Years of Academic and Christian Excellence* (Atlanta: Bookhouse, 2011), 8; Michael Arrington, *Ouachita Baptist University: The First 100 Years* (Little Rock: August House, 1985), 68; Bledsoe, 269; Hall, 141–42.

47. Steelman's position was officially called "Special Presidential Advisor," which after several name changes is now known as Chief of Staff. See Hall, 139–140; William Wagnon, "John Roy Steelman: Native Son to Presidential Advisor," *Arkansas Historical Quarterly* 27 (Autumn 1968): 206, 220.

Chapter 3

The Arkansas Soldier in the Great War

By Michael D. Polston

"All the Arkansas boys are rated as good soldiers."
—William Jackson, Independence County

hen the tragic events of 1914 quickly progressed into world war, the United States attempted to avoid involvement by declaring official neutrality. However, on April 6, 1917, after three years of anticipation, the Great War was brought to the front door of the United States—and Arkansas. By the time the war ended in November 1918, approximately 72,000 sons of what was then known as the Wonder State had, in some way, been involved in the daily life-and-death struggle in the "War to End all Wars." Of those thousands serving in the U.S. military, almost 300 were killed in action, with over 100 more dying of battle wounds. Wartime Arkansas soldier deaths—attributed to all causes—totaled almost 2,200.[1]

When war was declared in April 1917, the nation was ill prepared to enter a modern war that had been raging for three years. America's last "real" war, the 1898 conflict with Spain, had lasted only a few months and had resulted in fewer than 400 battle deaths. By the time the United States entered this war, millions were already dead.

How would America raise an army sufficient to turn the tide in favor of the allies? In 1917, the regular army numbered approximately 140,000, not nearly enough to make a difference by any standard.[2] There was an initial surge of patriotic volunteering, but even that was clearly not enough.

Conscription in the form of the Selective Service Act would fill the ranks of the American army. On June 5, almost ten million men across the nation between the ages of twenty-one and thirty were officially registered for the draft.[3] Soon, American armed forces were teeming with new untrained volunteers and draftees. Whether a volunteer or draftee Arkansan, many recruits expressed patriotic fervor. For instance, early in the war, Ranzie Adams, a soldier in the 154th Infantry from Greene County, sent a telegram to his mother, stating: "I will give the last drop of my blood for my country, gladly, before I would see those Huns overrun our land." On May 28, 1918, Adams became the first soldier from Greene County to die of battle wounds.[4]

Within a few weeks, the railroad depots in small-town Arkansas were alive with the sights and sounds of young men saying their goodbyes to their loved ones. Many a tear was shed by both recruit and family member as trains departed stations and headed for one of the training camps established throughout the United States.

To train these new citizen soldiers properly, the United States was divided into sixteen districts based on population, with each district having at least one training facility.[5] Arkansas was home to an infantry training base in North Little Rock named Camp Pike, while in neighboring Lonoke County there was a pilot-training facility named Eberts Field. For approximately two months, the new soldiers were put through the rigors of proper military training. (See the previous chapter for more information on the state's military installations.)

Arkansas recruits were assigned to a number of training camps across the United States. For many, this separation from family and community was new. As Guy Lewis of Sevier County observed, "[I]t was the first Christmas many of us boys ever spent from home."[6] Mail from home was a very important factor in combating this separation anxiety. "We were one happy bunch while the mail was being called off," wrote Arkansas recruit Tom Wofford.[7] Eighteen-year-old Chicot County resident Clifton Barnett, serving with Seventh Infantry in France, told his sister that "a letter from home is worth a million dollars to me."[8] Steady contact with home was vitally important to the new recruits.

After arriving in camp, recruits across the nation were put through the same regimen of a ten-day quarantine, physical examinations, shots, issuing of uniforms, and assigning to barracks. The training consisted of long days of conditioning and military drill designed to teach the use of modern weapons and combat techniques. It did not take long for the men to settle into the military routine. Much of the instruction was under the supervision of veteran British and French officers who had been sent to the United States to prepare the American recruits for the rigors of twentieth-century warfare. Many of the Arkansas soldiers were hardly fazed by the hard work. After only a short time at Camp Pike, in the summer of 1918, Woodruff County recruit Robert Clayton stated, "I am beginning to feel like a real soldier."[9] Others, however, quickly became disillusioned by the routine and likely would have agreed with three Baxter County soldiers stationed at Camp Pike that the "soldier's life...is not to be sought in preference to civilian life."[10]

Once properly trained, the soldiers were transported by train to the East Coast, where they boarded troop-transport ships bound across the Atlantic Ocean for Europe. This trip, over what was often referred to as the "big pond," made a lasting impression upon the Arkansas soldiers. Many eagerly anticipated departure. Homer Phillips of Sharp County wrote from Camp Stuart, Virginia, in 1918: "We have been getting our overseas clothes this morning...don't know when we will sail, but will not be long off."[11] In January 1918, Aubra Bunn from Ashley County wrote from Louisiana's Camp Beauregard: "We are becoming more reconciled to cross the 'Big Pond' each day we are in the army."[12]

To transport the American Expeditionary Force (AEF) to the battlefields of Europe was no easy task. All serviceable vessels—including cargo craft, luxury liners, cattle boats, and confiscated German ships—

were pressed into service. Many Arkansans had never seen a ship or even a boat larger than what was necessary to navigate the streams and rivers back home. Fortunately, the trip was uneventful for the most part, aside from seasickness. Writing home from France, Leo Long of the 154th Infantry stated that he "had a good trip on the transport, what time I was not seasick."[13] James E. McGuire of Baxter County wrote that he "could neither sleep or eat nor find a place on the boat where [he] could rest."[14] Zemry Sawyer of Ashley County stated that he "had almost decided that the boat must be going round and round as there wasn't anything to be seen but water and other ships."[15]

The Atlantic crossing normally took ten to fourteen days, depending upon weather conditions and enemy interference. Upon arrival at the French port of St. Nazaire, the soldiers were quarantined for several days before being transported by small railroad cars to a selected training ground.

For the next three to four months, for six and a half days a week, they endured intensive combat instruction under the direction of French officers. The intense routine was designed to prepare the new soldiers for what they would encounter at the front. It even included massive mock battles. Once properly trained, the soldiers were rotated into what was called a "quiet sector" at the front. Though considered quiet, such sectors remained dangerous places, where lives were constantly at risk. Still, no eminent enemy attack was expected there, so the soldiers could become accustomed to the sights and sounds of the war before being once again rotated to an active combat sector. But no amount of training could have adequately prepared the civilian soldiers for what they would face on the European western front.

Soldiers from Arkansas participated in almost every campaign involving American forces from 1917 through 1918. Early in the war, Paul Johnson of Baxter County told his family back home: "Believe me they sure will kill you up there. But it is what makes it interesting."[16] A frontline Cleveland County soldier jokingly stated that "we had our good friends with us, that is our machine gun...and the other friend is our gas mask and the steel hat which we take good care of."[17]

While many of the Arkansas soldiers spoke lightly about the war, many of them saw things that were nothing like they had ever witnessed before. Claude Barden of Randolph County stated that he had been in "action long enough to know that 'Sherman was right.'"[18] "They have not made it appear as bad as it is," said Charles Cox of Johnson County. "It is some scene," he continued, "to see where the Germans have gone through the country leaving everything to waste and even going further than that to rob the graves and vaults of the dead."[19] Luther Woodall of McCrory described action at the front as "tornado and lightning." On a more personal note, he described the death of a friend: "[S]hell went off and knocked a hole in his side, you could see he had to hold his entrails. He could barely talk. He told me about his mother and sister. That got next to me."[20] Similar experiences were confronted by those at the front on a daily basis. Memories of those experiences would haunt many of the Arkansas soldiers for the remainder of their lives.

November 11, 1918, was the day that combatants on both sides eagerly waited, the end of the bloodshed. Both boisterous and quiet celebrations followed the official announcement of the armistice. (See chapter 10 for additional information on the celebration of the armistice in Arkansas.) Hugh Coody of the Forty-Seventh Infantry told his sister in southeastern Arkansas that "shortly after the firing ceased the boys began to celebrate. It was something like an Xmas chivaree."[21] Marvin Sullivan of the 116th Infantry told the folks back home in Jackson County that he would "never forget this day for I was on my way to the front lines...marching on into the very jaws of death. But suddenly the firing from rifles and the roar from cannons ceased and the good news reached us that the armistice had been signed...words are insufficient to express the extacy [sic] and the joy which thrilled our hearts."[22] Finally, the bloody conflict was over.

Even with the excitement of the war's end, attention turned almost immediately to the issue of getting home. Ernest Cantwell of Baxter County wrote his father that "the main thing we look to now is when we sail for the USA."[23] How long would it be before they would return to the States? Many saw no reason for the army to remain in Europe and expected to be boarding ships homeward in a matter of days. Unfortunately for many of the Arkansas soldiers, it would be months before they returned home, as thousands of American soldiers remained behind as part of the occupation forces in Germany. In December 1918, Guy Glover of Lonoke County informed his uncle and aunt that "there is no telling when I ever will get back home."[24] While a temporary occupation was understandable, it did not lessen the eagerness of the sons of the Wonder State to return home. Richard McHenry of Independence County spoke for many when he wrote, "Oh how anxious I am to get back to the states. I have had enough of France."[25] In time, families back in Arkansas would learn that their loved ones were soon returning. In February 1919, Luther Jackson of Clay County wrote, "Kick the rust off the plows and give the mules a couple of extra ears of corn each morning, for Jess and I are coming."[26]

Eventually, the Arkansas veterans would return to their stateside homes. Many of those arrived wiser and stronger than when they had left, while others were maimed and scarred for life. Many of the dead were left behind, never to return to Arkansas. Upon arriving home, many veterans expressed pride in having done their bit. Perhaps Harl Jones of western Arkansas summed it up best when he wrote, "Don't think I am still a kid... for I have been where real men have been and have done my duty."[27]

Notable Arkansas Veterans

A number of Arkansas soldiers received recognition for their service during the war. Those include a brigadier general, common soldiers, flying aces, and Medal of Honor recipients. But although they performed distinguished service, their actions have mostly faded into obscurity.

From a national perspective, Little Rock–born Douglas MacArthur is probably the most famous Great War soldier from Arkansas. A career military man, MacArthur saw service during the U.S.-Mexican border troubles in 1916. When the United States officially entered the European war in 1917, MacArthur, as chief of staff, assisted in raising and training the soon-to-be-famous Forty-Second Division, known as the "Rainbow Division."[28] He soon rose in the ranks and was promoted to brigadier general; later, he briefly commanded the division.[29] By war's end, he was one of America's most decorated soldiers.

Perhaps the best-known common soldier from Arkansas was Herman Davis of Mississippi County. Few, if any, Arkansans were aware of Davis's war exploits until a statewide newspaper reported that he was included on a list of the top 100 soldiers of the war, released by American Expeditionary Forces commander General John J. Pershing. Davis was drafted in 1918 and went through his initial training at North Little Rock's Camp Pike. In June, he was transported to Europe as a private in Company A, 113th Infantry, Twenty-Ninth Division. Davis participated in the last major offensive of the war, the Meuse-Argonne Offensive. He was credited with single-handedly killing more than thirty German soldiers and, for his actions, was awarded the Distinguished Service Cross by the United States, as well as the Croix de Guerre with Palm and Gilt Star and the Medaille Militaire by the French government.[30]

Davis was discharged in 1919 and returned to eastern Arkansas. While on active duty, he had been exposed to poisonous gas, which likely contributed to tuberculosis in subsequent years. He died at the Veterans Hospital in Memphis, Tennessee, on January 5, 1923. Davis was buried in the Manila Cemetery, but his body was reinterred in 1925 at the base of a twenty-five-foot-tall granite monument fronted by a life-sized statue of Davis. In 1953, the monument and the small surrounding area were established as a state park. A restored fountain in front of the Old State House Museum in Little Rock is also dedicated to his memory.[31] (See chapter 12 for the state's efforts to memorialize the war.)

Since it was first presented in 1863, the Medal of Honor, the nation's highest military honor, has been awarded to twenty-one Arkansas natives. Marcellus Holmes Chiles, Oscar Franklin Miller, and John Henry Pruitt were all posthumously honored for their actions during World War 1.[32]

Eureka Springs native Captain Marcellus Holmes Chiles was awarded the medal for his actions while leading a battalion of the 356th Infantry during the Meuse-Argonne Offensive on November 3, 1918. Chiles assumed command of the battalion after all of the ranking officers were struck down. He picked up a rifle and led his unit forward until a wound to the abdomen prevented him from going any farther. He refused to be taken from the battlefield until the command could be passed on to the next senior officer. He was removed to a hospital, where he died a few days later.[33] His Medal of Honor citation stated that "under the inspiration of his fearless leadership his battalion reached its objective."[34] His remains lie buried in the Meuse-Argonne American Cemetery and Memorial at Romagne, France.

Franklin County native Major Oscar Franklin Miller of the 361st Infantry was also awarded the medal for his actions while leading his men in the Meuse-Argonne offensive on September 28, 1918.[35] Wounded twice, Miller continued to push forward until a third wound in the abdomen prevented his further advance. He was removed to a dressing station, where he died on September 29.[36] His Medal of Honor citation stated: "Major Miller inspired his men by personal courage."[37] He is buried in the Meuse-Argonne American Cemetery and Memorial at Romagne, France.

John Henry Pruitt, born near the small Newton County settlement of Fallsville, is just one of nineteen soldiers in the history of the U.S. military to be twice awarded the Medal of Honor. After enlisting in the U.S. Marine Corps shortly after the United States entered World War I, Pruitt was shipped to the European front as a member of the Second Division. On October 3, 1918, at Blanc Mont Ridge, France, Corporal Pruitt single-handedly captured two enemy machinegun nests. Continuing to move forward, he captured forty additional German soldiers. The next day, October 4, he died of wounds received during his heroic actions. On May 10, 1919, he was posthumously awarded the Medal of Honor by both the U.S. Army and the U.S. Navy. Pruitt is the only Arkansas recipient of two such medals. His body was returned to the United States and is buried in Arlington National Cemetery.[38]

While motorized aviation was new to military combat in World War I, Arkansas played an important role. In addition to the Lonoke County flying school, Eberts Field, Arkansas was home to one of the war's notable combat pilots.

Field Kindley was born in 1896 near the famous 1862 northwestern Arkansas Civil War battlefield of Pea Ridge. He moved to the Philippine Islands with his father in about 1903, living there for about five years before moving to Gravette (Benton County) to live with his uncle.[39] After moving to Kansas as a young man, he enlisted in the National Guard. Shortly after his induction, he transferred to the Army Signal Corps aviation branch. By the fall of 1917, about five months after the United States' declaration of war, he became a member of the first class of American pilots to be transferred to England for flight training.[40]

He received his first combat assignment to the Royal Flying Service's Sixty-Fifth Squadron, with which he downed his first enemy plane. But it was with the United States' 148th Squadron that Kindley saw the balance of his wartime service. Before the end of the war, he had assumed command of the unit. By the signing of the armistice in November 1918, Kindley was officially credited with twelve downed enemy aircraft, making him the third-ranked American pilot. Among the decorations he received for his service was the Distinguished Service Cross. Kindley remained in the service following the war and was killed in a flying accident at Kelly Field near San Antonio, Texas, in February 1920. His body was returned for burial in Gravette.[41]

Reminders of Arkansas's role in the Great War are scattered across the state. While much of the area where Eberts Field was located is now a golf course, a portion of the National Guard installation Camp Robinson still carries the name Camp Pike. A handful of towns are home to impressive Doughboy statues dedicated a few years after the armistice. Moreover, there are many other monuments dedicated to soldiers who served in all of America's wars, the Great War included. But the most reminders of the long-ago war are in the cemeteries. Walk through almost any cemetery, and there you will find the young dead of a generation resting under simple marble or bronze headstones provided by the U.S. government.

1. Dallas T. Herndon, *Centennial History of Arkansas*, Vol. 1 (Chicago: S. J. Clarke Publishing Company, 1922), 724.

2. Edward G. Lengel, *To Conquer Hell: The Meuse-Argonne, 1918* (New York: Henry Holt and Company, 2008),18.

3. *Second Report of the Provost Marshal General to the Secretary of War on the Selective Service System to December 20, 1918* (Washington DC: Government Printing Office, 1919), 22.

4. Ray Hanley, *Images of America: Camp Robinson and the Military on the North Side* (Charleston, SC: Arcadia Publishing, 2014), 87.

5. Michael D. Polston, "Time Doesn't Count Here: Letters of a Camp Pike Doughboy," *Arkansas Historical Quarterly* 45 (Spring 1986): 55.

6. Letter of Guy Lewis, *De Queen Bee*, January 11, 1918, p. 2.

7. Letter of Tom Wofford, *De Queen Bee*, December 18, 1918, p. 2.

8. Letter of Clifton Barnett, *Dermott News*, August 19, 1918, p. 5.

9. Letter of Robert Clayton, *Home News*, July 5, 1918, p. 3.

10. Letter of Edney, Ernest, and Arthur, *Baxter Bulletin*, November 2, 1917, p. 1.

11. Letter of Homer Phillips, *Sharp County Record*, August 23, 1918, p. 4.

12. Letter of Aubra Bunn, *Ashley County Eagle*, January 3, 1918, p. 2.

13. Letter of Leo Long, *Newport Daily Independent*, September 10, 1918, p. 2.

14. Letter of James McGuire, *Baxter Bulletin*, May 3, 1918, p. 1.

15. Letter of Zemry Sawyer, *Ashley County Eagle*, September 12, 1918, p. 1.

16. Letter of Paul Johnson, *Baxter Bulletin*, May 17, 1918, p. 1.

17. Letter of Jewel Pratt, *Cleveland County Herald*, August 22, 1918, p. 1.

18. Letter of Claude Barden, *Pocahontas Star Herald*, June 21, 1918, p. 2.

19. Letter of Charles Cox, *Lamar Democrat*, October 11, 1917, p. 1.

20. Interview with Luther Woodall, 1988.

21. Letter of Hugh Coody, *Ashley County Eagle*, March 6, 1919, p. 1.

22. Letter of Marvin Sullivan, *Newport Daily Independent*, January 30, 1919, p. 2.

23. Letter of Ernest Cantwell, *Baxter Bulletin*, January 17, 1919, p. 1.

24. Letter of Guy Glover, *Lonoke Democrat*, January 2, 1919, p. 1.

25. Letter of Richard McHenry, *Newark Journal*, January 9, 1919, p. 1.

26. Letter of Luther Jackson, *Clay County Courier*, February 18, 1919, p. 3.

27. Letter of Harl Jones, *De Queen Bee*, January 10, 1919, p. 2.

28. Douglas MacArthur, *Reminiscences: General of the Army* (New York: McGraw-Hill, 1964), 51.

29. Ibid., 71.

30. Michael David Polston, "Arkansas's Forgotten Hero," *Arkansas Gazette*, November 6, 1988, p. 1C.

31. Ibid.

32. Mike Polston, "Medal of Honor Recipients," *Encyclopedia of Arkansas*

History & Culture, http://www.encyclopediaofarkansas.net/encyclopedia/entry-detail. aspx?entryID=4348 (accessed December 23, 2014).

33. Gordon Hale, "Marcellus Holmes Chiles," *Carroll County Historical Society Journal* 52 (December 2007): 4.

34. "Marcellus H. Chiles," Congressional Medal of Honor Society, http://www.cmohs. org/recipient-detail/2511/chiles-marcellus-h.php (accessed December 23, 2014).

35. John Allen Johnson, "Oscar Franklin Miller: Arkansas's Forgotten Hero," *Arkansas Historical Quarterly* 31 (Autumn 1972): 274.

36. Ibid., 273.

37. "Oscar F. Miller," Congressional Medal of Honor Society, http://www.cmohs.org/ recipient-detail/2565/miller-oscar-f.php (accessed December 22, 2014).

38. Mike Polston, "John Pruitt," *Encyclopedia of Arkansas History &Culture,* http:// www.encyclopediaofarkansas.net/encyclopedia/entry-detail.aspx?entryID=5776 (accessed December 14, 2014).

39. James J. Hudson, "Captain Field E. Kindley Arkansas' Air Ace of the First World War," *Arkansas Historical Quarterly* 18 (Summer 1959): 4.

40. Ibid., 6.

41. William M. Smith Jr., "Field Eugene Kindley," *Encyclopedia of Arkansas History & Culture,* http://www.encyclopediaofarkansas.net/encyclopedia/entry-detail. aspx?entryID=1689 (accessed November 11, 2014).

Chapter 4

Resistance to the Great War in Arkansas: A Brief Overview

By Phillip Stephens

The Great War, while having considerably less of an impact on Arkansas than World War II, is notable for the state as a defining moment for resistance and civil disobedience, culminating in one of the most prevalent instances of organized socialism in the state's history. Ultimately, resistance to World War I was never more than a fringe phenomenon during a time when progressivism was pushing the state toward a new sense of social conformity, but these political elements made inroads into state politics nonetheless, offering a platform for discontented citizens who did not conform to Arkansas's cultural and political majority.

At the onset of war in Europe in 1914, the United States was committed to maintaining an isolationist attitude with regard to outside conflicts. President Woodrow Wilson's reelection in 1916 was partly on the basis that he had kept the country out of war. This position was reflected by Arkansas politics as well: former governor and U.S. senator James P. Clarke was a famed anti-imperialist, and his successor, William F. Kirby, was so committed to isolation that he filibustered the Wilson administration's Armed Neutrality Law.[1] (See chapter 6 for more on Arkansas's congressional delegation during the war.) Arkansas was not, overall, interested in international affairs, and the small size of the German immigrant community kept domestic tensions low, for a time. Of course, the national mood would rapidly shift, leading up to the declaration of war on Germany on April 2, 1917; German attacks on American ships and the furor over the Zimmerman Telegram (which revealed a German proposal to form a military alliance with Mexico in North America against the United States) had successfully fomented a surge of patriotism throughout the nation that cannot be understood without a look at the concurrent thrust of intolerance for those who did not conform to the ideals of that patriotism.

Political resistance in Arkansas prior to the declaration of war largely centered around the Socialist Party, which had had a small but noticeable presence in third-party politics since the turn of the century. The first state party convention took place in Little Rock in 1903, operating on a platform of collective ownership of industry, reduced working hours, a national insurance and pension program, free and compulsory education, and equal rights for women.[2]

There would also prove to be a strong socialist presence in the western region of the state, particularly in Fort Smith and Huntington in Sebastian County, where miners' affiliation with the powerful United Mine Workers union established a presence for workers' rights.[3] The Arkansas Socialist Party also benefited from support by the American Federation of Labor and, in 1903, put forth William Penrose as its first candidate for governor.[4] By 1906, the party began to shift away from mining and toward agrarian populism, which included affiliation with the Industrial Workers of the World (IWW) and saw an increase in membership throughout the state.

The Socialist Party was able to successfully run candidates for governor from 1908 to 1918, with its high point occurring in 1912, when G. E. Mikel received more than 13,000 votes in the general election, the strongest showing the party would ever manage in a state election.[5] These developments are strikingly similar to those taking place in the nation at large, with Eugene V. Debs and the Socialist Party of America seeing an apex of support in the 1912 presidential election with six percent of the popular vote.[6] Debs would visit Arkansas regularly at the behest of local socialists.

Party opposition to America's entry into the Great War would prove to be a near death knell for organized socialism in the face of a patriotic public majority and federal persecution. The socialist position both in the United States and internationally was that the war would mean the deaths of workers in service to the interests of the ruling classes, but socialists worldwide failed to put forth a strong united front when the fighting actually broke out—the Second International dissolved in 1916 when individual socialist parties preferred to support their nation of origin rather than opposing the war as planned.[7] Those American socialists who remained with the party called an emergency national convention on April 7, 1917, in St. Louis, Missouri, to discuss the party position on the war, ultimately deciding to confirm an anti-war stance; the convention also voiced stern opposition to the forced conscription introduced by the Selective Service Act of 1917.[8]

Among those in attendance at the St. Louis convention was Arkansas delegate Clay Fulks. Fulks, who would become an iconic figure in Arkansas's radical labor community for the next several decades, was a native of Pearson in Cleburne County. He was later a public school teacher in Beebe, where he ran for state representative for White County under the Democratic ticket in 1912.[9] Fulks never settled into one occupation, working as a teacher, journalist, and haphazard student. His prolific correspondence during this time shows a growing affiliation with religious skepticism and radical labor.[10] In 1918, Fulks was the Socialist Party's candidate for governor; he was able to secure 4,792 out of 72,984 total votes against the otherwise unopposed incumbent Charles Brough.[11]

Opposition to America's participation in World War I was met with overwhelming suppression on both a popular and federal level. The Espionage Act of 1917, passed on June 15, 1917, shortly after the U.S. entry into the war, was ostensibly passed to prevent spying but also criminalized desertion or refusal of duty to the armed forces under penalty of a fine of up to $10,000, twenty years in federal prison, or both.[12] Throughout the course of the war, thousands of political dissidents and conscientious objectors (mainly Christian pacifists) were arrested for anti-war activities and draft evasion, including Eugene Debs himself on June 30, 1917, for a speech he gave in Canton, Ohio, urging resistance to conscription.

In Arkansas, support for the war effort was prodigious. Senators Joe Robinson and William Kirby (previously a staunch isolationist) urged their fellow Arkansans to support the government and agitated against "slackerism"[13] in the form of draft evasion. By June 5, 1917, a total of 149,207 citizens had registered for military service, with only about 600 eligible men failing to do so; when the age limit was increased to forty-five the next year, 199,857 Arkansans registered.[14] Overall, the mood in the state was of strong patriotism and support of the war effort, but with it came a strong intolerance for those who did not conform culturally, politically, or ideologically.

Arkansans were frightened of enemies in their midst; anything Germanic was viewed with suspicion and intolerance, occasionally subject to state persecution. On April 13, 1917, concerned officials arrived at Subiaco Abbey in Logan County with the intention of destroying a radio they feared was being used for the purposes of spying for the German government. The following year, a German pastor in Lutherville was driven from his home by an angry mob. Many German congregations, both Lutheran and Catholic, ceased worshiping in their native tongue and used English. Similarly, many institutions changed their names to minimize their connection to anything un-American: the Little Rock–based German National Bank and German Trust Company changed their names to the American National Bank and American Trust Company, respectively. The town of Germania in Saline County became Vimy Ridge.[15] (See chapter 8 for more on the German experience in Arkansas during the war.)

The Green Corn Rebellion in neighboring Oklahoma further spurred fears, when a group of mostly black and Native American tenant farmers—seen as supported by the Socialist Party and the IWW—agitated against the draft. They enacted a short-lived rebellion against local authorities, resulting in the deaths of three people.[16] The incident amplified most Arkansans' antipathy toward socialists and radical labor, particularly in regards to draft resistance. The official total of 8,732 men in Arkansas who either evaded the draft or deserted[17] should be regarded as an estimate, but it illustrates a significant minority who were unwilling to contribute to the national war effort.

Government efforts to find and arrest draft evaders began in earnest in early 1918 and attempted to stifle "slackerism" throughout the year. A small fraction of these draft evaders resisted with violence. These so-called Draft Wars typically occurred in the mountain or hill regions of the state where socialism and organized labor had a stronghold. On May 18, 1918, the sheriff of Polk County assembled a posse in Mena to apprehend a gang of evaders in the surrounding countryside. The following morning would witness a shootout between the two groups that resulted in the death of a deputy sheriff. After the gunfight, the presumed leader of the evaders, Ben Caughron, was caught, and his followers surrendered soon thereafter.

Caughron was sentenced to death for his role in the shooting, while several other members of the group received lengthy prison sentences unrelated to draft resistance after their cases were tried in state courts rather than federal.[18]

Caughron asserted that socialism had led him into opposition against the war, but he demonstrated a poor understanding of it; in interviews with the *Arkansas Gazette* during the summer before his hasty execution, he cited the socialist periodical *Appeal to Reason*, which had, in 1917, lent its support to both the war and the draft.[19] Further statements Caughron made seemed to indicate that he and his gang's resistance was more cultural than political, as the kin-based "mountain folk" had always been defiant of central authority.[20]

A similar incident occurred in Leslie in Searcy County when, on June 5, 1918, a shootout with local authorities and the Goodwin family resulted in the death of draftee Steve Goodwin and the incarceration of his father, Eli, for resistance to law enforcement. The previous year, another member of the family, Miller Goodwin, had committed suicide rather than enter military service. Suicides by draftees were reported across the state.[21] The Goodwins were identified by locals as socialists, but there is no strong evidence as to the motivation behind their resistance.[22]

The next month would witness the most famous of the Draft Wars when, on July 7, 1918, Sheriff Jasper Duke assembled a posse near Heber Springs in Cleburne County in an effort to round up a group of draft delinquents believed to be hiding in the home of Tom "Old Man" Adkisson, whose son Bliss had been delinquent since the following year. A shootout erupted, leaving posse member Porter Hazelwood fatally wounded. Sheriff Duke retreated to Heber Springs and gathered a larger and more heavily armed group. Tom Adkisson, in turn, recruited his own band of draft evaders (eight in total) to await Duke's inevitable return. The two groups met again, and a larger shootout took place, after which Adkisson's gang set fire to the surrounding underbrush and escaped.[23] By the end of the day, 100 men, including officials and volunteers, were in pursuit of the group between Rosebud and Pearson. This number would double by July 9, including soldiers from the Arkansas National Guard. Authorities spent the remainder of the week combing the countryside not just for the Adkisson group, but for other resistors and sympathizers to their cause.

Eventually, starved and exhausted members of the Adkisson group began surrendering individually beginning on July 13 in both Pearson and Rosebud. In addition to crimes relating to evasion and resistance of the draft, both Tom and Bliss Adkisson were charged with the murder of Porter Hazlewood. Tom admitted to killing Hazlewood to protect his son, but he was found guilty only of voluntary manslaughter. Bliss Adkisson, on the other hand, was found guilty of second-degree murder and given twenty years in prison.[24]

The so-called Cleburne County Draft War received more attention than any other incident during the war,[25] and although it appears little

different than the earlier outbreaks of violence in Polk and Searcy
Counties, there are crucial aspects that set it apart. On July 10, authorities
searching the Adkisson compound discovered several copies of Charles
Taze Russell's *The Finished Mystery*, a religious tract that had been
banned by the Espionage Act as seditious literature. So-called Russellites,
known after 1931 as Jehovah's Witnesses, were doctrinally opposed to the
draft and violence on behalf of country, a position that earned them fierce
persecution in Arkansas. Russell had died in 1916, and the Russellites' new
leader, Judge Joseph Rutherford, was tried in violation of the Espionage
Act and sentenced to twenty years in prison (although the sentence would
eventually be reversed) for his role in publishing and distributing *The
Finished Mystery*, a tract which damned those who committed violence in
war to hell.[26]

The Cleburne County Draft War is significant in that the Adkisson
clan professed no affiliations with socialism; their motivations appear to be
purely religious.[27] The repressive, occasionally violent, responses by locals
and authorities to the Russellite movement would persist throughout the
war. Earlier that year, on April 29, 1918, five Russellites were imprisoned
in Walnut Ridge because of their resistance to the war effort. Later, an
angry mob descended on the group, whipping them, tarring and feathering
them, and finally driving them out of town.[28] Russellite preacher Houston
Osbourne and his family were jailed for supposedly instigating the
Adkisson debacle, while friends and family of the outlaws were held in
the Edwards Hotel in Heber Springs to prevent them from aiding the
resistance.[29]

On August 8, 1918, yet another draft war erupted in the area around
Logan County and the slopes of Mount Magazine. Following circumstances
similar to the other outbreaks, a group of draft resisters fired upon local
officials, killing one.[30] The resisters, including Oscar Scott and his two
brothers, would eventually be taken into custody and made out to be
connected to the Green Corn Rebellion in Oklahoma, although this proved
to be a tenuous connection at best. One important distinction between
the Oklahoma draft resistance and that of Arkansas was that the former
was made up of organized poor sharecroppers, while the latter consisted
of isolated incidents involving hill-folk without coherent ideals or ties to
political organizations.

The final incident in the Arkansas Draft Wars occurred in Cecil Cove
in Newton County, one of the state's most isolated regions. A handful of
so-called slackers defied authorities by hiding out in the near-inaccessible
area terrain of caves and cliffs. The Cecil Cove incident is interesting
in that it was largely bloodless and resulted in something of a victory
for the resisters. In September 1918, as the war neared its end, the War
Department arranged a meeting with relatives of the gang and offered
amnesty if they gave themselves up for military service; no charges for
desertion would be filed. Interviews with the resisters revealed by-now-
familiar motives of muddled socialism and desire for independence from

outside rule.[31]

The Draft Wars reveal the bilateral character of resistance to World War I in Arkansas—organized political movements represented by Clay Fulks and other socialists fought involvement with the war and conscription through campaigns and labor organization, while intransigent mountain folk from more isolated parts of the state fought with violence and evasion. While many of these rebels claimed a connection to socialism, they had neither a sophisticated understanding of that ideology nor a real affiliation with local or national representatives of the party. Ultimately, their resistance was to modernity itself and to their existence in and participation with a larger polity; law and authority were an unwelcome interference in their hardscrabble, self-sufficient lives.

Resistance in either form, while not insignificant, was doomed in the face of almost universal support for the war. Perhaps if local officials had made a greater effort toward communicating with draft resisters instead of engaging in posse-led confrontations, there would not have been violence. The non-political resistance of religious groups such as the Russellites was unlikely to be placated by any means, but it is also true that groups like this suffered considerably through popular and official persecution (and this would continue until World War II).[32]

The Great War would, for Arkansas, ultimately bring triumph for the progressive drive toward greater national conformity.[33] But this drive also exacerbated a divide between those who did and those who did not adhere to that broader vision, be they religious, political, or fiercely independent of any central authority. The clashes and bloodshed that resulted from these ideologies illustrate the powerful fear created by the war. Arkansans were just as fearful of enemies at home as of those abroad.

1. Michael Dougan, *Arkansas Odyssey: The Saga of Arkansas from Prehistoric Times to Present* (Little Rock: Rose Publishing Company, 1994), 376.

2. Cindy Grisham, "Socialist Party," *Encyclopedia of Arkansas History & Culture*, http://www.encyclopediaofarkansas.net/encyclopedia/entry-detail.aspx?search=1&entryID=4788 (accessed November 18, 2014).

3. Michael Pierce, "Great Women All, Serving a Glorious Cause: Freda Hogan Ameringer's Reminiscences of Socialism in Arkansas," *Arkansas Historical Quarterly* 69 (Winter 2010): 293–324.

4. Grisham, "Socialist Party."

5. Ibid.

6. Nick Salvatore, *Eugene V. Debs: Citizen and Socialist* (University of Illinois Press, 1982), 265.

7. Ibid.

8. Howard Zinn, *People's History of the United States* (New York: Harper Collins, 2003), 364.

9. Phillip Stephens, "Clay Fulks," *Encyclopedia of Arkansas History & Culture*, http://www.encyclopediaofarkansas.net/encyclopedia/entry-detail.aspx?entryID=5536 (accessed November 18, 2014).

10. Ibid.

11. Grisham, "Socialist Party."

12. David M. Kennedy, *Over Here: The First World War and American Society* (New York: Oxford University Press, 2003), 26.

13. Judith Sealander, "Draft Resistance in Arkansas to World War I," *Ozark Historical Review* 2 (Spring 1973): 1.

14. Ibid., 2.

15. Steven Teske, "World War I," *Encyclopedia of Arkansas History & Culture*, http://www.encyclopediaofarkansas.net/encyclopedia/entry-detail.aspx?entryID=2401   (accessed November 18, 2014).

16. Nigel Anthony Sellars, "Green Corn Rebellion," *Encyclopedia of Oklahoma History and Culture*, http://digital.library.okstate.edu/encyclopedia/entries/G/GR022.html (accessed November 18, 2014).

17. Sealander, 1.

18. Ibid., 3.

19. Ibid., 4.

20. Ibid.

21. Ibid., 2–3.

22. Ibid., 4.

23. James F. Willis, "The Cleburne County Draft War," *Arkansas Historical Quarterly* 26 (Spring 1967): 27.

24. Sealander, 6.

25. Ibid.

26. Ibid., 5–6.

27. Ibid., 5

28. Steven Teske, "Jehovah's Witnesses," *Encyclopedia of Arkansas History & Culture*, http://www.encyclopediaofarkansas.net/encyclopedia/entry-detail.aspx?entryID=3694 (accessed November 18, 2014).

29. Ibid.

30. Sealander, 6–7.

31. Ibid., 8–9.

32. Teske, "Jehovah's Witnesses."

33. Dougan, 377.

Chapter 5

Persuading Arkansas for War: Propaganda and Homefront Mobilization during the First World War

By J. Blake Perkins

omorrow your neighbor or your neighbor's boy may give his life for our country," read a large ad in the *Marshall Mountain Wave* in March 1918. "Are you a Patriot or a slacker?" it asked. "If you are a Patriot, rally around 'Old Glory.'" By the next month, the patriotic citizens of Searcy County, Arkansas, had answered the call. Among other contributions to the war effort, Searcy Countians had gone "over the top" in buying $16,050 worth of Liberty Bonds, which exceeded their quota by $4,050. Students at the local high school also raised an additional $1,250 in liberty bond subscriptions.[1] This homefront mobilization effort in Marshall represented thousands of others like it that were conducted nationally during 1917 and 1918 as the United States fought in the "Great War," and the enthusiastic response speaks to the deep patriotic sentiments that swept America. The level of dedication to and sacrifice for the cause exhibited by these Searcy Countians was remarkable, especially in a relatively poor and resource-strapped state like Arkansas.

In many respects, the story of wartime mobilization and the campaigns waged to win over the hearts and minds of the public in support of the U.S. war effort in Arkansas mirrored the broader national experience during World War I. Government officials and public institutions, as well as private citizens and organizations, devoted considerable time, resources, and energy to helping persuade American citizens to contribute to the United States' "total war," with its mission to "fight for things which we have always carried dearest in our hearts," as President Woodrow Wilson put it. This mobilization of the citizenry and the nation's abundant resources succeeded in furnishing invaluable war materiel and important military forces that played key roles in helping to tip the scale for an allied victory. Moreover, the U.S. war effort's successful outcome helped solidify America's place on the world stage as a leading political, economic, and cultural powerhouse. It also helped transform America at home by assisting many middle-class "progressives" to achieve a number of history-making social reforms for which they had long advocated, such as national prohibition and women's suffrage, to name two of the most significant.

But in other respects, the story of homefront mobilization and wartime propaganda in Arkansas, much like that of other southern states, is a distinctive one. In fact, today's popular memories and assumptions about the rural South's long and unchanged militaristic "tradition of soldiering" and unique "fighting spirit" have produced a monolithic and one-dimensional narrative that distorts historical reality and leaves out important nuances in Arkansas's early-twentieth-century and World

War I experience.[2] In Arkansas, particularly in the vast number of rural communities across the state, many citizens even by 1917 remained either staunchly opposed to or unconvinced and apathetic about the U.S. government's decision to involve the nation abroad in the Great War. War supporters attempting to rally their communities and state for the military crusade in 1917 and 1918 found themselves squaring off against a strong antiwar political and ideological tradition that, as historian William J. Breen noted, "had been unleashed in the populist-progressive upheavals in the two decades prior to the war."[3] A timber operative from Mobile, Alabama, for example, captured the popular mood facing wartime mobilizers in the rural South. He wrote that he had discovered during his business travels through Arkansas and a few other southern states that "a great majority of the people [are] opposed to the great military propaganda that is now exciting this country."[4]

Probably more than in any other region, war supporters in the rural South—who were mostly led by middle-class urbanites and townsfolk—had to work harder and more diligently to persuade common citizens to contribute to and sacrifice for the U.S. war effort.[5]

To wage the tough battle at home for people's hearts and minds in rural southern states like Arkansas, propaganda and mobilization campaigns frequently adapted their messages and movements to familiar social traditions and southern cultural norms. They framed the nation's war effort in absolute, clear-cut terms as a battle between "Americanism" and "un-Americanism," but they hoped to convince skeptical and apathetic citizens in Arkansas that the U.S. mission to "make the world safe for democracy" was not only a worthy cause for the nation but also an urgent and worthy cause for their state of Arkansas, their own local communities, and their own families.

Citizen mobilization proved inherently difficult in a southern state whose past experiences with and perspectives on war differed in many ways from those of the broader nation. Attempts at persuasion, therefore, did not always succeed. Many in Arkansas continued to oppose—and some even resisted—the nation's war effort and the great demands it placed on its citizens. When war supporters failed at persuasion, they or their rhetoric often encouraged the use of repressive tactics against dissenters to force compliance. But the propaganda and mobilization efforts, especially through the technique of blending with the region's culture and customs, did succeed in convincing many in Arkansas that supporting the war effort was not only their obligation as U.S. citizens but that it was also the *only* genuinely American opinion and morally righteous course of action.

War propaganda and homefront mobilization efforts in Arkansas helped serve the greater national and allied cause in 1917 and 1918—and, thus, helped shape a new American and international order, for better or worse. Wartime organizers' activities also helped spur many popularly supported violations of dissenters' civil liberties and led to several incidents of violent oppression that held both short- and long-term consequences. Patriotic propaganda and mobilization campaigns during World War I helped produce a historic watershed that, with some important exceptions, opened an important door in Arkansas and the South, where mainstream opinions about the use of U.S. military force abroad began to change significantly. This transformation in a region as politically influential as the South would hold far-reaching implications for the future trajectory of American and global history in the twentieth and twenty-first centuries.

By early 1917, a broad swath of the nation's public opinion had shifted from a commitment to peace and neutrality toward preparedness and a readiness to employ U.S. military force abroad. This change of mood developed in large measure in response to Germany's aggressive use of unrestricted submarine warfare in the Atlantic, which had killed several Americans, and Britain's interception of the Zimmerman Telegram in February 1917, which unveiled a German proposal to strike a military alliance with Mexico in North America against the United States. With pro-allied British and American propaganda helping to color these dramatic stories, a great many Americans by the spring of 1917 had become convinced that the Kaiser and his belligerent nation needed to be stopped and that the time had come for the United States to step in. But many rural southerners still remained suspicious at best about American military intervention abroad. Historian Jeanette Keith's recent study of dissent in the South during World War I, in fact, shows that the region was home to some of the most determined opposition and impassioned resistance to the war effort in the nation. Many rural and working-class residents saw the conflict as an unrighteous "rich man's war and poor man's fight."[6]

Many rural people in the South and some of their political representatives in Washington DC stood among the stiffest critics of fellow Democrat Woodrow Wilson's war preparation policies.[7] One of Arkansas's U.S. senators, Joe T. Robinson, had emerged as one of the most loyal and outspoken supporters of the president's war plans and a "leading proponent of all measures necessary to win the crusade, damning all who opposed the war efforts."[8] Likewise, Arkansas's governor, Charles H. Brough—who himself bore a striking resemblance to the highly educated, southern-born president—assured the Wilson administration that it had his and the Arkansas governor's office's whole-hearted endorsement.[9] But some of Arkansas's other leaders, particularly several of those who had launched their political careers during the agrarian-populist insurgency in the 1890s and first years of the twentieth century, exposed the sharply divided mind in the state about U.S. military intervention, even by April 1917. While Senator Robinson stayed in lockstep with President Wilson's positions on the war throughout, Arkansas's other U.S. senator, James P. Clarke—a member of the old agrarian-populist, Jeff Davis faction of Arkansas's Democratic Party—worked to impede the administration's early drift toward preparedness and allied support before he died in

October 1916. Clarke joined a number of the South's other agrarian Democrats, such as James K. Vardaman of Mississippi, who warned against the danger of the U.S. being "drawn into the brutal conflict which disgraces the civilization of Europe today just to gratify the speculative spirit[,] vanity[,] greed[,] and stupidity of a few American citizens," namely corporate business interests.[10]

Clarke's successor in the U.S. Senate, William F. Kirby, wasted no time in taking up the torch of his predecessor's populist antimilitarism. In a 1913 political campaign, Kirby had given hints to his position on the issue of U.S. military interventions abroad when he, along with condemning the "imperialism" of past and present Republican leadership, questioned the thinking of fellow Democrat Woodrow Wilson as the new president pondered whether to interfere in the Mexican Revolution to advance U.S. interests. Warning against it, Kirby crowed that the Monroe Doctrine did "not require that we shall regulate the internal affairs of Mexico to protect any financial interest of any of our citizens."[11] (See chapter 6 for more on Arkansas's congressional delegation during the war.)

Populist antimilitarism in the rural South was nothing new in the 1910s. This deeply averse attitude toward U.S. military intervention abroad had arisen forcefully amid the agrarian-populist political revolt in the 1890s, as popular rural and working-class protests condemned rising economic inequality and corporate capitalism's dominance of national affairs. Many rural populists had particularly abhorred the *laissez-faire*, gold-standard-defending Republican president William McKinley and his imperial foreign policy in Cuba and the Philippines during the Spanish-American War. In 1898, for instance, the *Marshall Mountain Wave* in Searcy County (perhaps ironically, considering that newspaper's future devotion, as we have seen, to the national war effort in 1917 and 1918) chastised those pro-interventionist war hawks who, it argued, proposed to blindly lead the nation into a senseless war and had the audacity to question the patriotism of their antiwar political opponents:

> The man who hastens to answer the call of his country and fights her righteous battles is a patriot—but he who refuses to bear arms for his country in an unjust cause is a greater one. The man who respects and loves his flag is a patriot—but he who tears it from its staff when unfurled for an unholy cause exhibits a patriotism of purity....This so-called patriotism [espoused by interventionists]—pure shoddy, warp and woof—that causes men to be silent and pass by unnoticed wrongs against their country because the perpetrators are high in office, have a political pull or are big guns in the community—is the veriest [sic] rot, the essence of anarchy and the seeds of ruin.[12]

In November 1899, furthermore, the *Wave* reported with approval on the populist, anti-imperialist Democratic leader William Jennings

Bryan and his recent condemnation of a war supporter who attempted to justify the U.S. seizing control of the Philippines because it would benefit the American economy. Bryan's "eyes flashed fire," the paper proudly explained, "as he thundered: 'I dare you to measure the lives of American boys and the heart aches of American mothers by the paltry dollars and cents of commerce; I dare you do it!'" Bryan continued, "You are not preaching the gospel of the Prince of Peace," Bryan continued. "You're preaching the infernal gospel of conquest and murder and death."[13] Bryan, the three-time Democratic nominee for president (who won overwhelming support from Arkansas voters in each election), was appointed U.S. secretary of state by Woodrow Wilson in 1913. But Bryan resigned his cabinet position in June 1915 in protest against the administration's increasingly antagonistic policy toward Germany after the sinking of the British ocean liner *Lusitania*. Bryan feared that the president's hostile handling of Germany would inevitably lead to U.S. military involvement in the world war. Many Arkansas populists joined other rural and working-class Americans in standing behind Bryan and his bold, principled stance of antimilitarism.[14]

Though Bryan was no longer the nation's secretary of state, like-minded political leaders such as Senator Kirby of Arkansas aimed to continue the fight against America's steady drift toward involvement in the war. As relations worsened between the U.S. and Germany by February 1917, Senator Kirby joined four other senators to cast the only votes against a resolution supporting the president's decision to sever diplomatic relations with Germany after the Central Powers announced the resumption of unrestricted submarine attacks. Then, after the Zimmerman Telegram was revealed and the Senate began debating the president's request for a congressional authorization to arm American merchant and passenger vessels, Kirby even lent his support to populist, antiwar Republican Robert La Follette of Wisconsin and his efforts to block the bill's passage in the Senate. Amid the debates in early March, Kirby rose to the Senate floor to deride the administration's dangerous course toward militarization. Germany's recent actions, truth be known, had little to do with the growing clamor for U.S. intervention in the war, he argued. Instead, the economic opportunity promised to American corporations as a result of U.S. military involvement, he claimed, was the real driving force behind this dangerous and unjust scheme. Big-moneyed capitalists were the ones "crying for war...in order that their profits may continue safe," he alleged, and *that* was the unvarnished "reason for engaging in war," notwithstanding the façade of patriotic rhetoric about America's duty to the world. Wall Street was behind this push to intervene in the war, Kirby warned, "the same Wall Street that revels yonder in the coining of money and that would revel in the coining of blood and patriotism of the Nation into dividends."[15]

The editor of Little Rock's *Arkansas Gazette* blasted Kirby's obstinacy and urged the people of Arkansas to "repudiate before the nation, by every means that may be immediately to hand, the action of Senator W. F. Kirby." Kirby may well have considered the *Gazette* among what he called corporate America's "hireling sensational press—that ought to be in hell" for having inflamed public opinion to back Wall Street's demand for war.[16] But the Arkansas senator, along with a number of like-minded southern agrarian colleagues such as Congressman Tom Watson of Georgia, increasingly found himself among fewer and fewer "willful men" in the fight to keep the United States out of war.

After President Wilson's war message on April 2 and subsequent call for a vote in the Senate for a declaration of war two days later, Kirby painstakingly made the decision to cast a "yea."[17] He wanted to make clear for the record, however, his deep reservations and reluctance. Speaking before the Senate, Kirby grumbled that he would grudgingly vote for the declaration of war for the sake of national unity but stated that "if there was the slightest chance on God's earth that my vote against it would defeat it, I would stand here and vote a thousand years if it might be that we do not go to war."[18] Kirby and many of his populist constituents continued to concur with a number of rural and working-class war critics, including several popular Farmer's Union spokesmen who vehemently protested U.S. involvement in the war: "We are driven to war by the munitions mongers, the bankers, speculators, the jingo press and the devil, and all for their profit," one of the union's North Carolina leaders lamented, "while all that is expected of the farmers is that they furnish the men to do the fighting and then pay the great bulk of the war taxes for the next hundred years."[19]

Kirby's nose-holding vote for war, though, also reflected the response of many rural southerners after April 1917. Once the United States issued a formal declaration of war, most of Arkansas's residents, despite their previous reservations, apparently fell into line. "Whether intimidated or acquiescent," wrote historian George Brown Tindall, "most of the peace advocates retreated into silence after April, 1917."[20] Many Arkansans probably responded the way many heretofore reluctant rural folk did in the Cumberland Mountain region of Tennessee. There, "regardless of whether people in the Upper Cumberland would have chosen to go to war with Germany in 1917," wrote Jeanette Keith, "once the war began and American troops were committed, many felt obligated to help 'the boys.'"[21]

Merely falling into line, though, was not enough for government officials and private wartime organizers. After all, as historian John Patrick Finnegan put it, "along with the decision for war came the decision for total war," whereby all Americans and all facets of society were expected to mobilize for an array of contributions to the nation's war needs.[22] "The war effort," wrote another historian, "demanded not only passive acceptance but active support in thought and deed." Thus, homefront mobilizers and propagandists charged with persuading the population to go above and beyond in supporting the American war effort still had their work cut out for them in Arkansas. They needed to make certain that "patriotic ventures overwhelmed the antimilitarism," and they did—whether by persuasion or force.[23]

Senator Joe T. Robinson helped set the tone for Arkansas and the rest of the nation in a speech he made in October 1917:

> There is no compromise....There are only two sides—Germanism and Americanism....Pro-Germans in this country, hired agents of the German government, those who are foolish enough not to know their duty had better get to cover....The hour has come for loyal Americans to assert their manhood. I don't want any half-hearted support of that flag hanging yonder. You had the right to question...the war if your honest judgment doubted it. But when Congress declared war, then instead of going about the country stirring sedition, gathering the Socialists and disventented [sic] elements and seeking to inflame them against your flag, your country and your president—by God you ought to stand here and support the flag and the president and help bring victory to American arms.[24]

Leaving no room for lukewarm or nuanced opinions, America's individuals, families, and communities were either decidedly with their country or against it; they were defenders of American greatness or accomplices to its foreign enemy and the evils that sought to destroy it. "That person who does not stand back of the President in this crisis is a traitor, and should be treated as such," echoed the Arkansas Council of Defense.[25]

This urgent and absolute theme of two opposing sides persisted throughout the duration of the war and characterized propaganda campaigns at all levels—federal, state, and local. In June 1918, David King, a lawyer and local political leader in the town of Hardy in Sharp County, announced that "every county officer, every road overseer, every food administrator, every justice of the peace, constable and every school director in the county" was required to attend a series of patriotic meetings in order to "receive instructions on the great work we are called on to do." King sought to rally his fellow citizens throughout Sharp County:

> We are engaged in the most gigantic struggle in blood and arms the world ever knew; nearly a million of the gallant sons of America are now on the fields of carnage spilling their blood and giving up their lives for you and for me;—that your home and my home—that your life and my life—that your country and my country may be spared the fiendish and damnable outrages of the brutal Huns! It is no time to quibble; our country calls; he who fails to respond and do his duty will be listed; none will escape. Our people have never failed to do their duty in every emergency; we have heroically met every demand in the past, both in men and

in money; and when our report goes in on, or just after the 28th [of June], I confidently expect Sharp County at the head of the list. "He who is not for us is against us."[26]

King's call to duty in Sharp County represented the all-or-nothing character of wartime mobilization throughout America in this total-war environment. The Wilson administration created an unprecedented mass of federal agencies to manage the home front for war, including the Committee on Public Information (CPI), which aimed to employ virtually all tools imaginable to carry out the "process of stimulation" among the masses, including the "printed word, the spoken word, the motion picture, the telegraph, the cable, the wireless, the poster, the sign board."[27] The War Industries Board, the War Labor Policies Board, the U.S. Railroad Administration, the U.S. Fuel Administration, the U.S. Shipping Board, the U.S. Food Administration, and other federal agencies were developed to organize and administer the nation's economic and social functions for the war with utmost efficiency. The federal government also formed the National Council of Defense to oversee a layered and comprehensive "nationwide network" of civilian contributions to the war effort that reached into virtually every community in the nation.

Nevertheless, despite immense organization at the top, Washington's efforts greatly depended upon and were even shaped by local and state officials and organizers. "Cooperation and not coercion [by federal bureaucracies] was the overriding motif," wrote historian William J. Breen.[28] The state, county, and local councils of defense, in fact, led the civilian wartime efforts. After the federal government created the National Council of Defense and its ancillary state and local system in May 1917, Governor Brough appointed thirty-three board members, mostly middle- and upper-class businessmen, to head the state council. Upon the state council's organization, the national office declared the Arkansas Council of Defense as "the supreme authority within the State, during the term of the war, to mobilize and conserve resources and co-ordinate all activities within the State for effective National service." It further explained that the state council's "scope of activity is comprehensive and reaches out into every phase of the life of the people of Arkansas." In addition to the state council in Little Rock, each of Arkansas's seventy-five counties formed councils of defense, as well as nearly 5,000 community councils that were organized at the local school district level. Designed as an "efficiency board," the Arkansas Council of Defense and its county- and community-level offices were broadly charged with spearheading and organizing any activity that might contribute to the nation's war effort. Run primarily by prominent town businessmen and local political elites, the state and local councils aimed to inform the public about "what mobilization of every resource means, the necessity for moral and physical solidarity, and the readjustment of individual life and effort."[29]

Local businessmen and political elites in Arkansas such as David

King in Sharp County served as the foot soldiers on the ground in this "war for the American mind," where propaganda and homefront mobilization campaigns would either succeed or fail.[30] Indeed, while most other states allocated public funds for wartime propaganda and mobilization organizations, the Arkansas Council of Defense relied solely upon donations and money "borrowed from wealthy individuals to finance the work."[31]

Genuine patriotism without a doubt moved many southern elites from their prior opposition or indifference to a dedicated support for the war effort, but historians such as George Tindall and Jeanette Keith have also noted the importance of economic interests in the shift, especially among southern businessmen and "urban middle-class southerners." The outbreak of war in Europe in 1914 had initially disrupted and severely damaged the South's cotton exports. Cotton prices plummeted from thirteen cents a pound to between eight and five cents by the end of 1914, resulting in an overall loss of about $500 million. The market crisis had combined with the region's traditional populist antimilitarism to help illicit deep animosities toward the world war in the South, largely across class. By March 1915, however, Britain's and their fellow war-torn allies' increasing dependence on American trade to supply their war effort drove cotton prices back up to nine cents, and "after that they rose steadily to much higher wartime and postwar peaks," along with the prices of virtually every other American farm product. Between 1917 and 1919, average cotton prices reached twenty-seven cents, the best prices ever. Moreover, many of the region's extractive industries, such as timber and mining operators, saw increased demand and improved markets for their products as a result of international wartime trade with the allies.[32] Stronger and more direct U.S. involvement in the Great War, which many southern businessmen and town elites began to foresee by 1917, presented the opportunity to combine a united commitment to national service with the promises of local economic and social progress that they had long championed.[33] (See chapter 1 for more about the effort to put the state on a war footing.)

In Arkansas and other southern states, town and business elites who headed the local homefront mobilization efforts worked to supplant old sentiments of antimilitarism among many residents by appealing to traditional sensibilities and customs of the state's rural and working-class majority. The community gatherings and rallies held to disseminate propaganda and fire up local support for the war effort, in fact, bore a striking resemblance to the style and venues of the old Farmers' Alliance and populist political rallies of the 1890s. Local war-effort leaders in 1917 and 1918 even billed many of the events they organized as "farmers' patriotic rallies." Such rallies almost always featured a plethora of social entertainment for the whole family and offered the best speakers in the area, much like the Independence Day festivals and Election Day picnics that had long been staples of rural social and political life.[34] Local churches, schools, and lodges—the meeting places of core community institutions in rural and small-town Arkansas—were also common venues for patriotic assemblies during the war. Local leaders of the war effort, moreover, mixed traditional tactics such as charismatic speeches and soul-stirring pamphlets with new methods like sensational film reels to reach the common citizens of Arkansas.[35]

Enemy portrayal proved highly important for informing Americans about who they were fighting and why it was necessary. Hence, demonizing the German enemy was crucial. Imagery and tales of German-inflicted atrocities and the imposition of their "barbaric kultur" upon innocent peoples loomed large in the state, just as they did throughout the rest of the nation. In Arkansas, though, depictions of the "dreaded Hun" as a rich, undemocratic aristocrat bent on subjugating the common masses to his will may have also struck a similar nerve that had long denounced America's own liberty-stifling robber baron and his northeastern monopoly. "If the peoples of the earth are not to become toiling millions for the Prussian Junkers [Germany's aristocratic class] and the Prussian Krupps, if they are not to be terror-ridden slaves at the mercy of a German Kaiser's will," read one such propaganda ad in the *Arkansas Gazette*, "Prussianism must be driven back within its own borders and kept there."[36]

America's fight against "Prussianism" aligned nicely with longstanding demands from Arkansas's populist rural and working classes for the people's power to rein in greedy profiteers for the sake of the common good. Wartime propaganda and mobilization drives frequently seized the opportunity to arouse popular, widespread condemnation of greedy and self-serving merchants and businessmen who failed to comply with the nation's wartime demands. At the national level, William Jennings Bryan represented this populist dynamic. Although, not surprisingly, he never became truly enthusiastic about U.S. military involvement in the world war, Bryan had offered President Wilson his helping hand for the nation's cause after Congress declared war in April 1917. The president never appointed Bryan to any official role, but he made patriotic speaking appearances and helped the national cause in other ways as a private citizen. According to his most recent biographer, Bryan adapted his longtime anti-corporate populism to the wartime mobilization effort, like "mingl[ing] anodyne pleas for conserving food with more spirited attacks on businessmen who sought to profit from the economic boom."[37]

In this same mold, wartime organizers in Arkansas worked to stir up popular grassroots pressure against business profiteers, eliciting familiar rural and working-class passions. In July 1918, Hamp Williams, Arkansas's head federal food administrator, issued a news release to the *Arkansas Gazette* that reported that, although most of Arkansas's counties had clean records, he had cited about sixty-six violations against the Food Administration's rules in fourteen counties, where businessmen were discovered making "illegal sales" of products such as flour and sugar. Though five were restaurant owners, "the majority of violators were proprietors or managers of retail stores," and Williams assured readers that they had been justly penalized and reprimanded.[38] Such publicized reports may have reassured many rural and working-class Arkansans, especially agrarian-populists. It also implied to common citizens that their own refusal to do their part for the war effort essentially placed them in the same camp with the greedy profiteers they had long despised.[39]

The state food administration updated Arkansas citizens again in November and expressed regret that some recent complaints made against profiteers were simply out of the reach of its agency's authority, insinuating that it was now up to private citizens to hold accountable and reprimand such "un-Americanism." The Arkansas Food Administration told the *Arkansas Gazette* about a poor working-class woman who alleged that her wealthy landlord—"the owner of about 30 four-room cottages"— had raised his tenants' monthly rent by more than twenty-five percent in order to capitalize on the current wartime shortage of rental property, probably in the North Little Rock area near Camp Pike. In disgust, it calculated that, with interest, this particular landlord stood to rake in an additional $36,000 in ill-gained profits for the year. Similar reports were made about a landlord in central Arkansas exploiting the housing needs of a young woman and her two roommates, as well as a greedy druggist capitalizing on medicine shortages by charging nearly five times his regular prices for filling prescriptions. The food administrator stated that, unfortunately, some cases lay outside their jurisdiction and explained that "all I could do was to prescribe publicity and the turning of the complaints over to the State Council of Defense."[40] Indeed, he must have expected that publicizing such stories would go a long way to ensure that the pressure of the people would take care of these sorts of problems in Arkansas.

That same November, as the war came to a close, local food administrators in Chicot County reported to the public that they had severely punished merchant J. Theo Smith of Luna for using wartime shortages to gouge excessive profits from his rural customers on food and other basic commodities. They released to the press the exorbitant prices that Smith had been charging and assured readers that officials had ordered Smith's store closed for ten days and required him to contribute $100 to the United War Work fund. Smith, however, tried to defend his actions—and probably hoped to deflect immense public scorn from his white neighbors and customers—by claiming that he had been left with no choice but to raise his prices drastically. Blaming local African Americans, Smith told reporters, "I have lost a lot of money on negroe customers."[41]

Wartime mobilizers strove to tap traditional rural and working-class populist ideas and emotions about the greedy rich exploiting the masses, but prosperous middle-class homefront organizers also hoped to take the opportunity amid this patriotic atmosphere to distinguish between the selfish and the selfless wealthy. Just as organizers utilized peer pressure among the masses to inspire support for the war, they also made

Arkansas's business elites plainly aware of one another's contributions
and obligations, lest any of them become "slackers" like J. Theo Smith. In
October 1917, one newspaper article explained how both the good country
people and prominent and patriotic businessmen alike in the state were
making substantial contributions to the war effort by purchasing war
bonds. While humble common folks were doing their part—like Mrs.
Will Dorough of Granite Springs Mountain, who purchased the first war
bond in her community for her three-year-old granddaughter—a number
of well-to-do business owners were also stepping up to the plate. The
owner of one Arkansas grocery company, it boasted, bought a whopping
$25,000 worth of war bonds in one transaction, and another Little Rock
businessman "of very substantial income" vowed to live on just $50 a
month for the entire year, donating the rest to "the purchase of Liberty
Bonds and other patriotic movements."[42] Another editorial, which urged
readers that "Arkansas Must Do Her Part" for the 1917 Red Cross
Christmas war drive, asserted that "we have few people in this state too
poor to join." If, however, there were a few among the poorest of the poor
who failed to contribute, it asserted that the "more prosperous" patriots
would dutifully purchase extra subscriptions to make up for it. Indeed, it
went on, "one of the state's most prominent attorneys" who had selflessly
given up his business to lead the drive would see to it, along with his cadre
of "soldiers, business men and professional men, some of whom have gone
over the state in a special train which was donated by the railroads."[43]
Many bankers and other financial men, another editorial explained to
readers, were also "patriots first and financiers next," men of means who
stood apart from the un-American, money-grubbing slackers out there.[44]

Propaganda and publicity about unpatriotic profiteers, in some cases,
helped drum up populist violence and vigilante justice against local
merchants suspected of not contributing their rightful share to the war
effort. In May 1918, for instance, an angry mob in Trumann "scoured the
town searching for slackers of any kind." First, the patriotic vigilantes
"rushed to the public square and whipped" two local sawmill laborers
who did not make donations to the Red Cross for the war. They then
set their sights on a local merchant who had also "steadfastly refused to
donate." They intended to administer some just, flag-waving "correction"
to this stingy businessman. When the mob seized him to carry out his
punishment, however, the merchant pleaded with them for mercy and
quickly handed over a $100 contribution. Luckily for the merchant, the
mob decided to spare the rod.[45] In another incident a few days later,
nearly 100 masked men in Malvern pressured the local sheriff to hand
over a salesman incarcerated in the county jail who had been arrested for
"making disloyal utterances" about the war. This businessman was not so
lucky. The mob "whipped, tarred, and feathered" the man and then forced
him to kiss the flag.[46]

Merchants who also happened to be German American were especially
scrutinized. In March 1918, a mob of about thirty in the small community

of Jamestown near Clarksville beat a German-born merchant who had refused to erect an American flag at his store and had failed to buy any war savings stamps. The posse also broke into his store, "threw his goods into the street and ordered him to leave town."[47]

Indeed, it seemed especially useful for pro-war propagandists in populist Arkansas if the so-called greedy profiteers turned out to be German Americans. The Arkansas Council of Defense's "Americanization Committee" kept a particularly close eye on supposedly disloyal German Americans and their business ventures in the state. The Crawford County Council of Defense, for instance, investigated one of its local residents, John Kohn, who owned a grocery store in Van Buren. The council branded Kohn an "alien enemy" and reported that he held "stock in the Citizens Bank and Trust Company" and also had "quite a lot of valuable real estate, [a] store building and two or three residences in the town of Van Buren."[48]

Homefront organizers during the war also employed wartime propaganda that perpetuated stereotypes about a German drunkard culture, a characterization dually convenient amid rising sentiments for prohibition. In July 1918, in an article located just above a headline about the recent arrest of several "enemy alien" bankers in New York, the *Arkansas Gazette* published an investigative report from New York alleging that the rich German-American Busch family of St. Louis, Missouri, the owners of the Anheuser-Busch Brewing Company, had bought "at least $1,000,000 worth of the German war bonds." Moreover, it charged that much of the Buschs' money had been put to use by the Germans for buying and influencing various American newspapers and other media to circulate "pro-German" sympathies and ideas. While the Buschs insisted that they had, in fact, purchased only $500,000 worth of bonds from the German government—all before the United States had declared war in April 1917—and had no knowledge that the money was being used for pro-German propaganda in the United States, the finer details probably mattered little amid the flood of hostile propaganda.[49] More than a month earlier in Arkansas, the chairman of the Crawford County Council of Defense had reported to his state-level superiors that the wealthy Busch family's St. Louis beer company owned property in his county, suggesting that it ought to be investigated.[50] The inference propagandists expected everyday Arkansans to draw from such reports seems clear: anyone purchasing or consuming the Busch family's beer might as well be in the Kaiser's army aiming a rifle at U.S. troops in Europe.

German Americans frequently faced other forms of discrimination in wartime Arkansas as well. As in other states, anti-German sentiments fueled by pro-American and pro-allied propaganda became so strong in Arkansas that many residents of German ancestry opted to anglicize their given and family names.[51] Many school boards throughout the state demonstrated their supposed patriotism by removing German language classes from the curriculum. In August 1917, war supporters' spirited scorning of Curtis Ackerman, the editor and publisher of a weekly German newspaper in Little Rock, even led to his arrest. Accusing him of disloyalty for printing pro-German material, authorities transferred Ackerman to a federal prison in Georgia, where he remained for the duration of the war.[52] (See chapter 8 for more on the experiences of German Americans during the war.)

At the same time that wartime propaganda warned against subversive German influences at home, it informed Arkansas residents that they were duty-bound as virtuous and honorable citizens to comply with and contribute to the various homefront campaigns for the American war effort. While wartime propaganda's appeals to duty were in no way exclusive to the South, they may have effectively tapped into deep cultural traditions of honor in a southern state like Arkansas.[53] In January 1918, the *Arkansas Gazette* told the citizens of Arkansas that purchasing Liberty Loan subscriptions was their duty. "If every man did his duty the country would absorb the Liberty loan issues with the greatest ease, but selfishness stands in the way," the newspaper explained. "Too many men jeopardize their fortunes and their country by failing to do their duty, hoping that other and nobler men will do their duty so well that the slackers will be carried through to safety," it scolded. Similarly, the *Cabot Herald* published a short but stirring piece in June 1918 titled "In the Performance of Duty." It reminded its readers of the many families who were receiving the painful news from authorities "announcing the death, on the field of battle, of a brave American boy who has sailed three thousand miles at the call of 'duty'...the brave soul who saw his duty and went bravely to meet it." Urging civilians in Lonoke County to "think soberly for a minute," the *Herald* asked, "And what shall we say of ourselves, we who were not called to go 'over there,' yet were called to an equally honored task here at home?" "Have we not 'died'—but LIVED 'in the performance of duty'?" it continued. "The boy gave all he had—his life. He gave it like the hero that he was," the newspaper reminded locals. "Are we giving LIFE?"[54]

Such preaching on duty corresponded with literal religious exhortations on patriotism and service to country in 1917 and 1918. Many Christian churches in Arkansas integrated wartime propaganda and civilian mobilization efforts into sermons, Sunday services, and special events. In February 1918, for instance, the First Presbyterian Church in Little Rock held a large flag celebration service to honor twenty-seven servicemen who were members of the church and to raise donations for army chaplains ministering to U.S. soldiers in Europe. Contrasting "David, the young soldier" who had taken a stand against Goliath without the confidence and support of his fellow Israelites with the American soldiers fighting in Europe who had behind them "our country's care," Dr. Van Lear, the pastor, vowed that his church "will do more and yet more until victory brings them home and disbands them." The service also included a musical program led by Mrs. C. W. Gray, which featured such songs as "Onward, Christian Soldiers" and "God Save Our Boys."[55] Other Christian denominations likewise held patriotic services throughout the war. In November 1918, a number of churches in the Little Rock area held special services honoring the troops and the U.S. war effort, including the First Methodist Church, the Winfield Methodist Church, the Forest Park Methodist Church, the Twenty-Eighth Street Methodist Church, the Church of Christ at Twelfth and Valmar streets, the Capitol View Methodist Church, the Second Presbyterian Church, and the Immanuel Baptist Church.[56]

Christians in Arkansas, however, were divided over the war. Historian Jeanette Keith has shown that deep antiwar convictions were held by many rural church members throughout the South, particularly in many small fundamentalist congregations such as the Churches of Christ, Holiness churches, and independent Baptist and Methodist churches. War proponents in Arkansas, especially those who were members of mainline denominations in towns and cities, condemned the antiwar sentiments of such "churches of the disinherited" and questioned the authenticity of their Christianity. The opposition and resistance to the war mounted by Russellite Christians (later known as Jehovah's Witnesses) in Cleburne and Lawrence Counties, for instance, raised the ire of state and local officials and patriotic journalists who, in addition to attempts at violent repression, labeled their faith as erroneous, seditious, and dangerous.[57]

But the Russellites were not the only "misguided" Christians in Arkansas, according to self-styled patriots. In late June 1918, Albert Duane Swift, the twenty-two-year-old son of a prominent Batesville family and a star football player and recent graduate of Arkansas College (now Lyon College), made press headlines for failing to report for military duty. Noting that Swift claimed that his Christian faith made him a conscientious objector to war, one reporter alleged that Swift was merely a "self-appointed preacher" who could not claim membership in any legitimate denomination and had only been preaching for about a year and a half "wherever he can get an audience."[58]

In many instances, patriotic citizens took it upon themselves to suppress such "un-American" Christians. In August 1918, the *Fayetteville Democrat* reported that F. D. Davidson, a "preacher of the Holy Roller faith"—a derogatory label referring to the Holiness movement—had been apprehended by Dr. W. T. Blackburn, who was a member of the local Lincoln Council of Defense. Blackburn told local reporters that he had seized Davidson after the preacher made an impassioned speech in which he compared President Wilson to the beast referred to in biblical scriptures about the End Times and asserted that women Red Cross workers were "no better than harlots." Similarly, a Baptist preacher in Sheridan who had scolded his congregation and others for "devoting too much of their time to the Red Cross and the Y.M.C.A. work" and had remarked that the Red Cross had "originated in hell" found himself facing charges of espionage.[59]

In addition to their efforts to conflate patriotism with religious sensibilities, war propagandists and mobilizers in Arkansas sought to tap residents' pride in their local communities to raise contributions for the war effort. The state and local defense councils, Red Cross administrators, food administration officials, and newspaper editors kept and published running tallies and comparisons of the amounts that the citizens of individual counties had contributed to various homefront campaigns. Hoping to ignite a deeper commitment to a Red Cross drive in Pulaski County, for example, the *Arkansas Gazette* informed its readers in December 1917 that "while some counties are far ahead" in working toward meeting their quotas, such as Sebastian County, "Pulaski is not half way." Like a modern-day sports commentator at a NASCAR race, the *Gazette* diligently kept readers posted on who the front-runners were and when the lead changed.[60]

War supporters in Arkansas also thoughtfully worked to contend with and absorb southern nationalism and Civil War remembrance. Old animosities between North and South needed to be suppressed in order to unite in national solidarity for victory in World War I. In August 1918, the *Helena Shield* regretted that some fellow southerners, such as the editor of the Memphis, Tennessee, *Commercial Appeal*, were complaining that the European press had taken to referring to all American soldiers, including southern boys, as "Yanks." The Helena writer, who claimed to remember firsthand the Civil War experience, argued that the Union army did, indeed, inflict horror and suffering upon the South, including "robbery and raping." But he alleged that more than two-thirds of the perpetrators were actually "foreign soldier[s], hired and brought over here to help overpower and subjugate the south," a great many of them Germans. He claimed to recall from his boyhood during the Civil War that, in fact, one such foreign mercenary—"who could scarcely talk English enough to be understood"—"cursed and abused" him when the Union army came into his community. Luckily for him, though, a more "civilized" native-born American soldier in the Union army intervened and scolded the foreigner. Instead of re-opening old wounds between Northerners and Southerners, the Helena resident contended that in this current world war, "Dixie and Yankeedom will join hands in opposing this dangerous [foreign] foe."[61]

Still, homefront organizers could also, at times, find the culture of southern pride useful. In an obvious but unspoken attempt to help deter draft resistance, which proved a particularly large problem in rural Arkansas, the *Gazette* published a short overview of the 1863 draft riots in New York. Those Yankee draft resisters during the Civil War produced "turbulent scenes" and a "reign of anarchy" in New York, the paper explained. In the current world war, though, by comparison, the *Gazette* claimed that America's patriotic boys "have accepted their assignments" in a "quiet and orderly way."[62] In truth, rural southern states like Arkansas produced some of the staunchest resistance to military conscription in the nation in 1917 and 1918.[63] By implying a comparison with cowardly

Yankees during the Civil War era, and by asserting that any negative thoughts about the contemporary draft were abnormal, propagandists and mobilizers hoped to shame potential war critics and draft resisters in Arkansas into complying with federal conscription. Similarly, after what it called a "recently disclosed taint of disloyalty and false teaching in the public schools of New York City" regarding the nation's war history, another Arkansas newspaper asserted with confidence that once the nation was set right on its rich and honorable war history, the nation ought to actually "look to the past to win the war!"[64]

Wartime propaganda and mobilization efforts in Arkansas also sought to inspire frugal and self-sacrificing behavior for the national cause, traits that poor and middling Arkansans had long deemed to be essential virtues of American "commoners" who had contributed to a thriving republic since 1776. Similar to the way that local agrarians had called for conservative consumption habits and a self-help strategy to protect the common people from predatory capitalists in the late 1800s, wartime newspaper ads and posters promoting the Food Administration's mission to conserve food for the war effort stressed how a mere "saving of two cents per meal each day by every man, woman and child in the U.S.A. totals a saving of Two Billion Dollars." "Anybody that doesn't save serves the Kaiser as effectively as if he were carrying a gun in the German army," one ad declared.[65] "Use a fraction of an ounce or so less of food a day," read another ad, "...to keep the allied armies and our own soldiers in fine fighting fettle."[66]

Homefront mobilizers asked women in Arkansas, as the primary consumers of household products, to play a particularly large role in promoting the virtues of frugality and national service during the war. In June 1918, L. M. Guthrie, the chairman of the Franklin County Council of Defense, urged merchants and consumers—women and men, but primarily women—to "unite in patriotic movement." In particular, Guthrie urged women to "set the fashion" on dress in accord with the needs of the war, lamenting that "I have never seen [people] dress so extravagantly." "[S]ome of the people who purchased those garments," he continued, "could have bought some of these Liberty bonds if they had been content with cheaper and more sensible clothing."[67]

Women played major roles in homefront contribution campaigns, especially in Arkansas's towns and cities. Many borrowed organizational skills pioneered by woman activists for progressive causes in the late nineteenth and early twentieth centuries and adapted them to wartime mobilization drives.[68] Two days after President Wilson delivered his war message to Congress, the Arkansas Democrat reported a "large increase in registrations by women" in the Little Rock chapter of the National League for Women's Service. The patriotic women quickly organized a drive to erect American flags throughout the city. They also sold flags to raise money at the Arkansas Travelers' season-opening baseball game. The Democrat honored their work by publishing the names and addresses of each participant.[69] In July 1917, the Arkansas Council of Defense formed a women's committee and appointed Mrs. Joe Frauenthal, a well-to-do Conway socialite, to lead it. County- and local-level committees soon followed. Women helped the war effort in various ways, ranging from the administration of Red Cross and Liberty Loan drives to helping with draft registrations in their communities.[70]

While under the leadership of predominately urban middle-class women, many rural and small-town women also participated in the war effort in significant ways. Woman homefront organizers typically succeeded most when they brought small-town and country women together in familiar rural social gatherings, such as quilting parties. Resource conservation drives also tended to work best when organizers tried to amalgamate their efforts with local cooperative institutions, such as community canneries and laundries and home demonstration gatherings. The Woman's Committee Council of Defense, for instance, estimated that about fifty percent of Arkansas's farm women had participated in a program conducted through local home demonstration groups to teach women how to make their own soap in lieu of buying it. Governor Brough bragged on the Woman's Committee and, more generally, the patriotic women of Arkansas: "With a meagre fund,...this organization has thoroughly mobilized the woman power of our state, until it is now a vital dynamic force in our midst, battling to make the world safe for democracy."[71] (See chapter 7 for more on women during the war.)

Homefront leaders also expected Arkansas's black residents to contribute to the national cause, though they also expected them to remain within the racial boundaries ascribed by Jim Crow laws. While the national office of the Council of Defense recommended that states form "Negro councils of defense," most southern states balked, fearing that such organization of blacks might challenge established racial mores.[72] Instead, the Arkansas Council of Defense sought to address the need for mobilizing black residents for the war effort by partnering with what was known at the time as the state education department's Negro division. It enlisted African American education department employee P. L. Dorman to integrate patriotic education with his regular duties. Dorman traveled to black schools and communities across Arkansas to deliver speeches and meet with local residents about their duties to serve the nation's wartime needs. But the national defense council continued to insist that states adopt a more comprehensive approach to organize blacks for the war effort. Finally, the Arkansas Council of Defense created what it called a colored auxiliary state council in September 1918. White council leaders, however, ensured that they controlled appointments to the black auxiliary and that those African American men chosen to lead their black communities for the war effort were "conservative in the views and good representative men with considerable influence among their people." These black men appointed by the Arkansas Council of Defense also established some county- and local-level auxiliaries before the war ended in November.[73]

While many of Arkansas's black residents joined the war effort, many others remained unconvinced that this was truly *their* war. After all, while U.S. officials and war supporters expected black Americans to both serve in the military and in homefront campaigns, African Americans encountered segregation and discrimination at every turn. Black antiwar dissenters became so alarming to a white plantation owner and the deputy prosecuting attorney in Lake Village in 1917 that they reported the dissenters to the federal government's Bureau of Investigation, alleging that the local blacks were trying to form an alliance with Germany and were plotting an insurrection. The local prosecutor informed the bureau that the patriotic white men of Lake Village had already formed a home guard to see to the matter, but he urged the feds to undertake a serious investigation of the seditious activities. In the meantime, the deputy prosecutor stated that he and fellow white patriots in Lake Village would see to it that the local blacks would come to "the full realization of the fact that at all times they will be kept under strict surveillance." Moreover, they would order any black dissenter to "Obey the law and keep his mouth shut"; if he did not, he would "be dealt with accordingly."[74]

War supporters in Arkansas complained especially about black draft evaders and deserters. Governor Brough even saw the need to comment on blacks who were "slacking" on their duties for the war effort, particularly those evading the draft and deserting from military service. In a likely attempt to help defuse white alarm about defiant and rebellious blacks in Arkansas, Brough insisted that high black desertion rates were probably "due to the general illiteracy of that race and their roving disposition and not to lack of patriotism or intention to evade the draft on their part."[75] Nevertheless, in the racially charged atmosphere, black deserters became synonymous with sedition and slacking. Thus, many local whites, working through their county and state council of defense organizations, capitalized on the wartime condemnation of slackers to strengthen local anti-vagrancy laws, which were typically aimed at African Americans. Stronger laws against vagrants were needed, according to one member of the state council, in order to go after those "generally known in the community in which they live as consumers and not as producers."[76] Likewise, the Arkansas Council of Defense aimed to help deal with slothful "slackers" by passing a resolution in July 1918 to pressure local officials to stop issuing licenses for new pool halls and to pass ordinances to close those already operating.[77] (See chapter 8 for more on African Americans and their experience of the Great War.)

The popular image of blacks as slackers belied the fact that whites made up the vast majority of dissenters and deserters in World War I Arkansas. Indeed, although "Arkansas did more than most southern states...to round up deserters," the state had one of the highest desertion rates in the country.[78] While the national desertion average stood at 12.24 percent, military officials classified 15.5 percent of Arkansas's inductees as deserters or delinquents, and these statistics did not account for those

who had refused to register for service in the first place.[79] Many who
evaded the draft were discontented rural and working-class whites who
continued to see the U.S. war effort as an unrighteous and unjust cause,
despite all of the patriotic propaganda that attempted to convince them
otherwise. After several small farm families banded together to resist
the draft in mountainous Newton County, for instance, one of the local
dissenters contended that "the good book says: 'Thou shalt not kill.' We
didn't want our boys takin' nobody's life. It ain't right 'cause it's contrary
to the Bible and the good Lord's teachin's." Another explained, "We don't
want our boys fightin' them rich fellers' battles and gettin' killed just to
make a lot of money for a bunch of millionaires."[80]

High desertion rates and incidents of draft resistance indicate that
wartime propagandists and homefront mobilizers in Arkansas failed
to achieve absolute conformity to their fervent support for the war. As
historian Jeanette Keith wrote, "A close look at southern rural dissent
indicates that people's minds were not nearly as malleable as or as simple
as [the architects of pro-war propaganda] supposed."[81] The vast majority
of Arkansans, of course—whether they were convinced by propaganda
and homefront campaigns about the worthiness of the cause—did not go
so far as to openly defy conscription laws or actively attempt to sabotage
wartime efforts in their towns and communities. Even so, a number of
Arkansas's "un-persuaded" encountered the punishing wrath of some war
supporters for merely expressing uncertainty or making critical remarks
about the war in private. Local war supporters in Helena, for instance,
had a man jailed because he "uttered sentiments disloyal to the United
States." Another man in Earle was locked up because "when he was offered
a small flag to wear on his collar he threw the emblem down and cursed
the government." Similarly, a Newport man found himself in trouble after
making "unpatriotic remarks" and for saying that he believed many "men
volunteered in the army and bought war savings stamps because they
were forced to do so and [for] selfish motives, rather than from patriotism."
Luckily for him, local authorities put him in jail before a pro-war vigilante
mob got its hands on him.[82]

Such intolerance and abuse of dissenters in the name of patriotism
was rampant in Arkansas. In Hartford, a group of residents seized a man
for ques tioning the virtues of the nation's war effort and "forced [him]
to get on his knees, apologize and to kiss the flag several times." They
did the same to three other men who had "made adverse comment[s]." In
Jonesboro, a civilian mob publicly whipped a night watchman at a factory
who was accused of "making some of the remarks against the government,
the Red Cross and other war activities." A soldier who had recently
returned from Europe after losing both of his legs in combat was "one
of the first to apply the whip." In Pocahontas, an employee at a button
factory offended a fellow worker—who, perhaps ironically, happened to
be a German American—for allegedly saying that "he hoped the Germans
would whip the whole world." The furious German-American employee

hurried to request permission from the county sheriff "to beat the stuffing out of a blamed traitor," who obliged him "to go to it." Back at the factory, he assaulted his colleague, beating him until his "face is said to have resembled jelly when the young German finished with him." He then made his bruised and battered victim "kiss a Wilson button several times" and "salute the Stars and Stripes."[83]

The combination of wartime propagandists' and homefront mobilizers' actual persuasion and the activities their messages frequently inspired effectively silenced all but the most idealistic and defiant critics of the war in Arkansas. Adapting patriotic war messages and organizing efforts to traditional cultural and social norms helped move many Arkansans from their initial skepticism. Home-front efforts galvanized war supporters in an enthusiastic all-or-nothing, with-us-or-against-us fight to harness the minds, resources, and actions of Arkansas's population. Those who remained unconvinced encountered hostility, derision, and, in numerous cases, even violent oppression. By the war's end, a great many Arkansas towns and communities, such as Marshall in Searcy County, had gone "over the top" for the war effort. By most accounts, wartime organizers in Arkansas had met or exceeded most of their goals by the fall of 1918, despite the major obstacles they had faced when they had first begun in early 1917.[84] Through suasion, manipulation, or forceful suppression, Arkansas made its contribution to the Great War.

World War I mobilization also produced important long-term consequences in Arkansas. The impact of war propaganda and homefront campaigns during the First World War also helped open the door to major political and ideological changes in Arkansas concerning the nation's involvement in and use of military force in foreign affairs. In Arkansas's 1920 U.S. Senate election, Thaddeus H. Caraway made his opponent William F. Kirby's "anti-war" record prior to April 1917 the centerpiece of his campaign's effort to oust the old populist, anti-imperialist incumbent. It worked. Arkansas voters rejected Kirby's bid for reelection, marking the important political and ideological swing.

In the 1930s, Arkansas did, however, join the nation's overwhelming mood for American isolationism during the Great Depression. Maybe Wall Street's "merchants of death," many Americans had come to wonder, had hoodwinked the nation into a world war back in 1917, after all, just as their greedy behavior had now, apparently, wrecked the nation's economy. In 1932, Kirby hoped to capitalize on this mood to retake his old Senate seat, focusing his campaign on an I-told-you-so message that recent events had justified his former antiwar stance back in the spring of 1917. Nevertheless, Kirby's campaign to regain his old seat failed, as he and several other candidates fell to Hattie Caraway, the wife of the recently deceased Thaddeus Caraway.[85] Even in the isolationist political climate of the 1930s, Kirby had apparently overestimated the popular appeal of an anti-interventionist message that had once stirred roaring ovations and helped win votes in Arkansas. Times and minds had changed.

Indeed, representing Arkansas in the U.S. Senate, "Mrs. Caraway," as she preferred to be called, supported internationalism and new policies to beef up the U.S. military when the storm clouds of foreign conflict and war began rolling in again in the early 1940s.[86]

With only a few exceptions (most notably, Arkansas's U.S. senator J. William Fulbright in the 1960s and early 1970s), Arkansas and the rest of the South would never again produce the kind of broad-based political pressure for antimilitarism that populist-progressives like William F. Kirby had once represented. Conversely, southerners, or at least their political representatives, have generally stood among some of the greatest and most eager advocates for employing U.S. military intervention abroad since World War I. The southern bloc in Washington, in fact, would wield major political influence in shaping the United States' interventionist foreign and military affairs during World War II, the long Cold War era, and the nation's post-Soviet international policies of the 1990s and early twenty-first century, including the so-called War on Terror.[87] In Arkansas, the World War I experience, and particularly the fight for the minds and souls of the citizenry, played no small role in helping effect this remarkable transformation, one that literally helped shape the course of American and global history in the twentieth and twenty-first centuries.

1. *Marshall Mountain Wave*, March 8, 1918; ibid., April 12, 1918.

2. On popular imagery and assumptions, see James Webb, *Born Fighting: How the Scots-Irish Shaped America* (New York: Broadway Books, 2004), 253–56.

3. William J. Breen, *Uncle Sam at Home: Civilian Mobilization, Wartime Federalism, and the Council of National Defense, 1917–1919* (Westport, CT: Greenwood Press, 1984), 112.

4. Walter O. Ernest, quoted in George Brown Tindall, *The Emergence of the New South, 1913–1945* (Baton Rouge: Louisiana State University Press, 1967), 41.

5. See, for instance, Tindall, 40–49. On populist rural resistance to the draft and other mobilization efforts during the war, see Jeanette Keith, *Rich Man's War, Poor Man's Fight: Race, Class, and Power in the Rural South during the First World War* (Chapel Hill: University of North Carolina Press, 2004).

6. Keith, *Rich Man's War, Poor Man's Fight*.

7. Historian George Brown Tindall documents how the majority of southern political leaders increasingly fell in behind President Wilson's foreign policy agenda during the early months of 1917, although he notes that "a widespread if largely latent rural-progressive opposition continued up to the time of the declaration [in May]." Tindall, 45–47.

8. Cecil Edward Weller Jr., *Joe T. Robinson: Always a Loyal Democrat* (Fayetteville: University of Arkansas Press, 1998), 75.

9. Brough's support of President Wilson's increased shift toward military intervention is mentioned in Richard Leverne Niswonger, "William F. Kirby, Arkansas's Maverick Senator," *Arkansas Historical Quarterly* 37 (Autumn 1978): 261.

10. On Clarke's anti-interventionist politics, see Michael B. Dougan, *Arkansas Odyssey: The Saga of Arkansas from Prehistoric Times to Present* (Little Rock: Rose Publishing, 1994), 376. Vardaman is quoted in Tindall, 44.

11. Kirby quoted in Niswonger, 259.

12. *Mountain Wave*, April 8, 1898.

13. Ibid., November 4, 1899.

14. On William Jennings Bryan, see Michael Kazin, *A Godly Hero: The Life of William Jennings Bryan* (New York: Anchor Books, 2006).

15. Quoted in Niswonger, 260.

16. Ibid., 260–61.

17. For a useful discussion of Wilson's war message, see Robert H. Zieger, *America's Great War: World War I and the American Experience* (Lanham, MD: Rowman and Littlefield, 2000), 52–55.

18. Quoted in Niswonger, 262.

19. Quoted in Tindall, 47.

20. Ibid., 48.

21. Jeanette Keith, *Country People in the New South: Tennessee's Upper Cumberland* (Chapel Hill: University of North Carolina Press, 1995), 161.

22. John Patrick Finnegan, *Against the Specter of a Dragon: The Campaign for American Military Preparedness, 1914–1917* (Westport, CT: Greenwood Press, 1974), 187.

23. Tindall, 48–49.

24. *Arkansas Gazette*, October 7, 1917.

25. Quoted in Gerald Senn, "Molders of Thought, Directors of Action: The Arkansas Council of Defense, 1917–1918," *Arkansas Historical Quarterly* 36 (Autumn 1977): 284.

26. *Hardy Herald*, June 21, 1918.

27. George Creel, the head of the CPI, quoted in Joseph Carruth, "World War I Propaganda and Its Effects in Arkansas," *Arkansas Historical Quarterly* 56 (Winter 1997): 386.

28. Breen, xvii.

29. Senn, 281, 283.

30. On propaganda and mobilization as a "war for the American mind," see David M. Kennedy, *Over Here: The First World War and American Society* (New York: Oxford University Press, 1980), 45–92.

31. Breen, 98.

32. Tindall, 33–37, 55–60; Keith, 36–37. On the dramatic rise in agricultural prices during World War I, see Gilbert C. Fite, *Cotton Fields No More: Southern Agriculture, 1865–1980* (Lexington: University Press of Kentucky, 1984), 94–96; and James H. Shideler, *Farm Crisis, 1919–1923* (Berkeley: University of California Press, 1957), 10–19. More broadly, on the war's impact on the national political economy, see Kennedy, 93–143.

33. See Michael Pearlman, *To Make Democracy Safe for America: Patricians and Preparedness in the Progressive Era* (Urbana: University of Illinois Press, 1984).

34. For an example of a "Farmers' Patriotic Rally and Picnic" during the war in Searcy County, see *Marshall Mountain Wave*, July 26, 1918.

35. Carruth, 388.

36. *Arkansas Gazette*, April 6, 1918.

37. Kazin, 254–55.

38. *Arkansas Gazette*, July 25, 1918.

39. Davis quoted in Raymond Arsenault, *The Wild Ass of the Ozarks: Jeff Davis and the Social Bases of Southern Politics* (Philadelphia: Temple University Press, 1984), 167.

40. *Arkansas Gazette*, November 7, 1918.

41. Ibid., November 10, 1918.

42. Ibid., October 24, 1917.

43. Ibid., December 21, 1917.

44. Ibid., January 4, 1918.

45. Ibid., May 27, 1918.

46. Ibid., April 1, 1918.

47. Ibid., March 29, 1918.

48. Quoted in Senn, 288.

49. *Arkansas Gazette*, July 12, 1918.

50. Quoted in Senn, 288.

51. On the anglicanization of names, see, for instance, *Arkansas Gazette*, February 4, 1918.

52. Carruth, 392–93.

53. On the cultural significance of "honor" in the South, see Bertram Wyatt-Brown's classic *Southern Honor: Ethics and Behavior in the Old South* (New York: Oxford University Press, 1982).

54. *Cabot Herald*, June 28, 1918.

55. *Arkansas Gazette*, February 4, 1918.

56. Ibid., November 9, 1918.

57. On Arkansas Russellites and their antiwar positions, see James F. Willis, "The Cleburne

County Draft War," *Arkansas Historical Quarterly* 25 (Spring 1967): 24–39; *Arkansas Gazette*, July 14, 1918; and Steven Teske, "Jehovah's Witnesses," *Encyclopedia of Arkansas History & Culture*, http://www.encyclopediaofarkansas.net/encyclopedia/entry-detail.aspx?entryID=3694 (accessed January 27, 2015).

58. *Arkansas Gazette*, June 28, 1918.

59. *Fayetteville Democrat*, August 22, 1918; Carruth, "World War I Propaganda and Its Effects in Arkansas," 396–97.

60. See, for instance, *Arkansas Gazette*, December 21 and 28, 1917.

61. *Helena Shield*, August 10, 1918.

62. "Draft Drawing Started Riots in New York in 1863," undated clipping from the *Arkansas Gazette*, Subject Files (microfilm), 4.775, Arkansas History Commission, Little Rock.

63. On draft resistance in the rural South, see Keith, *Rich Man's War, Poor Man's Fight*. On draft resistance in Arkansas, and particularly in the Ozarks, see J. Blake Perkins, "Dynamics of Defiance: Government Power and Rural Resistance in the Arkansas Ozarks" (PhD diss., West Virginia University, 2014), 111–64.

64. "Setting the Country Right on War History," undated/unnamed newspaper clipping, Subject Files (microfilm), 3.4131, Arkansas History Commission, Little Rock.

65. *Arkansas Gazette*, February 24, 1918.

66. Ibid., March 3, 1918.

67. Ibid., June 16, 1918.

68. For an overview on women's political activism in Arkansas during the era, see Jeannie M. Whayne, et al., *Arkansas: A Narrative History*, 2nd ed. (Fayetteville: University of Arkansas Press, 2013), 287–92, 305–11.

69. *Arkansas Democrat*, April 6, 1917.

70. Senn, 289.

71. Ibid., 289–90.

72. Breen, 107–8.

73. Senn, 288.

74. Keith, 144.

75. Brough quoted in ibid., 180.

76. Breen, 107.

77. *Arkansas Democrat*, July 20, 1918.

78. Keith, 181.

79. These statistics from *Final Report of the Provost Marshal to the Secretary of War on the Operation of the Selective Service to July 15, 1919* (Washington DC: Government Printing Office, 1920) are transcribed in Willis, "The Cleburne County Draft War," footnote 3, p. 25.

80. "Uncle Sam's Little War in the Arkansas Ozarks," *Literary Digest* (March 8, 1919): 107–11.

81. Keith, 11.

82. Carruth, 394.

83. Ibid., 395–96.

84. Historian William J. Breen generally gives the homefront campaign in the states of the South and Southwest, particularly the work of the councils of defense, a "lackluster" assessment. He said, though, that eventually and "well into 1918...the overall quality of state councils in the South and Southwest began to reach satisfactory levels." Within the South, Breen notes that federal officials frequently commended the work of Arkansas's state council and considered it among the best in the region. Breen, 112. Historian Joseph Carruth likewise wrote, "Despite numerous expressions of resistance to America's participation in the Great War, the government program to arouse American public opinion was highly successful....Thus, Arkansas—and virtually all America—went 'over the top.'" Carruth, 397–98.

85. Niswonger, 263.

86. Leo J. Mahoney, "Hattie Ophelia Wyatt Caraway," in *Arkansas Biography: A Collection of Notable Lives*, ed. Nancy A. Williams (Fayetteville: University of Arkansas Press, 2000), 52–53.

87. On the American South's powerful influence on U.S. foreign policy, see Joseph A. Fry, *Dixie Looks Abroad: The South and U.S. Foreign Relations, 1789–1973* (Baton Rouge: Louisiana State University Press, 2002).

Chapter 6

Politics, Partisanship, and Peace: The Arkansas Congressional Delegation and World War I

By William H. Pruden III

World War I represented a very different type of conflict for the United States. Not surprisingly, then, the road to war, as well as its aftermath, revealed much about the nation's ambitions and its changing political currents. Forced to assess anew the validity of its longtime neutrality stance—a foreign policy that traced its roots back to President George Washington (and which was perhaps honored more in the breach than in the observance)—President Woodrow Wilson found himself having to navigate a previously untraveled path in an altered international landscape. Throughout this period, the Arkansas congressional delegation, especially its senators, played a substantive and important role in the discussions and debates that ultimately resulted in the nation going to war. They continued to be at the forefront of, first, the effort to win the war, then, the later effort to achieve a peaceful resolution to the conflict, and, finally, the attempt to determine the role of a politically divided America in the postwar world.

In a time of great uncertainty, the make-up of the Arkansas congressional delegation was very stable. As the war broke out in Europe in the summer of 1914, the state's U.S. House of Representatives delegation included Thaddeus Caraway of the First Congressional District, William Oldfield from the Second, John Floyd from the Third, Otis Wingo from the Fourth, Henderson Jacoway from the Fifth, Samuel Taylor from the Sixth, and William S. Goodwin from the Seventh. With the exception of John Floyd, who chose not to run for reelection in 1914 and was succeeded by John Tillman as the representative of the Third District in March 1915, every member of the House who was representing Arkansas when the conflict began in Europe was still in office when the armistice was reached in 1918—and even in 1920 as the Senate wrangled over the Treaty of Versailles.[1] This stability undoubtedly affected the delegation's responses to the challenges posed by this first global conflict.

In contrast, things on the Senate side of the delegation were a good bit less stable. In a quick succession of events, Joseph T. Robinson, who had represented the Sixth District in the House for a decade, was elected governor in 1912. But only days after Robinson had assumed the governorship, the state's junior senator, Jeff Davis, died of a sudden heart attack. Using his considerable influence as governor, Robinson persuaded the legislature to choose him to succeed Davis, making him the last Arkansas senator to be chosen by the legislature.[2] Meanwhile, the man Robinson joined in the Senate, James P. Clarke, would beat back a spirited challenge by state supreme court justice William F. Kirby in

1914 to secure a third term, only to die on October 1, 1916, after a short illness. With the national election approaching, Governor Charles Brough called for a special election, and on the same day that Woodrow Wilson was reelected president, Arkansas voters chose Kirby as their new junior senator.[3]

The pairing of Robinson and Kirby proved to be a volatile one. Indeed, the state's senators were in many ways polar opposites in their approaches to the Senate. Few members in Senate history were more loyal to their party's interests than senior senator Joseph T. Robinson, a fact that was ultimately rewarded with his selection as the party's Senate leader in 1922. Serving as majority leader beginning in 1933, he shepherded countless pieces of New Deal legislation to fruition until his sudden death in 1937.[4] In contrast, throughout his career, whether at the state or national level, William F. Kirby, a populist/progressive, had established himself as, in the words of one historian, "a maverick," one who showed no hesitation in going counter to party orthodoxy.[5] These differences were brought into sharp focus by the issues confronting the nation as the conflict in Europe widened. Indeed, as their parallel Senate careers unfolded and as tensions increased in Europe, no issue better illustrated their differences than preparedness for a possible war.

Before Kirby had arrived in Washington DC and before tensions in Europe had arisen, Robinson—still the state's junior senator—demonstrated his loyalty to Wilson and the president's foreign policy. In 1914, he supported the president's dispatch of troops to Veracruz, Mexico, in order to protect American financial interests and citizens, and two years later, he backed the Jones Act, under which the administration laid out the groundwork for Philippine independence. He also approved the use of troops in dealing with Mexican marauder Pancho Villa in 1916.[6] And yet, while Robinson proved to be no less supportive of the Wilson administration once the conflict in Europe began to affect American interests directly, he was an early opponent of any efforts to build up the American military, an effort he saw as premature. Indeed, in April 1916, he denounced the effort to increase the U.S. Army's ranks to 250,000 members, although he did support a measure that called for an increase to 150,000. However, once that passed, he supported a subsequent measure that spring to roll it back to 100,000.[7] Later in the summer of 1916, Robinson voted on four separate occasions for amendments that would reduce the number of ships the U.S. Navy was planning to build. He also sought to lengthen the timeframe in which they would be constructed.[8] However, his whole approach changed in early 1917 after the president met with the Senate leadership and shared a message from the Germans that they would be resuming unrestricted submarine warfare on all shipping. While others urged the president to send a message of protest to the German ambassador, Robinson, apparently having concluded that war could not be avoided, argued for a more aggressive approach, recommending that the president break off diplomatic relations with Germany—the path Wilson, in fact, did take, although it appears that he had determined to do so prior to his meeting with the congressional leaders.[9] With this decision, Robinson became a firm proponent of military preparedness, a stance that put him at odds with his colleague, Senator Kirby.

Indeed, a contrast to Robinson's approach was presented by William F. Kirby, who was elected on November 7, 1916, the same day that Woodrow Wilson, running on the slogan "he kept us out of war," was narrowly elected to a second term. Arkansas's junior senator wasted no time making his views known, and while the extent of his opposition to the president's preliminary wartime activities may have surprised many observers, anyone who had listened closely to Kirby's campaign speeches should have recognized that he was not heading to Washington DC intent upon leading the nation into war. Rather, his campaign rhetoric made it clear that he was determined that the Democratic Party's declaration that "he kept us out of war" would ultimately represent more than just a campaign slogan to be cynically discarded once the president's reelection had been secured. Indeed, during his effort to oust Clarke, Kirby had been outspoken in his opposition to American international intervention.[10] Kirby was a strong progressive voice, one that reflected and represented the agrarian interests of the state, and during his 1914 campaign, he had made clear his belief that the Monroe Doctrine did not require that "we shall regulate the internal affairs of Mexico to protect any financial interests of our citizens."[11] Like many progressives who sought a limited foreign involvement, Kirby feared that it would distract the government from more pressing domestic issues, like currency reform, one of his greatest concerns. During the campaign, he had also expressed the fervent hope that Wilson could avoid war with Mexico. He cautioned that it must "be done with honor and dignity of the nation," but after expressing this cautionary note, he declared, "I believe it can be done."[12] While unrealized at the time, that sentiment proved to be a preview of his views on the developing European conflict and America's role in it. Consequently, it was not surprising that once in the Senate, Kirby took an increasingly active role in keeping the United States out of what he saw as a European conflict.

The split in the Arkansas ranks became clear after Wilson's decision to break off diplomatic relations with the imperial German government. Following that decision, on February 7, 1917, Missouri senator William J. Stone offered a resolution expressing the Senate's support of the president's action.[13] Kirby's response to the resolution offered an early indication of his independent outlook. Joining the group that Wilson biographer Arthur Link termed the "agrarian radicals or advanced progressives"—a disparate collection that included James K. Vardaman of Mississippi, Robert M. LaFollette of Wisconsin, John D. Works of California, and A. J. Gronna of North Dakota—Kirby was one of only five who voted against the resolution.[14] Not surprisingly, the populist in Kirby led him to question the motivation for U.S. involvement, and he joined those who argued that pressure from Wall Street interests as well as munitions manufacturers was playing no small role in the growing pressure for the United States to intervene.[15] This debate was played out in February 1917 when, after Germany's resumption of submarine warfare, the president proposed arming U.S. merchant ships. This bid for armed neutrality was buttressed by the accompanying release of the Zimmerman Telegram, a communiqué in which Germany sought Mexican assistance in a conflict with the United States. This news heightened anti-German sentiment across the nation, while also providing additional public support, and the House responded quickly. Giving swift consideration to the Armed Ships Bill, it passed by an overwhelming vote of 403–13.[16]

However, the reception in the Senate was more muted. A small group of senators led by Robert LaFollette and joined by Kirby was opposed to the effort and sought to filibuster the bill until the congressional session ran out on March 4. This effort ran counter to the general sense of the Senate, a fact that was made clear by the seventy-four members—a group that included all but two southern senators, one of whom was Kirby—who had supported a "round robin" introduced by Robinson that called for a vote on the bill.[17] While Kirby did not participate in the filibuster led and organized by his Wisconsin colleague, Robert LaFollette, he did support the effort, while strongly opposing the bill.[18] Kirby made that fact clear when, in a forceful statement on March 2, 1917, he declared his opposition to arming American ships, announcing, "The time has come when we should tear aside cant and hypocrisy and sham."[19] He asserted that he did not believe that the Sussex Pledge had constituted an agreement that the Germans had now violated; rather, in Kirby's view, the Germans had always retained the right to resume U-boat activity.[20] The senator all but mocked the administration's claim that Germany's action represented the abandonment of a "solemn promise."[21] He went further, asserting that it was not Germany but the American business community that was "crying for war...in order that their profits may continue safe."[22] He made clear his belief that the only thing being protected were the profits of those engaged in the sale of supplies and munitions to belligerents.

To Kirby, ever the southern populist, an irresponsible press, which was doing the bidding of Wall Street interests, had inflamed public opinion to such an extent that it was impossible for the Senate to be the reasoned, thoughtful, deliberative body it was intended to be.[23] That was a bold statement in a Senate whose intention was made clear by Robinson's "round robin." However, the filibuster was successful, bringing down the curtain on a legislative session that ended on March 4 and forcing the president to authorize the arming of American ships unilaterally while also calling Congress back for a special session in which, on April 2, 1917, he asked for a Declaration of War.[24] The intransigence of LaFollette and those, like Kirby, who supported his cause if not the specific tactic—a group that Wilson denounced as a "little group of willful men, representing no opinion but their own"—did yield a historic change in Senate procedures:

the adoption of Rule 22, which for the first time offered a mechanism to end a filibuster.[25]

For all Kirby's efforts, there is little evidence that they had much impact on the views of his constituents. The House delegation remained firm in its support of the president's ongoing efforts, and the Arkansas press was outspoken in its criticism of the senator's efforts. Indeed, much was made back home of the contrast in the relationships each Arkansas senator had with the president's nemesis, Robert LaFollette. In fact, the full extent of the state's unhappiness with Kirby's role in the pre-war debates became clear in the weeks following the filibuster; less than six months into his time as a member of the "world's greatest deliberative body," the state's junior senator found himself being pilloried by many of his constituents.

After the Senate standoff on arming American ships, Governor Charles Brough sent a message to the Arkansas General Assembly that offered congratulations on President Wilson's second inauguration as well as support for his policies. He urged the assembly to express the state's support for the president's efforts to protect the nation.[26] In a clear rebuke to their senator who had worked so hard to block the president's efforts, the legislature voted to forward on to the president Brough's eloquent message of support and commendation. In fact, at the same time, the state Senate offered kudos in support of Robinson's efforts, passing a resolution recognizing him for being "true to the people of Arkansas and the Armed Neutrality Resolution."[27] In contrast, in one of many actions that served only to rub more salt in the wound, the editorial writers of the *Arkansas Gazette* urged the people of Arkansas to "repudiate before the nation, by every means that may be immediately at hand, the action of Senator W. F. Kirby."[28] Meanwhile, in addition to the resolution from the state legislature condemning his efforts, a citizens' committee made up of his fellow Arkansans had labeled Kirby the reincarnation of Judas Iscariot, sending along thirty pieces of silver to reinforce the message.[29] Although Kirby did receive support from former governor George Donaghey, who even advised the president of his stand, it was clear that Kirby's antiwar stance was out of step with his constituents, especially the state's farming population.[30]

Following the debate on arming the ships and severing relations with Germany, the decision to go to war was almost anticlimactic. While the Arkansas House delegation was unanimous in its support for the president's request, the senators were less united—and definitely not speaking with one voice. Robinson, as expected, was a solid supporter of the president. However, Kirby's path was more tortured. While all his actions and words up to that point had made clear his deep desire to keep the United States out of the conflict, with the die cast, it appears that he did not want to further the divisions that had marked the earlier deliberations and for which he had had been so roundly criticized. Whether all of the abuse and criticism had an actual impact on Kirby's thinking is hard to know, but the reality is that once it was clear that U.S. entry into the war was a certainty, Kirby switched gears and, unlike LaFollette and some of his other previous allies, voted in support of the war resolution, which passed the Senate with only six members in opposition.[31] It was not an easy decision for Kirby, nor one made without regret, for as the junior senator from Arkansas declared, "If there were the slightest chance on God's earth that my vote against it would defeat it, I would stand here and vote a thousand years if it might be that we do not go to war."[32]

As the nation turned its attention to winning the war, an incident in the Senate later that spring served as a reminder of the divisions that had been evident in both the Senate and the Arkansas delegation in the months leading up to the declaration. Indeed, few things revealed more clearly the split between Robinson and Kirby than the senior senator's exchange with LaFollette in the spring of 1917 as the United States began its war effort. Having already been frustrated by LaFollette's leadership of the filibuster effort at the end of the previous legislative session in March, Robinson went after the Wisconsin progressive, who was still expressing his opposition, in what one historian termed "one of the angriest exchanges in the history of the United States Senate."[33] Blaming LaFollette for the war and incensed that the Wisconsin legislator had refused to apologize for his opposition but instead had reminded his colleagues that the likes of Abraham Lincoln and Daniel Webster before him had opposed earlier U.S. war efforts, Robinson attacked LaFollette, declaring, "If I entertained your sentiments, I would be applying to the Kaiser for a seat in the Bundesrath."[34] He asserted that LaFollette was responsible for the expansion of the war, announcing his view that in blocking the bill to arm the merchant ships, LaFollette had, in fact, prevented the allies from offering a united front that might have discouraged German aggression. Livid at the attacks on his patriotism and character, LaFollette had to be restrained as the fiery Robinson taunted him, offering to "settle it outside."[35] The exchange shone a spotlight on Robinson and raised his national profile considerably.

Most exemplified by the encounter with LaFollette was Robinson's full-scale commitment to winning the war. From the moment Congress adopted the Declaration of War until well after the fighting had ended, Joseph T. Robinson was in the thick of the political battles that marked the war and the peace. As a member of the Senate leadership team, Robinson had a substantive role in supporting the president's program and, as always, was a loyal supporter of all the administration proposed.

Meanwhile, although he was low on the ladder in terms of seniority, Kirby's membership on the Military Affairs Committee did give him a platform from which to observe and influence the developing war effort. The committee, chaired by Senator George Chamberlain of Oregon, undertook a vigilant approach to its responsibilities and often clashed with the administration. However, Kirby was seldom a critic. In fact, once the war was under way, Kirby was, by all accounts, a strong supporter of the nation's efforts, often tangling with some of his fellow committee members. Indeed, later, in an effort to rebut the stinging attacks made by Congressman Thaddeus Caraway as he challenged Kirby for the Senate nomination in 1920, Kirby secured a letter from Secretary of War Newton D. Baker in which the secretary praised Kirby's "zeal and fine discernment" as a member of the Military Affairs Committee.[36] And in a letter to Wilson after the war, Baker acknowledged that in the early stages of the international crisis, "Kirby acted badly and joined forces with our adversaries," but the secretary further asserted that "from the moment we declared war until now he has been as stalwart and as constant a defender of the War Department and advocate of its policies as we have had."[37]

With the United States at war, the nation and Congress turned their attention to winning the conflict, and that effort played out both at home and abroad, with the Arkansas delegation substantively involved in both areas. The major issues that Congress addressed during the war were the draft; the Espionage and Sedition Acts; the Railroad Act, which enacted the federal control of the nation's railroads; the Overman Act, which shifted substantive powers from Congress to the president; and the Lever Food Control Act, which gave the government power to control both the production and the distribution of food, fuels, and other necessities. It also dealt with the two other major anti-filibuster measures that arose after the controversial filibuster conducted against Wilson's Armed Ships Bill.

Southern congressional delegations represented a solid bloc in support of the president with only twenty-one total votes—none from Arkansas—being cast in opposition to the administration-backed measures.[38] The draft law was the most contentious, for the South's military tradition, going back to the Revolution and reinforced in the Civil War, coupled with concerns about potentially integrated units, made the notion of forced service a difficult one in some quarters. Too, early draft calls seemed to have a disproportionate effect on farm labor—and thus the southern population. However, in the end, the region came around, with the Arkansas members standing as one in supporting the president's request for a conscription bill as the way to supply the needed manpower.[39] Indeed, despite his early opposition, as well as his concern that it could come to typify the old adage about "a rich man's war and poor man's fight," Senator Kirby was a forceful advocate.[40] In the midst of the Senate debate, he declared that it was critical that the nation wake up and begin "to understand what had to be done." He added: "We must get down to business. Men must be trained. We have embarked on an enterprise and we must do something to get all the men we can over to France." He closed by asserting, "We've got to draft men from every walk of life to do it. Let's get at it and do less talking about it."[41]

No less controversial were the Sedition and Espionage Acts. In an attempt to ensure public support of the war in a nation in which the pre-war debate had shown the wide range of ethnic and national roots (as the country was populated by an increasingly immigrant-bred citizenry),

Congress passed legislation in 1918 aimed at preventing any citizen from straying from the path of total support for the allies' effort to achieve victory. The laws were stringent enactments aimed at ensuring a united national voice and increased internal security. This had the full support of the Arkansas delegation; the ultimate congressional vote on the legislation was overwhelmingly in support.

As Congress navigated its way, seeking to prosecute the war while not ignoring issues at home, few men were more influential than Arkansas's senior senator. Regardless of the issue, Robinson remained loyal to the president and the administration's efforts, often carrying their banner in the legislative process. On issues ranging from the Sedition Act to Prohibition—not a difficult issue in the South, but also one that was framed, in some circles, as a conservation issue in wartime—Robinson could be counted on for both his support and his active efforts to bring others along. His experience and expertise as a member of the Interstate Commerce Committee were particularly important to both the government's takeover of the railroads during the war—a measure deemed necessary to ensure uninterrupted and efficient rail service—and the fair compensation due the railroads when the war was over. Robinson crafted a bill that secured appropriate compensation for the railroads while being mindful of the national economic interests involved.[42]

Throughout the war, the Arkansas delegation remained almost slavishly loyal to the president. It had voted with the president in support of the Sedition and Espionage Acts, and while Goodwin on the House Committee on Foreign Affairs, Wingo on the House Committee on Expenditures of the War Department, Robinson on the Senate Foreign Relations Committee, and Kirby on Senate Military Affairs all had some measure of oversight responsibility, none appeared to be anything other than supportive. Indeed, after his early opposition to almost all things Wilsonian, Kirby appeared to have been one of the president's staunchest supporters on the Military Affairs Committee, a panel that was chaired by Senator George Chamberlain and that was never shy about questioning the president's efforts.

In April 1917, Secretary of War Baker went to the House Committee on Military Affairs to urge passage of the president's Selective Service law at a time when many, including Wilson nemesis Theodore Roosevelt, were pushing a volunteer army, and he found virtually no opposition. However, on the other side of the Capitol, the Senate Military Affairs Committee not only undertook an investigation of the War Department, but Chairman Chamberlain's speech to the Senate in January 1918 bemoaning the poorly managed war brought some senators to tears.[43]

With critics decrying the way the administration was managing the war, one major effort to improve things was a proposal for the creation of a War Cabinet, a body that would provide for the executive and the legislative branches to share the responsibility for the war effort.[44] Senator Gilbert Hitchcock was the prime mover behind this idea. However, in the course of Hitchcock's major Senate speech on the subject, Kirby challenged the Nebraska lawmaker, accusing him of failing to consult with the administration before seeking to curb the president's constitutional role as commander in chief. While Hitchcock denied the allegation, Kirby remained firm in his opposition, and the proposal ultimately died.[45]

In April 1918, as part of its vigorous (in the White House's view, meddlesome) oversight of the war effort, the Senate Military Affairs Committee issued a report calling the nation's developing aviation program a failure, but Kirby refused to sign the report, aligning himself with a group that defended the administration, asserting that it faced tremendous difficulties that constituted an ongoing challenge.[46] Too, with the war on, Kirby worked hard to make Arkansas a part of the war effort, helping bring the U.S. Army's Camp Pike training facility to North Little Rock, a move that helped the local economy and also served the senator's political interests.[47]

Meanwhile, on the House side, the greater stability in the delegation's membership was mirrored in a virtual consensus of opinion on the major issues relating to the war. Unlike the early Senate clashes between Robinson and Kirby, there had been no discord or opposition within the Arkansas delegation as the president steered the nation on the cautious path of neutrality before events forced his hand. At the same time, unlike Robinson, there was no member of the state's House delegation who was a part of the leadership group with which the president consulted. But that lack of inside influence in no way undermined their loyalty, and from the beginning of hostilities, they were strong and consistent supporters of the administration-directed war effort.

At the same time, during the war, William Goodwin's congressional responsibilities included service on the Committee on Foreign Affairs, and he was one of a select group of congressmen who went to Europe at Christmastime in 1917 in an effort both to assess the war effort and to start the process of facilitating better relations between the United States and foreign powers following the war. Similarly, both Thaddeus Caraway and John Tillman were part of a seven-member House delegation that traveled to France, England, Italy, and Ireland in June 1918 looking at economic changes that had taken place in these allied countries in an effort to learn lessons that might benefit the postwar economy.[48] Too, at the height of the action, from 1915 to 1919, the state was represented by the ever vigilant Otis Wingo on the Committee on Expenditures of the War Department. However, in this time of crisis, the often combative Wingo offered nothing but support to the War Department and its efforts to achieve victory in Europe.

In the midst of the war effort, Robinson found himself facing reelection. As the 1918 midterm contest approached, Robinson believed the best strategy was to simply do his job in an effort to convince the voters that he was irreplaceable. While he was no more happy than any other Democrat over the president's decision to make the election a referendum on his wartime leadership and the war effort, he did not shrink from his close association with the president. In fact, he had received an enthusiastic letter of support from President Wilson early in 1918, but the shrewd and savvy Robinson did not release it to the public until the campaign was well along, at which time it reinforced the case for the senior senator and undoubtedly contributed to his overwhelming reelection.[49]

However, neither the president's nor the party's electoral fortunes fared as well in other parts of the country. In October 1918, word leaked out that there had been an exchange of notes between Wilson and Germany asking about armistice terms, bringing about a public outcry. The president was denounced in many quarters, and unconditional-surrender clubs soon dotted the landscape. Ironically, given his early opposition to the president (but reflective of the nation's changing political landscape), Senator William Kirby criticized the effort, declaring, "We are organized to whip Germany and I think we had better do it before we quit."[50] However, intent upon achieving a peace based upon his previously announced fourteen points, while no less determined to reshape the postwar international map, the president did not back down. Instead, with negotiations ongoing, and to the chagrin of Democratic candidates across the country, Wilson asked the American people to indicate their support of his work by electing a Democratic Congress that would provide the continued support he needed.[51]

Unhappily, the man who had failed to achieve a popular vote majority in either of his own presidential election victories saw his party's congressional contingent shrink significantly after the midterm elections. In the Senate, the Democrats lost five seats with their previous 52–44 majority having been transformed into forty-seven Democrats and forty-nine Republicans. Meanwhile, the House saw the Democratic membership drop from 214 to 198, while the new Republican majority counted 236 seats as its own.[52] With voters refusing to give Wilson's effort the stamp of approval he sought, the president found himself a likely lame duck, forced to work with a majority Republican Congress. One direct casualty of the realignment was Senator Robinson. The prized seat on the Senate Foreign Relations Committee that he had assumed back in December 1917 became a short-lived assignment when the mid-term election loss resulted in fewer Democratic committee slots and as the junior member Robinson was an odd man out.[53]

Shortly after the Democrats staggered out of the mid-term elections, the hostilities in Europe came to an end. However, while the armistice of November 11, 1918, marked the end of combat in World War I, Arkansas, like the rest of the country, and the world, would be affected by the war well beyond the official end of hostilities.

From the beginning of American involvement in the war, Woodrow Wilson had made clear his intent to make a world different from the one that had existed before the war. Consequently, once the war was over, Congress turned its attention to peace and the nature of the postwar world.

The main stage for this effort was the Senate, where a historic debate over the Treaty of Versailles, the League of Nations, and Wilson's vision for a postwar world was played out. The Senate debate over the treaty broke down into three conflicting camps. There was a small group, known as the "irreconcilables," who opposed the treaty under all circumstances. Another group, headed by Republican leader and Foreign Relations Committee chair Henry Cabot Lodge, was known as the "reservationists." At the other extreme were the Democratic loyalists, among whose leaders was Robinson, who gave their unwavering support to the president.[54]

From the beginning, Robinson and Kirby were staunch supporters of Wilson's League of Nations. In the early summer of 1919, Kirby placed in the Congressional Record a lengthy article trumpeting the value of the league.[55] Then, the following spring, prior to the final effort to ratify the controversial treaty, Kirby took to the Senate floor to defend the treaty and trumpet the virtues of the league, an institution, he reminded his colleagues, that had been created by the "greatest statesmen of the world" and that "embodies the greatest dream for the establishment of a permanent peace."[56] Robinson, meanwhile, had become the floor leader for the administration's effort to secure passage of the president's handiwork. In typical fashion, Robinson's efforts reflected his belief in collective security as well as his loyalty to both the party and the president who headed it. The senior senator from Arkansas showed little restraint as he castigated the Republicans, who, he asserted, had engaged in "shameful displays of partisanship," as well as "deliberate misrepresentations" and "falsehoods."[57]

From the outset of the Senate's deliberations, Robinson was an outspoken defender of the president. In fact, before the treaty was even formally presented to the body, in May 1919, the volatile and loyal Robinson attacked Missouri's James A. Reed, the only Democrat who had openly expressed opposition to the treaty. Outraged at what Robinson saw as Reed's lack of loyalty to president, Robinson publicly challenged him to test public opinion. Robinson proposed that they should both resign their seats, with the subsequent campaigns for reelection serving as a referendum on the treaty and the League of Nations. The stunned Reed termed the idea "impractical," but the incident was a telling indicator of Robinson's deep commitment to the president on this controversial issue.[58]

In the debates and political maneuvering that characterized the Senate's consideration of the Treaty of Versailles, Robinson was caught between his long-standing support for an organization dedicated to international peace, an idea he had advocated going back to his earliest days in the House of Representatives, and his loyalty to both the president and the party.[59] While U.S. membership, indeed leadership, in the League of Nations had been a central tenet of the original treaty, upon the adoption by the Republican majority of "reservations"—sponsored by Foreign Relations Committee chairman, Senator Henry Cabot Lodge— the president, suffering from the effects of a massive stroke, was adamant in his refusal to accept anything but the original treaty. He called upon loyal Democrats to hold the line, ordering them to refuse to accept any compromise or substitute. While he engaged in much parliamentary maneuvering, Robinson was unable to rescue the treaty, and when the time came for a final vote, both he and Kirby remained loyal to the president, voting against the reservation-encumbered document.[60]

While the league was strongly supported by the constituents back home, the support of Wilson and the League of Nations offered by Robinson and Kirby represented far more than representative politics.[61] For Kirby, it was the logical flip side of his earlier opposition. As much as he had opposed Wilson's advancing effort toward war in 1917, he saw the league as a vehicle to avoid further such events and was all for it. Not withstanding their earlier bitter differences, he was also behind the man who was pioneering it.

For Robinson, the league had the potential to bring to fruition an idea he had been advocating for a long time. Back in 1910, while in the House, he had supported a proposal calling for the creation of a world forum for peace, and the league represented a more comprehensive and potentially more effective manifestation of that idea.[62] His support for the league and the president was total, extending to the very last vote, itself the result of his own effort to resurrect the already defeated treaty and have one final—and ultimately unsuccessful—vote on the unencumbered treaty, a document containing no amendments, as the ailing Wilson desired.

While the defeat of the treaty arguably signaled the end of the war, the 1920 Arkansas Senate election offered a replay of many of the pre-war debates, as Senator William Kirby was forced to defend his actions against an aggressive challenge from Congressman Thaddeus Caraway. In the aftermath of the war, before a tired Arkansas populace, it was not a defense easily mounted. Indeed, Representative Caraway focused most of his attacks on Kirby's pre-war opposition, refusing to let the state's Democratic voters forget that it was Kirby, almost alone among southern senators, who had been part of "the group of willful little men" who had opposed the president's efforts to protect American ships and lives, as well as keep the nation out of war.[63]

As if that were not enough, the state press, which had so vilified Kirby's efforts in 1917, took up the cry again, with editorials like the one titled "Lest We Forget" in the *Jonesboro Daily Tribune*, typical of the ongoing vitriol aimed at Kirby's actions.[64] Kirby sought and received help from War Secretary Newton Baker attesting to his consistent support during the war. Baker wrote a letter of support to the *Batesville Record*, in which he praised Kirby's work as a member of the Military Affairs Committee, citing his "zeal and fine discernment," while a Kirby campaign ad included an excerpt from a Baker letter that asserted that, as a member of the Military Affairs Committee, Kirby had been an asset in the effort to successfully prosecute the war, while also expressing his gratitude for the senator's "constant support throughout these long and difficult months."[65]

However, such efforts fell short, as Caraway pounded home the message that Kirby had been out of step with his fellow Arkansans, as well as the nation.[66] In the end it proved a highly successful strategy against the man about whom a bitter Woodrow Wilson would write, "I do not know of any man who has more grievously disappointed me."[67] Kirby went down to a crashing defeat, with Caraway winning the Democratic primary with sixty-four percent of the vote. Caraway easily won the general election over Republican Charles F. Cole in November.[68]

The 1920 election marked a change, for despite Caraway's landslide election victory and Robinson's ever increasing stature in the Senate hierarchy, the Republicans' overwhelming across-the-board victories in the 1920 elections meant that the influence of Arkansas's Democratic delegation would be significantly reduced when Congress reassembled in 1921. They had played no small role in the events surrounding World War I, but like the rest of the party, they would be consigned to the sidelines while the Republican Party dominated the political decision-making process for over a decade.

1. *Historical Report of the Arkansas Secretary of State 2008* (Little Rock: Arkansas Secretary of State's Office, 20008), 48.

2. Cecil Edward Weller Jr. *Joe T. Robinson: Always a Loyal Democrat* (Fayetteville: University of Arkansas Press, 1998), 59–60.

3. Richard Leverne Niswonger, "William F. Kirby, Arkansas's Maverick Senator," *Arkansas Historical Quarterly* 37 (Autumn 1978): 259.

4. For the best look at Joseph T. Robinson's political career, see Weller, *Joe T. Robinson: Always a Loyal Democrat.*

5. For the best overview of William Kirby's public career, see Niswonger, "William F. Kirby, Arkansas's Maverick Senator."

6. Weller, 70.

7. Ibid., 70.

8. Ibid., 70–71.

9. Ibid., 70.

10. Niswonger, 259

11. Ibid.

12. Ibid.

13. Ibid., 260.

14. Ibid.

15. Ibid.

16. Justus D. Doenecke, *Nothing Less Than War: A New History of America's Entry into World War I* (Lexington: University Press of Kentucky, 2011), 271.

17. Weller, 70–71.

18. Doenecke, 272.

19. Niswonger, 260.

20. Ibid.

21. Ibid.

22. Ibid.

23. Ibid.

24. A. Scott Berg, *Wilson* (New York: G. P. Putnam's Sons, 2013), 438.

25. Berg, 426; Marin B. Gold and Dimple Gupta, "The Constitutional Option to Change Senate Rules and Procedures: A Majoritarian Means to Overcome the Filibuster," *Harvard Journal of Law and Public Policy* 28, no. 1 (2005): 205–72, 217–19.

26. Niswonger, 261.

27. Ibid.

28. Ibid.

29. Doenecke, 275.

30. Niswonger, 261.

31. Berg, 439.

32. Niswonger, 262.

33. Weller, 76.

34. Weller, 77.

35. "Joseph T. Robinson: The 'Fightingest' Man in the U.S. Senate," U.S. Senate: Art & History, Senate Leaders; online at http://www.senate.gov/artandhistory/history/common/generic/People_Leaders_Robinson.htm (accessed November 4, 2014).

36. Niswonger, 262.

37. Ibid.

38. Joseph A. Fry, *Dixie Looks Abroad: The South and U.S. Foreign Relations, 1789–1973* (Baton Rouge: Louisiana State University Press, 2002), 164.

39. Ibid., 164–65.

40. Jeanette Keith, *Rich Man's War, Poor Man's Fight: Race, Class, and Power in the Rural South during the First World War* (Chapel Hill: University of North Carolina Press, 2004), 85.

41. "Senators Leaning to Labor Draft," *New York Times*, March 3, 1918, p. 6.

42. Weller, 80.

43. Marybelle Donavan, "Woodrow Wilson's Relations with the Democratic Party, 1919–1924" (MA thesis, Loyola University Chicago, 1936), 20; online at http://ecommons.luc.edu/luc_theses/464 (accessed February 27, 2015).

44. "Need War Cabinet If We Would Win, Says Hitchcock," *New York Times*, February 5, 1918, p. 1.

45. Ibid.

46. "Senators Demand One-Man Air Control of Air Program," *New York Times*, April 11, 1918, p. 1.

47. Calvin R. Ledbetter Jr., "The Other Caraway: Senator Thaddeus Caraway," *Arkansas Historical Quarterly* 64 (Summer 2005): 132.

48. Ibid., 129–30.

49. Weller, 80.

50. Donavan, 29.

51. Berg, 504.

52. House Election History, http://history.house.gov/Institution/Party-Divisions/Party-Divisions/ (accessed November 4, 2014); Senate Election History, http://www.senate.gov/pagelayout/history/one_item_and_teasers/partydiv.htm (accessed November 4, 2014).

53. Weller, 81.

54. Weller, 82–83.

55. Michael A. Nelson, "Arkansas and the League of Nations Debate," *Arkansas Historical Quarterly* 56 (Summer 1997): 187.

56. Ibid., 187–88.

57. Nelson, 188.

58. Weller, 82.

59. Nelson, 188.

60. Fry, 172

61. Nelson, 188.

62. Ibid.

63. Ledbetter, 131.

64. "Lest We Forget," *Jonesboro Daily Tribune*, June 29, 1920, p. 2.

65. Ledbetter, 131.

66. Ibid, 131–32.

67. Niswonger, 263.

68. Ledbetter, 132.

Chapter 7

"A Service That Could Not Be Purchased": Arkansas's Mobilized Womanhood[1]

By Elizabeth Griffin Hill

In 1917, Arkansas's women had numerous distractions that could have drawn their attention away from their war work. For example, prominent suffragists visited Arkansas to rally support for passage of the Nineteenth Amendment to the U.S. Constitution. The Arkansas General Assembly in 1917 passed a law allowing Arkansas's women to vote for the first time in state primaries—if they had paid their poll tax. Telephone operators in Fort Smith and Little Rock walked off their jobs at Southwestern Bell Telephone Company as labor organizers encouraged them from the sidelines. Well-to-do women read syndicated columnists' recommendations as to the appropriate attire to purchase and wear during war time. Mothers puzzled over changing expectations and mores among their teenaged and young adult daughters' generation.[2]

However, Arkansas's women were perhaps the original multi-taskers. During the eighteen months in which the United States was engaged in active warfare in Europe, they gardened, canned, made cottage cheese, baked war bread, scrimped on sugar, learned war cookery, used leftovers, knitted and sewed for the troops, filled unfamiliar jobs, and made do. They also sold more than $14.5 million of war bonds, mostly through door-to-door canvassing to reach small donors. All of their patriotic efforts were for "the boys"[3] who were fighting in the trenches in France and to provide adequate food for the nation and its allies.

For its part—by establishing the National Council of Defense— the federal government had managed to create an army of volunteers throughout the country to carry on the government's work in support of its military and the many requirements of those remaining at home. In so doing, the government was able to standardize the states' contributions to the war effort, raise millions of dollars to fund the military, eliminate duplication of effort, and choreograph—and thus control—the activities of its citizens. By including women in the mix, the government had tapped into a segment of society that was organized, trained, and available for service.[4]

By April 1917, Arkansas's women had been working together for the betterment of their own communities for several decades. Women's historians have called the late nineteenth and early twentieth centuries "a veritable golden age of women's organizations, which multiplied rapidly in both number and membership and among every class, race, ethnicity, and region."[5] Social and benevolent organizations in every county collaborated under the umbrella of the Arkansas Federation of Women's Clubs, which had its own page in the *Arkansas Gazette* each Sunday.

According to an archival history of the organization through 1934, "The club women having had training in their different organizations were the leaders in all the work accomplished."[6] The simple fact is that the Arkansas Federation of Women's Clubs' communications structure, which was already in place throughout the state's seventy-five counties, made possible a significant, coordinated wartime effort by Arkansas's women.

Arkansas Woman's Council Organizes

On April 21, 1917, the Council of National Defense appointed the Woman's Committee of the Council of National Defense. The next step was for states to organize their own woman's councils. On July 1, Governor Charles H. Brough appointed the Woman's Committee, Council of Defense for Arkansas ("Arkansas Woman's Committee"), with his wife, Anne, as honorary chairman and Ida Frauenthal of Conway as temporary chairman. Eventually, other members of the Executive Committee were appointed, including six officers and sixteen departmental chairmen. Frauenthal became permanent chairman and received her appointment as the only woman member of the Arkansas Council of Defense as well.

Chairmen were responsible for the departments of legislation, child welfare, registration, food administration, home economics, health and recreation, publicity, training for service, education, women in industry, and home and foreign relief, as well as maintenance of existing social service agencies, the speaker's bureau, Liberty Loans, War Savings Stamps, and Americanization. The list of departments speaks eloquently to the variety and extent of the women's work.[7]

Even before the Arkansas Woman's Committee met for the first time, however, it was tasked with a huge responsibility. In a letter to chairmen of the state councils of defense, dated June 22, the National Woman's Committee provided instructions as to women's role in a food-conservation campaign scheduled to begin July 1—just nine days hence. Because of an unintentional leak to the press, there was obvious scrambling in Washington DC to get the campaign under way, despite the states' lack of preparation for such an endeavor. A portion of the letter provides insight into the national food situation during the summer of 1917 as well as an early glimpse into the federal government's methods of maintaining control over the citizenry:

It is literally true that there will not be enough food in the world to maintain the population if present methods are followed. Founded upon this fact, the program for food conservation is briefly stated as follows:

1st An exact survey of the amount of food on hand in this country, so that the amount available for home consumption and exportation to the allies may be accurately known.

2nd An investigation undertaken by the Department of Agriculture into the normal consumption of food by different families from representative groups of the population.

3rd Some control of food in storage, better methods of transportation, and the elimination of speculation in foodstuffs.

4th The enrollment of a league of women who will pledge themselves to carry out the wishes of the President, the National Government, and the Food Administration.

The last part of the program will be the first to be put into operation, and from July 1st to July 15th an intensive campaign will be undertaken through every possible medium of publicity. This is intended to create such a sentiment in favor of the Food Administration program that women throughout the country will gladly sign the pledge cards and promise to carry out the instructions of the Food Administration.[8]

The letter continued, noting that "since this matter chiefly concerns women, it is clear that leadership must in a large measure be given over to the women themselves."[9] The letter also stressed that the entire woman's committee of each state must work together on the food pledge campaign, even though there had likely been no time to appoint a chairman of food conservation—in other words, appointments could come later.[10]

An article that appeared on the Arkansas Federation of Women's Clubs' page of the Sunday, June 24, *Arkansas Gazette* announced a call for the heads of all women's societies throughout the state to attend an organizational meeting of the Arkansas Woman's Committee of the Council of National Defense at the Hotel Marion in Little Rock on Monday, July 2. At the meeting, twenty-five women learned of the impending campaign to register housewives for food conservation. By signing the cards, women would pledge to follow the federal government's conservation guidelines. Arkansas's goal was to send 250,000 signed cards to Herbert Hoover, national food administrator.[11]

As the one-day meeting continued, the women elected six permanent officers and the chairmen of three of the sixteen departments: education, welfare of women and children, and registration. Selection of other department chairmen was deferred to the executive committee. However, two women were appointed to confer with the representative of the army camp entertainment committee and with Governor Brough, "in an effort to protect the boys of the camp and the girls of the town and state from prostitution."[12] This concern continued throughout the war, particularly in Little Rock and North Little Rock, as citizens and governments accepted their roles as cantonment cities.[13]

Food Conservation Pledge Drive Takes Place

The Arkansas Woman's Committee's newly elected officers—selected from among the state's leading club women—wasted no time in organizing for the food pledge drive. Thirteen days later, an article appearing on the women's club page of the Sunday, July 15, *Arkansas Gazette*, explained the purpose and functions of the Arkansas Woman's Committee as well as the food pledge drive, including the organization in each county down to the township and school-district level. The registration date had been scheduled for Saturday, July 28, and the list of seventy-five county chairmen was published in the newspaper—for the benefit of those who did not receive a personal letter. Women were advised to look for their names on the list of county chairmen and then begin organizing immediately. Those who were unable to serve were directed to find a willing substitute. The article addressed the need for food conservation as follows:[14]

> Only a few reasons for this may be given: That we are to be called upon to feed the greater part of the world, and that at a time when something like one-fifth of our workers will be called into army camps and into industries that supply war materials, such as munitions and war vessels of all kinds; that the allies have food enough to last until September, only; that a soldier fed in France, means one less American soldier sent to France; that Belgian babies are carefully examined to see if they can live without being fed today, while our relief workers feed those who were not fed the day before, and that without a campaign of education to the situation, we may continue to waste our crumbs.[15]

Surely such compelling words would stir Arkansas's women to participate fully in this patriotic endeavor.

According to Emma Archer, chairman of the Food Administration Department, each county chairman appointed township chairmen throughout the county and ward chairmen throughout cities. Some women, however, were hesitant to sign. Although complaints of insufficient information topped the list of reasons not to sign, other excuses included lack of interest; belief that one could economize without signing; fear that the government would take the canned goods; and, finally, concern that families would be forced to eat cornbread.[16]

In an August 16 letter to Wallace Townsend, the chairman of the State Council of National Defense, Frauenthal evaluated the campaign: "We are working hard with the Hoover cards but it is uphill work as there seems to be a decided objection to 'signing anything' and most of the women say that their husbands have cautioned them against putting their names to any sort of paper."[17]

Arkansans' fears about signing the food conservation pledge cards would be repeated later during the women's registration-for-service campaign.

Some other states were obviously well ahead of Arkansas in organizing their food pledge campaigns. A newspaper article with a Washington, July 7, dateline boasted that one million women had already signed the food pledge cards, were now enrolled as official members of the food administration, and would receive the following instructions on food conservation to post in their kitchens:

One wheatless meal a day. Use corn, oatmeal, rye or barley bread and non-wheat breakfast foods. Cut the loaf on the table and only as required. Eat less cake and pastry.

Beef, mutton or pork not more than once daily. Use freely vegetables and fish. At the meat meal serve smaller portions and stew instead of steaks. Make dishes of all leftover food.

Conserve the milk. The children must have milk. Use buttermilk and sour milk for cooking and making cottage cheese. Use less cream. Save the fats. Use butter on the table, but not in cooking. Reduce use of fried foods. Use less candy and sweet drinks, but do not stint [sic] sugar in putting up fruit and jams, they will save butter.

Save the fuel. Use wood when you can get it.

Fruits and vegetables we have in abundance. As a nation we eat too little greenstuffs. Double their use and improve your health. Store potatoes and other roots properly and they will keep. Begin now to can or dry all surplus garden products.

General rules: Buy less, serve smaller portions, preach the clean plate; don't eat a fourth meal; don't limit the plain food of growing children; watch out for the wastes in the community; full garbage pails in America mean empty dinner pails in America and Europe.[18]

Archer reported that 35,000 women signed food pledge cards through the efforts of the women of the state.[19]

Food Production and Conservation Program Continues

Although the Arkansas Woman's Committee was tasked with overall coordination of food conservation, its members turned to the home demonstration program of the Cooperative Extension Service for the day-to-day education of the state's women. The fledgling Cooperative Extension Service—a collaboration between state land-grant colleges and the U.S. Department of Agriculture—was officially created by Congress through the Smith-Lever Act of 1914, with funding provided equally among three separate entities: county, state, and federal governments.[20]

The estimated value of food produced by women's home gardens, as well as family chickens and cows, was $500,000. During 1918, a total of 2,145 women received instruction in war cookery in sixty-eight home demonstration kitchens throughout the state. In less than three months' time, 1,003 women produced 18,000 pounds of cottage cheese, and in Crawford County alone, 700 women raised 100 fall chickens each, thus freeing up carloads of smoked meats to be sent to Europe.[21]

Women in Work Rooms Sew and Knit for U.S. Troops

For Arkansas's women, their food production and conservation activities were equaled only by their efforts to fill the fighting men's need for supplies. For leadership and guidance in constructing those supplies, women turned to the Red Cross work rooms in communities across the state. Early on in the war, the nation found itself unprepared to provide warm clothing for the thousands of men who would soon be mustered into service. The Red Cross coordinated and standardized much of the volunteer work required to clothe America's soldiers. Although women's organizations retained their social connections with their members, Arkansas's women cooperated under the auspices of the Red Cross to knit or sew for troops as they prepared to be sent to the battle front in France. The Woman's Missionary Union of the Arkansas Baptist State Convention, various chapters of the Daughters of the American Revolution, and members of the National Society of Colonial Dames of America, to name only a few representative groups, reported that their members spent untold hours in the work rooms to provide hospital supplies and knitted socks, sweaters, and wristlets for the fighting men.[22]

By June 1917, Arkansas's women were making thousands of pieces of hospital supplies as U.S. troops prepared to sail for France. In Little Rock, the Gus Blass and M. M. Cohn companies' display windows exhibited complete outfits needed for hospitalized soldiers. A newspaper article explained:

> One complete outfit consists of six sheets, four draw shirts, two spreads, four pillow cases, four pajama suits, three hospital bed shirts, one convalescent gown, four pairs of socks, two pairs bed socks, four bath towels, three face towels, one wash cloth, one pair slippers, one hot water bag cover, one ice water bag cover and six handkerchiefs.[23]

Thus, each hospitalized soldier required forty-six pieces of sewn or knitted supplies, thousands of which were made in Red Cross work rooms throughout Arkansas.

By late August, the Red Cross sent a rush order to its work rooms for knitted articles for soldiers on the front lines in France. The urgent request noted that U.S. and allied soldiers would suffer from the bitter cold during the winter, partly because of a lack of warm housing accommodations. Soldiers would need warm clothing next to their bodies—particularly woolen socks, sweaters, and wristlets. The letter requested that work rooms engaged in making surgical supplies switch immediately to knitting clothing articles instead. Women who were not part of an organized work room were asked to knit according to the Red Cross instructions published in the news article.[24]

In the meantime, the Navy League of the United States saw a need that its members could meet and immediately sent out representatives to establish branches in every state. The Arkansas branch's specific goal was to enlist recruits to prepare comfort kits and to knit woolen garments for the 1,600 men, including officers, of the USS *Arkansas* (BB-33). The organization was able to provide each crew member with a knitted sweater, helmet, and wristlet before December 1, 1917. Most of the organization's work ended as the Red Cross took charge of the bulk of knitting operations at the beginning of 1918. All in all, the Arkansas Chapter of the Navy League knitted about 6,000 garments.[25]

In early December, the St. Louis district of the Red Cross, which encompassed Arkansas, received orders to provide 600,000 surgical dressings—which were different from pads already being made—to be received in New York by January 1 for shipment to France. In order to meet the deadline, Arkansas's work rooms' hours were increased to include evening work as well as the daytime schedule.[26]

Arkansas's Women Take Unfamiliar Jobs

The summer of 1917 brought newspaper accounts of Arkansas's women training for and entering newly opened fields of employment. At Hardy, a military training camp for women and girls from Arkansas, Mississippi, and Tennessee provided training in military, hospital, and Red Cross work. Classes were held in home nursing, surgical dressing, fever nursing, dietetics, bacteriology, anatomy, first aid, life-saving, battalion drill, setting-up drill, and target practice. The two-week camp was approved by the American Red Cross; students completing the course were given certificates enabling them to volunteer to the government for Red Cross work.[27]

Women were filling other nontraditional roles as well. During the war, almost 1,000 Arkansas women worked in box factories, planing mills, sawmills, and certain lines of office and railroad work. Although women were urged to accept their patriotic duty by filling vacated positions, the process was not always smooth. At the Missouri Pacific Railroad's Fort Smith Crossing, fifteen yard clerks quit their jobs because nine women had been hired to labor alongside them. According to the general superintendent, the men said they were afraid the women might hear objectionable language. In Little Rock, the streetcar manager—who had announced two days previously his plans to hire women as conductors—purchased a large advertisement in which he assailed those who considered any honest employment to be beneath women's standards.[28]

Registration-for-Service Campaign Begins

By January 1918, women's leaders were chiding America's women to do more for their country. In a newspaper article on January 20, Florence King, a Chicago, Illinois, lawyer and president of the Woman's Association of Commerce of the United States of America, made her message clear: "Wake up, women, it's war."[29] King continued:

> Lots of women are knitting. Very well, but many of them have got to drop that to attend to wounded, grow food, enter business

and keep the factory wheels moving. I have little patience with able-bodied women who are content just to knit. Leave that to the women with children they cannot leave and to semi-invalids.[30]

In another section of the same Sunday newspaper, Lettie Dodge Gibson, president of the Arkansas Federation of Women's Clubs, rebuked the state's club women for not doing all they could do.[31]

Concurrently, the Arkansas Woman's Committee's Department of Registration was planning a women-only registration-for-service campaign. Governor Brough set aside February 18–26, 1918, as Registration Week. The registration cards were intended "to indicate the chief usefulness of the women of Arkansas in this crisis, to give strength to the government and mobilize the spiritual resources that did much to help prosecute this righteous war."[32] Although ten counties failed to turn in any cards, 43,000 Arkansas women registered for service. The complete report sent to Washington after the war showed total numbers registered in each of 155 trades and professions. Jobs were sorted into eight broad categories:[33]

Number Registered	Category
12,245	Agriculture, home gardens, apple picking, cotton picking, etc.
6,625	Clerical
32,237	Domestic
4,657	Trained for social service
3,576	Industrial
5,112	Professional
1,912	Public service, mail routes, telephone, telegraph
5,259	Red Cross work

As a result of the census, clerical help was supplied to local exemption boards, and stenographers were secured for businesses; retired teachers were located to help fill vacancies created as regular teachers took higher-paying professional positions; and practical nurses were placed at the disposal of the State Board of Health during the Spanish influenza crisis in the fall of 1918. However,

[t]he State only showed a ten per cent registration, many of the registrars reporting they could not induce the women of their county to register on account of the many false rumors spread that if women registered they would be conscripted. Many men refused to permit their wives to register, and although great publicity was given to the movement, it was met with half-hearted response and grave doubts.[34]

Just as in the food conservation registration the previous summer, women often exhibited fear of the government and refused to sign the cards.

Organizations Work as Advocates and Protectors for Women

By the end of July 1917, the state labor department had received reports that women were performing light duties in several sawmills throughout the state. This practice was not in violation of state labor laws regarding the employment of women, so long as the women did not work more than nine hours each day. However, the general manager of a lumber company in Kensett requested approval to hire women for ten hours of light duty a day, noting the women's willingness to work the extended hours. The deputy labor commissioner refused to allow more than nine hours' work. Instead, he cited a request from the Woman's Council of the National Board of Defense, asking the state agency "to rigidly enforce the laws relative to the protection of Women in Industry. The council takes the position that to grant longer hours would be drawing upon the vitality of future generations, and that at this time it is imperative to conserve not only the national resources, but the human as well." Thus, at the request of the National Woman's Council, the state government chose to protect women by limiting their hours of work. [35]

As the state Women in Industry department of the Arkansas Woman's Committee became functional, it was tasked with overseeing female employees to ensure that they were placed "where they would render most efficient service."[36] Women were urged to remain in their own localities, to stay in their positions without changing from one to another, and, in general, to prevent unrest among workers. The Women in Industry department was also charged with advocating for women and thus focused on ensuring appropriate working conditions. In a measure that strengthened the department, Governor Brough appointed Mary H. McCabe, state chairman of the Women in Industry department, as Secretary of Minimum Wage and Maximum Hour, an action that provided McCabe authority to meet the needs of Arkansas's women in the workforce.[37]

McCabe and her department labored to ensure that the Minimum Wage and Maximum Hour Law was enforced throughout the state. Partial inspections were made in Little Rock, Fort Smith, Fayetteville, Pine Bluff, and eight other cities. Findings and awards were made to women employed in laundries, restaurants, telephone companies, basket factories, millinery establishments, retail stores, cigar factories, hotels, and candy factories. Reports of findings of the commission were forwarded to the National Consumer League, among others. In her final report, McCabe noted:[38]

> The demand for the Minimum Wage and Maximum Hour Law is an expression of awakened social conscience of the people of Arkansas. Thinking men and women are everywhere realizing the individual and social menace of the low wage, and demanding that it be made possible for able-bodied, willing women to earn their living by their day's work.

The right to earn a living and the right to live are indistinguishable terms. We are told that wages of women need not be adequate for their support, as many of the girls and women live at home. When this fact is given by the employer, he admits he is not paying a living wage, as the brother or father has to supply what he refuses to pay.[39]

The Young Women's Christian Association (YWCA) advocated for women in the workplace as well. The organization was concerned that young women in first-time jobs—who were excited to earn any wage— might be exploited in the name of patriotism. An article in the weekly *Y.W.C.A. News*, dated April 3, 1918, insisted that responsible women in the community who were not knowledgeable of industrial situations had to educate themselves in order to make industrial situations right and fair for those who entered into employment.[40]

Cantonment Cities Create Special Needs

As has been noted, the Arkansas Woman's Committee wasted no time in appointing two women to confer with a representative of the army camp entertainment committee and with Governor Brough, "in an effort to protect the boys of the camp and the girls of the town and state from prostitution."[41] The cantonment cities of Little Rock and North Little Rock were of paramount concern as plans were made and perfected to build Camp Pike near North Little Rock. Women took an active role in attempting to alleviate issues of sexual and moral impropriety.[42]

On September 19, 1917, representatives of thirty-five central Arkansas organizations, including the Board of Commerce, Ministerial Alliance, women's clubs, and church groups, met in the gymnasium of the YWCA to form the Health and Recreation Association—an entity separate from the Arkansas Woman's Committee. All officers and committee chairmen for the new organization were women. Chairmen of committees on chaperones, curfew, city mothers, and mass meeting were appointed. The committee on chaperones also named presidents of all school improvement associations as members.[43]

The Reverend J. D. Hammons assured the women that they would have the cooperation of the Little Rock police department. Rev. Hammons commented that at Ministerial Alliance meetings, businessmen had expressed disapproval of the clothing in which many women appeared on the streets. In response, Annie Griffey, primary supervisor of the Little Rock schools, led a discussion on "chaperonage," which would be the primary work of the association. According to the newspaper article:

Miss Griffey emphasized the fact that it is necessary for each mother to protect her daughter. She spoke of the crowded condition in the city schools as evidence of the great influx of new residents in the city. She said that not only should girls be chaperoned on the streets after 6 o'clock in the evening and riding in autos—but [we] need to keep them off the streets on Sunday afternoons. "A short time ago," she said, "there was a sentiment in Little Rock against allowing a group of young girls to go laughing and chatting down Main Street, unchaperoned, on Sunday afternoons. Now, often, young girls from some of the best homes may be seen on the street unchaperoned on Sunday afternoon." Soldiers are no worse than other men, Miss Griffey said. "Girls should be chaperoned at any time when there are likely to be groups of idle men on the streets."[44]

As the discussion continued, the women talked about the need for a curfew—not as a law but as "an expression of sentiment"[45] because it was "bad form"[46] for young girls to be out alone after the streetlights were on. The women agreed that a speaker's bureau was needed to inform mothers in every school of the need to chaperone their daughters. Jennie Erickson, a probation officer, noted several cases of girls who had gone out without adult supervision, and she suggested that the women who were present endeavor to influence other mothers to keep watchful eyes over their own daughters.[47]

While the newly formed Health and Recreation Association sought to educate the community's mothers of the need to protect their daughters, employees of the Little Rock YWCA and volunteers were active in the cities—protecting, comforting, and guiding women of all ages as they came to central Arkansas in search of jobs, to be with their loved ones in military service, or for less laudatory purposes. In the December 19, 1917, edition of its weekly *Y.W.C.A. News*, the Little Rock organization provided a narrative of the situation: "What a challenge to us as Y.W.C.A. members, living in a cantonment city brings! Do you see around you the things that need righting, the needs of a city full of girls, a responsibility toward the 'little sisters' and the strangers daily thronging our streets?"[48]

In the General Secretary's Report for calendar year 1917, May F. Conway noted that, beginning in August, the army situation and the constant stream of young women into the city "brought a realization of war's effect upon the womanhood of the Nation."[49] The YWCA thus opened its doors wide for Red Cross classes and women's lodging, as well as for religious, social, educational, and recreational activities. In September, the organization sent its initial request to the YWCA's national office for the establishment of a Hostess House at the newly built Camp Pike. By December, the lovely house had been dedicated, and the assigned YWCA employees and volunteers from local women's organizations were providing comfort and guidance to hundreds of women visiting loved ones at the military post.[50]

Perhaps the greatest task before the organization, however, was aiding the thousands of women and girls who came by railroad to the city. Although many of the travelers had come to visit soldiers at Camp Pike, others thronged the city in search of jobs:

> After the declaration of war, and the beginning of the great demand
> for Red Cross workers, young girls came to the city without funds,
> friends, or knowledge of what the work meant. It was our duty to
> send those who could not secure employment back to their homes.
> A number of girls who could do other work were placed in desirable
> positions and are now self-reliant and independent.[51]

Four travelers' aid matrons were on duty at two railroad stations—as
they had been during the previous six years—but the increase in workload
was staggering. During the year 1916, a total of 10,918 women and girls
were aided; however, for 1917, the number had more than doubled to
22,803. Beginning March 1, 1918, the Red Cross began paying the salaries
for two additional matrons to serve at the Iron Mountain and Rock Island
stations. The six matrons had police authority, and their salaries were
paid by contributions from the City of Little Rock, the YWCA Board of
Directors, several local churches, the Rock Island and Missouri Pacific
railroads, and the Red Cross.[52]

The matrons were on eight-hour shifts, twenty-four hours a day. They
provided assistance to all travelers, but their reports were limited to the
girls, young women, and women with children whom they aided. The 1917
travelers' aid report provided insight into the situation in Little Rock as
it listed, in part, the matrons' assistance to 2,740 girls traveling alone;
1,071 women and children traveling alone; 1,543 girls and young women
accompanied or directed to hotels; 125 girls and young women protected
from the attentions of strangers; eleven insane and 266 sick cared for;
sixty-eight sent to United Charities; twenty-six inefficient unemployed
persuaded to return home; and fourteen accompanied or sent to police
station.[53]

Women in Counties Memorialize Their Contributions

Although the cantonment cities of central Arkansas had unique
situations with which women were confronted, women in counties
throughout Arkansas participated in the war work, and numerous counties
made significant contributions. Most county councils submitted reports,
which were included in the Report of the Woman's Committee, Council
of Defense for Arkansas, July 1, 1917–December 30, 1918. Each of the
county reports represented hours and days of work completed by women
of the county. In many instances, the reports were beautifully documented
accounts of the creativity and diligence of the women.[54]

Conclusion

Looking back from our vantage point nearly a century later, it would
be difficult to find much fault with our great-grandmothers' attempts to
help out the hungry people of Europe and the fighting men in the trenches.

As to their war efforts, Arkansas's organized women were not completely successful, but there were victories, too. Thousands of women refused to sign pledge cards for food conservation, yet individual women dutifully encouraged their families to clean their plates and avoid using the garbage pail. A disappointingly low number of women signed the service registration cards, yet the census provided names of retired teachers willing to fill classroom positions as well as practical nurses to help during the influenza epidemic.

Women advocated for other women as they entered new jobs; attempted to give protection and guidance to young women as they came to the big city with its enticements; and gave comfort to wives, sweethearts, and mothers as they visited their loved ones at the military post. Additional thousands of women spent hours upon hours in Red Cross work rooms throughout Arkansas, sewing and knitting enormous numbers of supplies for American and allied soldiers and sailors. Perhaps a report from one northwestern Arkansas county helps put many of those women's efforts into context:

> "As chairman of the Boone county branch of the Arkansas division of the National Council of Defense I appointed chairmen for each school district and called a meeting at Harrison. About 25 district chairmen attended the meeting and a permanent organization was formed. To show the interest these women have taken in the movement, one woman rode for sixteen miles on horseback from the southern border of the county, and another came from the extreme northern section, 18 miles, in her little Ford, to attend the meeting," said Mrs. J. W. Andrews, vice president of the State Federation of Women's Clubs and chairman of the Boone County Council of Defense.[55]

1. Report of the Woman's Committee, Council of Defense for Arkansas, from July 1, 1917, to December 30, 1918 (hereafter cited as Report of the Arkansas Woman's Committee), 6; on file at Arkansas History Commission, Little Rock, Arkansas (hereafter, AHC/LR). In his tribute to the organization, Adjutant General Lloyd England stated, in part, "[The record of the woman's committee] shows how volunteer workers rendered a service that could not be purchased."

2. "Suffragists Will Speak Here Today," *Arkansas Gazette*, May 7, 1918; "Wright Defeated by Women's Vote," *Arkansas Gazette*, November 14, 1917; "Fort Smith Phone Girls Resume Work," *Arkansas Gazette*, November 6, 1917; "Phone Company to Seek Injunction," *Arkansas Gazette*, November 14, 1917; "Economy Idea in Clothes Gives Way to Simplicity," *Arkansas Gazette*, June 17, 1917; "Women Organize to Protect Girls," *Arkansas Gazette*, September 20, 1917.

3. The term "the boys" was used throughout primary sources in referring to U.S. military troops.

4. Report of the Arkansas State Council of Defense, May 22, 1917, to July 1, 1919, AHC/LR; Ida Clyde Clarke, *American Women and the World War* (New York: D. Appleton and Company, 1918), 18–19.

5. Kirsten Delegard, "Women's Movements, 1880–1890s," in *A Companion to American Women's History*, ed. Nancy A. Hewitt (UK: Blackwell Publishers, 2002), 328.

6. Frances Hanger and Clara B. Eno, "The Administration of Mrs. H. C. Gibson, 1917–

1919," *The Story of the AFWC 1897–1934*, UALR.MS.0056, Federation of Women's Clubs, Center for Arkansas History and Culture, University of Arkansas at Little Rock (hereafter, CAHC). (The authors noted that the organization "went over the top in every war measure and were often the first, notably the sending of sugar to the boys at the front.")

7. Report of the Arkansas Woman's Committee, unnumbered front matter. AHC/LR.

8. Letter, Woman's Committee, Council of National Defense, to chairmen, state councils of defense, June 22, 1917, File 234, Council of Defense Records, AHC/LR.

9. Ibid.

10. Ibid.

11. "Call for Heads of Women's Societies," *Arkansas Gazette*, June 24, 1917; "Women Organize to Save Food," *Arkansas Gazette*, July 8, 1917.

12. Ibid., July 8, 1917.

13. Ibid.

14. "Arkansas Women Called Into Service by State Division," *Arkansas Gazette*, Sunday, July 15, 1917.

15. Ibid.

16. Report of the Arkansas Woman's Committee, 15. AHC/LR.

17. Letter, Ida Frauenthal to Wallace Townsend, Chairman, State Council of National Defense, August 16, 1917, Folder 234, Council of Defense Records, AHC/LR.

18. "Directions How to Conserve Food," *Arkansas Gazette*, July 8, 1917.

19. Report of the Arkansas Woman's Committee, 14. AHC/LR.

20. Elizabeth Griffin Hill, *A Splendid Piece of Work 1912–2012: One Hundred Years of Arkansas's Home Demonstration and Extension Homemakers Clubs* (N.p.:2012), 31.

21. Report of the Arkansas Woman's Committee, 7–8. AHC/LR; 1918 Annual Narrative Report for Northwest District Home Demonstration Agent, Record Group 33, Arkansas Cooperative Extension Service, National Archives and Records Administration, Fort Worth, Texas.

22. Minutes, Thirtieth Annual Meeting of the WMU, April 10–12, 1918, Arkansas Baptist State Convention Collection, Riley-Hickingbotham Library Archives and Special Collections, Ouachita Baptist University, Arkadelphia, Arkansas; Arkansas Society of the Daughters of the American Revolution Collection, MSS 97-21, Box 1, File 2, Butler Center for Arkansas Studies, Central Arkansas Library System, Little Rock, Arkansas (hereafter, BC/CALS); National Society of Colonial Dames of America, 1899–1999. UALR.MS.0054, Box 3, File 1, Record Book, Vol. II, 1912–1925, CAHC.

23. "Make 700 Articles for Army Hospital," *Arkansas Gazette*, June 17, 1917.

24. "To Rush Knitting for the Soldiers," *Arkansas Gazette*, August 26, 1917.

25. Report of the Woman's Committee, 64–65. AHC/LR.

26. "Local Red Cross Has Rush Order," *Arkansas Gazette*, December 5, 1917.

27. "Training Camp for Women at Hardy," *Arkansas Gazette*, June 11, 1917.

28. Report of the Arkansas Woman's Committee, 16–17. AHC/LR; "Quit When Women Workers Appear," *Arkansas Gazette*, September 21, 1917; "No Honest Work is Derogatory to Woman," *Arkansas Gazette*, January 11, 1918.

29. "Declares Women Should Wake Up," *Arkansas Gazette*, January 20, 1918.

30. Ibid.

31. "Message from the A.F.W.C. President," *Arkansas Gazette*, January 20, 1918.

32. Report of the Arkansas Woman's Committee, 9. AHC/LR.

33. Ibid.

34. Ibid.

35. "Women Working in State's Sawmills," *Arkansas Gazette*, August 1, 1917.

36. Report of the Arkansas Woman's Committee, 16–17. AHC/LR.

37. Ibid.

38. Ibid.

39. Ibid.

40. "What of the Industrial Day," *Y.W.C.A. News*, April 3, 1918, Y.W.C.A. (Little Rock) Papers, 1911–1990, CAHC.

41. "Women Organize to Save Food," *Arkansas Gazette*, July 8, 1917.

42. Ibid.

43. "Women Organize to Protect Girls," *Arkansas Gazette*, September 20, 1917.

44. Ibid.

45. Ibid.

46. Ibid.

47. Ibid.

48. "Our Wartime Responsibility," *Y.W.C.A. News*, December 19, 1917, Y.W.C.A. (Little Rock) Papers, 1911–1990, CAHC.

49. "General Secretary's Report," *Y.W.C.A. News*, December 26, 1917, Y.W.C.A. (Little Rock) Papers, 1911–1990, CAHC.

50. Ibid.; Arkansas Society of the Daughters of the American Revolution, MSS 97-21, Box 1, File 2. BC/CALS.

51. "General Secretary's Report," *Y.W.C.A. News*, December 26, 1917. CAHC.

52. Ibid.

53. Ibid.; "Traveler's Aid Secretary's Report for Year 1917," *Y.W.C.A. News*, December 26, 1917. CAHC.

54. Report of the Arkansas Woman's Committee, 22–63. AHC/LR.

55. "16 Miles on Horseback," *Arkansas Gazette*, August 5, 1917.

Northeast Arkansas recruits Martin Grady (left) *and Ward Croft pose for a photograph at Camp Pike.* Photo courtesy of Mike Polston.

Herman Davis of Manila was included on a postwar list of the 100 best U.S. soldiers. His gravesite in Manila is an Arkansas state park. Photo courtesy of the Museum of American History, Cabot Public Schools.

Perry County recruit Paul Strassell's Selective Service registration card. Courtesy of Mike Polston.

In later life James H. Atkinson became a leader in the promotion of Arkansas history. Many in the field referred to him as "Mr. Arkansas History." Photo courtesy of Mike Polston.

*Contact with home was a major factor in maintaining
high morale for Arkansas soldiers.* Postcard courtesy of
Mike Polston.

Eberts Field airplane hangar. Photo courtesy of
the Butler Center for Arkansas Studies, Central
Arkansas Library System.

*Many Arkansas citizens caught
their first glimpse of an airplane
at Eberts Field.* Photo courtesy of
the Butler Center for Arkansas
Studies, Central Arkansas Library
System.

*Eberts Field, pilot
training school
at Lonoke.* Photo
courtesy of the
Butler Center for
Arkansas Studies,
Central Arkansas
Library System.

Camp Pike under construction, 1918. Photo courtesy of the Butler Center for Arkansas Studies, Central Arkansas Library System.

Many soldiers mailed comical photographs to loved ones remaining at home. Photo courtesy of the Butler Center for Arkansas Studies, Central Arkansas Library System.

Camp Pike, 1918. Photo courtesy of the Butler Center for Arkansas Studies, Central Arkansas Library System.

Camp Pike, 1918. Photo courtesy of the Butler Center for Arkansas Studies, Central Arkansas Library System.

New recruits board troop transport train at the Paragould depot, June 1918. Photo courtesy of the Butler Center for Arkansas Studies, Central Arkansas Library System.

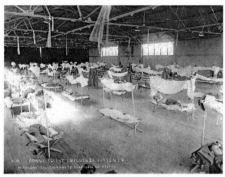

The 1918 flu pandemic took millions of lives worldwide. Patients convalesce at Eberts Field medical facility. Photo courtesy of the Butler Center for Arkansas Studies, Central Arkansas Library System.

The American Legion, a patriotic organization formed by Great War veterans, was chartered by the U.S. Congress in 1919. Among the many posts established in Arkansas was Gordon Gales Post 99 in North Little Rock. Photo courtesy of the Museum of American History, Cabot Public Schools.

Herman Davis memorial at Manila. Photo by Mike Polston.

Spirit of the American Doughboy sculpture by artist E. M. Viquesney was dedicated in 1930 by the Fort Smith American Legion Victor Ellig Post No. 31. Photo by Mike Polston.

Leon Kendall Bostwick was an actor in the early 1900s who enlisted during WWI and was a victim of the influenza pandemic in 1919. He seems representative of the vital young men who survived the war but were killed by the flu. Courtesy of Nancy Hendricks.

Chapter 8

Intolerance on the Homefront: Anti-German and Anti-Black Sentiment during the War Years and Beyond

By Shirley Schuette

World War I highlighted Arkansans' intolerance of two specific groups, ethnic Germans and African Americans, who both possessed a long history in the state. But there was a difference—prejudicial treatment of African Americans during the war was more a continuation of the oppression already in place than a response to issues directly related to the war, while wartime intolerance directed at people of German descent reflected distrust of their political loyalty and suspicion that their perceived loyalty to Germany was a threat to the United States.

In this time of Jim Crow laws, African Americans were discriminated against for reasons that had nothing to do with the war itself. The war merely provided a new venue for the ongoing struggle. At the same time, the war made some from the majority community consider moderation, at least in public statements. There was a need, expressed by both black and white leaders, to tone down routine expressions of animosity in order to ensure that African Americans would support the war effort and not use it as an opportunity to turn against their oppressors. Master John H. Harrison of the Masonic lodge in Pine Bluff expressed this need to encourage and appease when he said, "We are not stopping to discuss racial differences now, for when a foreign enemy approaches us, we are all one, and together we meet him and together we slay him, or together we die."[1]

Germans, on the other hand, were seen by the majority community as possibly having a stronger loyalty to the enemy than to the United States. In most cases, however, this was not the way German Americans themselves felt. Certainly, there would be struggles with actually engaging in battle with family members, should it come to that—especially among those who had immigrated more recently and still had strong ties to relatives still in Germany. For the most part, however, the political loyalty of German Americans was to their adopted country. After all, had they not left Germany in search of greater freedom and opportunity?

Negative attitudes toward the two groups came together at one point. Rumors abounded that German agents were attempting to persuade African Americans to support them in the war with promises for better treatment under a future German regime. A man from Magnolia, for example, was arrested for handing out German propaganda literature to African Americans in Columbia County in April 1917. Whites in Calhoun County were afraid that Germany was working through contacts in Mexico to stir up African Americans. Because of this, African Americans were arrested and told to stop holding meetings. Although they may not have stated it quite so frankly, the white majority feared that the anger of African Americans at the unjust treatment that defined their lives in the South was stronger than their political loyalty to their country.

Fear of Germans

Ironically, suspicions of disloyalty among people of German descent, felt from the president on down, led to laws that suppressed the very freedoms that drew immigrants to America. The Espionage Act of 1917, strengthened by the Sedition Act of 1918, outlawed speech, publications, or actions that would hinder military recruitment or other war-related activities. While public voices and official leadership often stressed tolerance within official channels, individual reaction and judgment frequently took the form of vigilante action. Disloyalty was frequently assumed, whether or not it had actually been demonstrated by German Americans. Small, relatively insignificant actions, such as declining to display a flag in a store window, were interpreted as signs that the individual was actively working in support of Germany and against the United States. Simply being of German descent or using the German language was often seen as proof of disloyalty and not infrequently met with violence.

The most prominent official voice to stress tolerance was the president himself. In his April 2, 1917, address to Congress asking for a declaration of war, President Woodrow Wilson acknowledged the challenge presented by the presence in the American population of many millions of people of German birth. America's fight, Wilson said, was with the German government and not the German people. As "the sincerer friends of the German people," Americans "shall desire nothing so much as the early reestablishment of intimate relations of mutual advantage between us." He called on Americans "to prove that friendship in our daily attitude and actions towards the millions of men and women of German birth and native sympathy who live amongst us and share our life."Americans of German birth, he continued, "are most of them, as true and loyal Americans as if they had never known any other fealty or allegiance....If there should be disloyalty, it will be dealt with with a firm hand of stern repression; but, if it lifts its head at all, it will lift it only here and there and without countenance except from a lawless and malignant few."[2]

In Arkansas, as in the rest of the country, native-born people always had a mixed reaction to the arrival of Germans, welcoming them in many ways and yet demonstrating fear and prejudice when Germans settled nearby, or when their numbers increased. On the positive side of this coin, in 1833, when a large group of German people arrived in Little Rock intending to settle in the state, *Arkansas Gazette* editor William Woodruff described the newcomers as being diligent and well educated. He encouraged Arkansans to welcome them and give them whatever assistance they needed. Following the Civil War, the state government recruited immigrants to help rebuild the state, and the railroads recruited them to settle the land and provide a customer base. These recruitment efforts reached out to Germans already settled in the United States, and also to German-speaking countries in Europe. Public relations pieces in the German language were published widely, and recruiters for the state and for the railroads traveled to Germany and Austria in search of immigrants.

This recruitment had modest success. The 1900 census recorded people of German birth in every county in the state, as well as German communities of significant size in several counties, especially along the route of the railroads and in the major cities.[3] The newcomers joined a small group of German Americans who had come to the state in the 1850s or who had returned to Arkansas after serving in the state during the Civil War.

The names of several businesses in Little Rock reflected this success in recruiting and also the respect often accorded businessmen of German descent. Papa Geyer's beer garden was for many years a popular gathering place, and German merchants controlled the grocery and bakery businesses in the city. When a new bank was formed in 1876, with German American Charles Penzel as president, it was named the German National Bank "largely because Germans were perceived in Arkansas in the late nineteenth century as thrifty, dependable, and trustworthy in financial matters."[4] John Gould Fletcher, in his history of Arkansas, lauded the German influence on the business and social community of Little Rock. Mardi Gras, a celebration first held by the German Turnverein, had grown by the early years of the twentieth century to be a highly anticipated social event.[5]

For three years beginning in 1908, Arkansas's German community followed the example of German-American communities around the country in celebrating German Day. First held in Philadelphia in 1883, the celebration marked the first German colony established in the New World, in October 1683. It also acknowledged the contributions of Germans to American society, as well as the loyalty of German Americans to their adopted homeland. According to Carl Schurz—a German revolutionary, Civil War general, and U.S. senator and diplomat—speaking at the St. Louis Exposition:

> German Day in the United States is the celebration of the friendship of the German and the American people. The German-Americans are the hyphen between Germany and America, presenting the living demonstration that a large population may be transplanted from one to another country, and may be devoted to the new fatherland for life and death, and yet preserve a reverent love for the old.[6]

The 1909 German Day in Arkansas was a cooperative effort of the German Roman Catholic Staatsverband (the Catholic Union of Arkansas) and the German-American Alliance of Arkansas. The alliance was formed on June 9, 1909, with the stated purpose to "protect the personal freedom and the freedom of conscience of the German Americans in Arkansas."

Essays in the 1908 and 1909 Arkansas German Day programs explored the reasons for the celebration in Arkansas. The author (probably Carl Meurer, editor of the German-language *Arkansas Echo*, which published the program) gave several reasons, among them the desire of the German people to express pride in their language and heritage, both to the community and to their children. However, the alliance felt strongly that Arkansas's political leaders had betrayed them. They had first persuaded Germans to come to Arkansas because it would be a good place to grow grapes, but the prohibition movement in the state and nation threatened to make viniculture impossible. The German community saw prohibition as a threat to their social and cultural life. Members of the German community also wanted to set the historical record straight, the author continued, as they felt that many historians failed to record their contributions, and, particularly, they wanted to document the fact that as faithful American citizens, they had supported the United States in peace and in war.[7] Such efforts to defend Arkansas's Germans continued throughout the war.

The German community in Little Rock at the time when World War I began was centered in St. Edwards Catholic Church and First Lutheran Church, both founded in the years following the end of the Civil War. Arkansas also supported two German-language newspapers, the *Arkansas Echo*, which had a strong connection to the German Catholic community, and the *Arkansas Staatszeitung*, strongly connected the Lutheran community. The third element of the German community was the German Jewish immigrant community.

The basic mistrust of all German immigrants, perhaps because of their nationality and perhaps because of their religion, was ongoing. Once the German Catholic communities were established, for instance, rumors abounded that weapons were stored in church basements, awaiting an order from the pope. With the coming of the war, this distrust was fed by other official voices, urging Americans to be on the lookout for elements within their communities that would be trying to undercut the war efforts.

The National Council of Defense, established by Congress in August 1916, provided publicity material to state and local councils to coordinate the message to citizens regarding support of the war. The Arkansas Council of Defense, which met for the first time within days of the official declaration of war, passed this information along through press releases and public speaking opportunities. The council was tasked with coordinating activity related to the war effort. Its mission included "the suppression of disloyalty and sedition..., [serving as] guardians of patriotism and civilian morale..., [stopping] sedition at home by reporting enemies of the Government to those legally in authority..., [applying] the lash of [local] condemnation to those who give aid and comfort to the enemy through failure to give their time, money or labor to the cause of the nation."[8] Council members called upon the public to help them by reporting those who failed to meet their high standard of loyalty.

The Council of Defense was active in a wide range of activities seen as critical to the war effort. What is of particular note here is the formation of the Americanization Committee, given responsibility for identifying "enemy aliens," which were non-citizens among the population who could be influencing others to resist war efforts in the community. Arkansas's committee identified three non-English-speaking communities of sufficient size to warrant oversight: in the western areas of the Arkansas River Valley, in Prairie County, and in Little Rock. Five Little Rock citizens who were part of the German community were appointed by the committee to spread patriotic education. They were the Reverend A. H. Poppe of the German Evangelical Lutheran Church (later First Lutheran); businessmen August Probst, Fred Rossner, and Andrew Karcher; and newspaperman Carl Meurer of the *Arkansas Echo*.

The Americanization Committee kept close watch on the German-speaking community, even to the point of asking libraries to remove books from their shelves that were perceived to be pro-German. Little Rock librarian Beatrice Prall thanked the council in a July 1918 letter for providing the list of books, saying, "I am very glad to receive an authentic list of such books, and by its aid we were able to remove a few books that we had not known about."[9]

The *Arkansas Echo* was unique among German-language newspapers nationwide in that it continued to publish through the war; in fact, it published through 1932, when longtime editor Meurer died. The fact that Meurer served on the Council of Defense Americanization Committee may have influenced the newspaper's survival. The *Arkansas Staatszeitung* was not so fortunate, however; its last issue was published on August 10, 1917, the day after editor Curtis Ackerman was arrested and charged with obstructing enlistments and encouraging disloyalty. He was charged under Title I, Section 3, of the Espionage Act, passed by Congress on June 15, 1917. This law prohibited speech or action that would interfere with the military or with recruitment or that would in any way encourage disloyalty or refusal of duty.

Curtis Ackerman was born on May 4, 1875, in Gera, Germany. He served two years in the German army before emigrating, arriving in the United States in October 1907. As required by law, he registered with the German Consul in St. Louis, Missouri, on August 7, 1914. Ackerman applied for naturalization as an American citizen on March 13, 1917, in Little Rock.

Ackerman served as editor of the *Arkansas Staatszeitung* for about five years. Few copies of it have survived, but one that has is the final one, issued August 10, 1917, the day following the editor's arrest. On the issue's editorial page, Ackerman gave a brief description of what had happened and expressed his surprise and confusion over the events of the previous week. Articles in the *Arkansas Gazette* gave brief descriptions of

Ackerman's trial, which took place in early September.

Charles Weber, an employee of the *Arkansas Gazette* and a friend of Ackerman, testified that the newspaperman had offered to give him a powder that would make him appear sick when he was called up for his draft physical. In addition, the prosecutor, Assistant District Attorney W. H. Rector, charged that an August 2 article in the *Staatszeitung* violated the Espionage Act by directly encouraging resisting the draft. The offending article criticized the president of Union Trust Company for taking out ad space to welcome a visiting Belgian commission to Little Rock, stating, according to a report in the *Arkansas Gazette*, that "the Belgians are a brutal people and that the Germans are not."[10] Unfortunately, the August 2 issue of the newspaper did not survive, and so the actual content of the editorial is not available today.

The only source for information on the incident from Ackerman's point of view is the editorial he wrote for the final issue of the *Staatszeitung*. Ackerman opened his August 10 editorial with a quote from Thomas Paine: "These are the times that try men's souls." "We want to press the hand of the righteous man," he wrote, "no matter what his ideology. And together we will fight the good fight, the fight for truth and right." This is how Ackerman saw himself, fighting for the truth:

> The affair with the Union Trust Company has really stirred up the dust. We have presented the facts and given our view of them, but not given advice on what should be done. This we have left to the good sense of our fellow citizens. They have acted, and we are proud of them. Not everyone belongs to the poor souls who put up with anything....But this thing has blown up terribly, and the anger of resulting criticism is enormous. We have been arrested. We will report details about this in our next number.[11]

Ackerman was not able to keep his promise to report about his arrest, because, of course, there was not another issue of the paper. Initially freed on bond, Ackerman was found guilty of the charges in his September trial and held in the county jail. The Espionage Law provided for a punishment of a fine and imprisonment, but because Ackerman was not a citizen of the United States but of Germany, he was also held as an enemy alien and his punishment was determined by the Justice Department. At that agency's direction, he was first transferred to Fort Roots in North Little Rock and then interned at Fort Oglethorpe and Fort McPherson, Georgia. The sentence was for the duration of the war, but many internees were not released for many months after the armistice.

Ackerman's wife and daughter moved to Chattanooga, Tennessee, where he had family, at the end of October 1917, following his internment. After the war, he initially requested to be paroled to Chattanooga, assuring officials that he would not return to his work as a journalist. His family was destitute, he said, and he needed to work to support them. When this request was denied, Ackerman decided to be repatriated. He was paroled on June 25, 1919, and on June 28 sailed for Rotterdam on the SS *Martha Washington*, under the sponsorship of the Swiss Legation. His wife, who had come to America at the age of two, and his daughter, who was born in the United States, accompanied him as he returned to Germany.[12]

Ackerman's experience was perhaps the most dramatic example of the prejudice and intolerance directed at Germans in the state. However, many other instances were reported. For example, business-owning members of the Lutheran church reported that formerly loyal customers refused to patronize their businesses; some individuals complained of personal attacks such as rocks thrown at their windows.

Two other voices in Arkansas can be seen as representative of the German community: the other German-language newspaper, the *Arkansas Echo*, and the *Southern Guardian*, predecessor to the *Arkansas Catholic*. The editors of both of these publications, given their European background, were able to provide well-thought-out analyses of the war. In the years before U.S. entry into the war, they generally expressed support for Germany, giving reasons for their statements. As it became obvious that the United States would not remain neutral, however, both editors expressed total support for America's war efforts and encouraged their readers to do the same.

Many examples could be given of accusations of German Americans supporting the enemy. Sometimes, however, the incidents that resulted in public charges were misunderstood or exaggerated in the retelling. For example, in April 1917, John Dorchich from Austria, while working at a stave mill in Bradley County, was arrested by a U.S. marshal. Several witnesses testified that he had told people about an offer of $200 to any who would enlist in the Austrian army. In court, Dorchich testified that he had merely read a newspaper article about the subject and talked to his friends about it. Charges against him were dismissed.

At the same time, a report came in to Governor Charles Brough from John R. Gibbons of Bauxite in Saline County that a Mr. Hoffman from the Collegeville area had raised a German flag over his home and was refusing to take it down. Considerable time passed while the governor tried to determine whether he could order a detail from the Arkansas Military Department to respond and demand the flag be taken down. In the meantime, some Bauxite residents decided to take matters into their own hands. However, when they arrived in the Collegeville area, they could find no one by the name of Hoffman, and no such flag flying. Adolph and John Hubman lived in the area, but they were Swiss, not German, and they had lived and done business there—even participating in local politics—for over thirty years.

In general, the German Americans in Little Rock and the rest of Arkansas made every effort to convince the larger community of their commitment to the United States and their determination to support the war effort. Shortly after the declaration of war, the Executive Committee of the German-American Federation of Arkansas, made up of more than forty local societies, passed a resolution and released it publicly, affirming that their oath of allegiance to the United States is a "sacred obligation": "We hereby renew our pledge of loyalty to support the government of this country and to assist in every way in our power to protect and maintain the present and future interest, honor and welfare of the people of the United States."

Such pronouncements, and indeed repeated examples of activity in strong support of war efforts on the part of Arkansans of German descent, could not silence the voices of intolerance and prejudice and the violent actions that too often resulted. Nevertheless, the great majority of the German people lived and served according to these promises of loyalty, possessing gratitude for the freedoms they now had as Americans.

Attitudes toward African Americans in Wartime

Official voices stressed that with America in a state of war, it was not the time to let longtime animosity and division rule. There is a threat from the outside, leaders said, and we must all work together to meet that threat. African Americans were also needed in the army. Black leaders echoed the official pronouncements from the white leaders: we are all Americans, this is our country, we must be willing to support the war effort and to fight for America. Black leadership speculated even before U.S. entry into the war that if African Americans supported the war effort—and were willing to fight to the death—whites could not help but grant them the freedoms they deserved.

Black Arkansans responded to the call to service. The Provost Marshal General's office reported that 33,217 white men were called up by the Selective Service in Arkansas and that 17,544 African American men were called. A number of black Arkansans participated in a ninety-day officer training camp in Des Moines, Iowa, and, on October 15, 1917, twelve were commissioned as officers—eight as second lieutenant and four as first lieutenant.[13]

Nevertheless, the discrimination common in civilian life continued in the military. While the law establishing the draft included African Americans, albeit with separate regiments, black soldiers were given the most menial work and were not allowed to be in command positions over white troops. Most southern whites agreed that blacks should be part of the draft and serve in the army but wanted this done within the framework of Jim Crow. Some, no doubt, feared the danger of putting guns in the hands of black soldiers.

The official policy of the War Department, that it would "brook no discrimination based upon race or color," was difficult to enforce.[14] Emmet Jay Scott, an associate of Booker T. Washington, served as special assistant for Negro Affairs to Secretary of War Newton D. Baker. He encouraged African Americans to consider first the needs of a country at war, with a promise that problems facing the black community could be dealt with when peace returned.

In the South, including at Camp Pike, there was resistance, in the military as well as civilian population, to the training and service of African American troops alongside white troops. While serving at Camp Pike, Captain Eugene C. Rowan, a white native of Georgia who then lived in Mississippi, refused a direct order to drill his troops alongside black troops. His defense was that this action would have destroyed the morale of the southern soldiers and reduced their efficiency. In May 1918, while Rowan awaited court-martial, the Mississippi Bar Association passed a resolution that it sent to the president, stating that "it is the sense of this Association that Captain Rowan has been guided in his conduct by the highest purposes and if punished at all, only the lightest penalty should be imposed."[15] This was indeed the outcome. Direct disobedience of an order was a serious offense and often carried severe punishment. Rowan was convicted, but his only punishment was to be discharged from the army. This was the first situation in which a white officer was charged with offenses that turned on the color question.[16]

Trouble came in some cases when African American soldiers from the North did not understand the restrictions of the South's Jim Crow system. A train carrying the Eighth Illinois, a black National Guard unit, stopped briefly in Jonesboro, Arkansas, on its way to Camp Logan in Texas. Walking in the town carrying their Springfield rifles, the black soldiers blew kisses at white girls and wrecked a store that refused to serve them. A black major and an armed guard prevented the local sheriff from boarding the train.[17]

The *Arkansas Gazette* attempted to provide a calming voice to encourage cooperation while both blacks and whites were being trained at Camp Pike. A September 6, 1917, editorial reminded readers that it was the policy of the War Department to train both groups at the same facilities, a policy they agreed with:

> The government could not afford to say in effect that it has not confidence enough in the discipline of its military establishment to train negro troops in the part of the country where most negroes live....If measures should be necessary against either whites or negroes to vindicate discipline and maintain peace and order, then let those measures be taken....The *Gazette* refuses to believe that the training of negro soldiers at Camp Pike involves any serious menace to the peace and order of Little Rock. We believe the good relations that have always existed between whites and negroes in this city, and generally speaking, throughout the state, will rule in this new situation.

A letter to the editor on September 8 from G. W. Hayman, a black doctor in Little Rock, agreed with the editorial: "The amicable relationship that has always existed between the races here will not be disrupted, we believe, by the training of negro soldiers....The negro is proud of being called to do his bit in defending Old Glory and will conduct himself as a soldier in an appropriate way." Both of these statements appear to reflect an optimistic view not in line with the reality of what was actually happening. At Camp Pike, as at other army posts in the South, barracks were segregated, and living conditions for the black soldiers were poor.

The National Council of Defense pressured states to also organize local councils within the black community, something that most southern states were reluctant to do. They feared that any statewide official organization within the black community would threaten their control. As in other areas, local leaders attempted to do the minimum possible to meet the requirements, while still being able to say they were providing adequately for the black people. To meet the request of the National Council of Defense to educate the black community about the need for support of the war effort, Arkansas gave P. L. Dorman, a black employee of the State Education Department, the task of visiting colored schools and giving patriotic talks. It was only in September 1918 that the Arkansas Council gave in and organized a "colored auxiliary State Council."[18]

Black church leaders, merchants, and leaders of black social and fraternal organizations were adamant in encouraging community members to do all the things presented as necessary to the war effort. This included such work as conserving food, purchasing Liberty Bonds, and sending material and contributions to the Red Cross.

African Americans called to action in response to the war effort did not easily step back into Jim Crow. After spending time outside of the South and even in Europe, the returning soldiers had seen what it was like to live where they did not have to step off the sidewalk when a white person approached them, where there were no signs restricting the use of public facilities, and where they were not automatically treated with hostility because of their dark skin.

Indeed, returning black soldiers were occasionally targeted by lynch mobs, with the year 1919 being a particularly brutal one for African Americans in the state. Frank Livingston of Union County, who had been stationed at Camp Pike for two years, was tied to a tree and set on fire by a mob on May 21, 1919, eighteen miles west of El Dorado for having allegedly murdered his employer, William Robertson Clay, as well as Clay's wife.[19] On June 13, 1919, Clyde Ellison was lynched at Star City for reportedly assaulting the daughter of a local farmer; however, reports that circulated nationally held that Ellison's real crime was refusing to work in the fields of local landowner David Bennett and that Bennett concocted the story, forcing his daughter to go along, in order to intimidate Ellison and his other workers.[20]

The incident that shows the extent to which whites could react with total violence to the slightest perceived transgression from returned black soldiers is probably the September 1, 1919, lynching of Clinton Briggs in Star City. Briggs, who had received the World War I Victory Medal and the World War I Victory Lapel Button, was walking down the sidewalk one day when he stepped aside to let a white couple pass. According to nationally distributed reports, the white woman brushed up against Briggs, saying, "Niggers get off the sidewalk down here," to which Briggs replied, "This is a free man's country." The woman's escort, incensed, seized Briggs until some associates could arrive with an automobile, after which he was driven out of town, chained to a tree, and shot. In response to this event, a Hot Springs newspaper editorialized: "For valor displayed in the recent war, it seems that the Negro's particular decoration is to be the 'double cross.'"[21]

But the year 1919 had more in store for returned black veterans. African Americans in Arkansas, as in other areas, had quickly realized that their white oppressors had no intention of changing the Jim Crow structure of southern life. They returned to Arkansas with more willingness to fight for their rights. In Phillips County, a group of black sharecroppers, some of whom had served in World War I, met on the evening of September 30, 1919, in a church at Hoop Spur. The organization behind the meeting was the Progressive Farmers and Household Union of America, which had been organizing sharecroppers in the area in order to get better payments for cotton crops from white landowners. Armed guards had been placed around the church in order to prevent the meeting being disrupted, but a shootout between these guards and three individuals in a vehicle that parked in front of the church resulted in the death of W. A. Adkins, a white security officer for the Missouri Pacific Railroad, as well as the wounding of a white deputy sheriff.

Soon, the alarm spread across the state and nation that African Americans in Phillips County were planning an "insurrection," intending to kill all of the county's whites. Some 500–1,000 armed whites, some from across the river in Mississippi, traveled to the area around Elaine in order to put down this rumored insurrection. Too, Governor Brough requested that the War Department send U.S. troops to the area, which permission was granted. More than 500 soldiers from Camp Pike, many of them having combat experience from World War I, traveled to Phillips County with the governor at the head, ostensibly to restore order. However, civil rights historian Grif Stockley asserts that these troops, like the mobs, probably participated in the indiscriminate murder of African Americans, along with engaging in acts of torture against black prisoners.[22]

Conclusion: German Americans and African Americans after the War

The number of African Americans killed in what has become known as the Elaine Massacre may number in the hundreds. Those deaths represent a particularly insidious nxus of race and class in America, especially as the Russian Revolution of 1917 sparked elite fears of Bolshevism in America, manifested most clearly in actions taken against labor unions. Of course, issues of race and class lay at the root of the American experiment. As has been observed by many scholars, European immigrants could eventually be integrated into the broader category of "white," a category that allowed general movement up into the middle class of American life.

Anti-German sentiment certainly arose in Arkansas, and the rest of the nation, during World War I, leading many German Americans to devote themselves to the project of Americanization all the more, so much so that few, if any, German-speaking communities survived in the state past the two world wars. The German desire to possess in full the rights and responsibilities of American citizens did not threaten the status quo to the extent that the same desire in African Americans did, and thus anti-German sentiment did not last as a cultural force past World War I. However, the attempt by black Americans not only to perform the responsibilities, but also to claim the rights, of full citizenship was a direct threat to the system of exploitation to which they were subject. It would be decades more—with bloodshed at home, rather than abroad—before the first tentative steps toward full citizenship on the part of African Americans could be achieved.

1. Quoted in Randy Finley, "Black Arkansans and World War One," *Arkansas Historical Quarterly* 49 (Autumn 1990): 258.

2. "U.S. Declaration of War with Germany, 2 April 1917," http://www.firstworldwar.com/source/usawardeclaration.htm (accessed October 25, 2014).

3. Shirley Sticht Schuette, "Strangers to the Land: The German Presence in Nineteenth-Century Arkansas" (MA thesis, University of Arkansas at Little Rock, 2005), 35.

4. Catherine Henderson, "German National Bank," *Encyclopedia of Arkansas History & Culture*, http://www.encyclopediaofarkansas.net/encyclopedia/entry-detail.aspx?entryID=5581 (accessed November 18, 2014).

5. John Gould Fletcher, *Arkansas* (Fayetteville: University of Arkansas Press, 1989), 223–24.

6. Quoted in Moritz Tiling, *German Element in Texas* (Houston, TX: 1913), 177–78.

7. Schuette, 130–34.

8. Austin L. Venable, "The Arkansas Council of Defense in the First World War," *Arkansas Historical Quarterly* 2 (Summer 1943): 119.

9. Gerald Senn, "Molders of Thought, Directors of Action: The Arkansas Council of Defense, 1917–1918," *Arkansas Historical Quarterly* 36 (Autumn 1977): 288.

10. Joseph Carruth, "World War I Propaganda and Its Effects in Arkansas," *Arkansas Historical Quarterly* 56 (Winter 1997): 393.

11. The editorial page is written partially in German and partially in English. Translation for the German portions are by this author.

12. RG 407, UD 56, WWI Prisons and Prisoners, 201 File for Kurt Ackermann (alias Curt), National Archives and Records Administration, Washington DC.

13. Emmett Jay Scott, *Scott's Official History of the American Negro in the World War* (Chicago: Homewood Press, 1919), 471; online at https://archive.org/details/scottsofficialhi00scot (accessed January 12, 2015).

14. Ibid., 102.

15. *Report of the Thirteenth Annual Meeting of the Mississippi Bar Association* 13 (1918): 15.

16. Scott, 104.

17. Gail Lumet Buckley, *American Patriots: The Story of Blacks in the Military from the Revolution to Desert Storm* (New York: Random House, 2002), 187.

18. Senn, 288–89.

19. Nancy Snell Griffith, "Frank Livingston (Lynching of)," *Encyclopedia of Arkansas History & Culture* http://www.encyclopediaofarkansas.net/encyclopedia/entry-detail.

aspx?entryID=8283 (accessed November 18, 2014).

20. Nancy Snell Griffith, "Clyde Ellison (Lynching of)," *Encyclopedia of Arkansas History & Culture*, http://www.encyclopediaofarkansas.net/encyclopedia/entry-detail. aspx?entryID=8252 (accessed November 18, 2014).

21. Nancy Snell Griffith, "Clinton Briggs (Lynching of)," *Encyclopedia of Arkansas History & Culture*, http://www.encyclopediaofarkansas.net/encyclopedia/entry-detail. aspx?entryID=8254 (accessed November 18, 2014).

22. Grif Stockley, *Blood in Their Eyes: The Elaine Race Massacres of 1919* (Fayetteville: University of Arkansas Press, 2001); C. Calvin Smith, ed., "The Elaine, Arkansas, Race Riots, 1919," Special Issue, *Arkansas Review: A Journal of Delta Studies* 32 (August 2001).

Chapter 9

A Letter from Home Is Worth a Million Dollars: World War I Soldier Correspondence in Local Newspapers

By Michael D. Polston

housands if not millions of the young men inducted into the U.S. military for service in Europe during the Great War had never been more than a few miles from home. Recruits from Arkansas were no exception. Homesickness quickly became a major issue confronted by these raw recruits. Letters from home served to help lessen their separation pains. While the soldiers eagerly requested letters from loved ones, they, too, wrote letters home describing their experiences while in the service of their country.

Topics addressed in such letters run the gamut from the mundane daily routine to heart-stopping descriptions of combat. However, much of what was written was filtered through a system of wartime censorship. Soldiers' mail was examined and edited to ensure that sensitive material that could be intercepted and used by the enemy was not relayed to the folks back home. As a result, many of the letters, especially those written before 1919, are lacking in detail. Still, many soldiers composed interesting and informative letters.

Fortunately, for the past nearly 100 years, untold numbers of Arkansas soldiers' letters have been preserved by families, collectors, and local archives. A special treasure trove of letters can also be found hidden away in the numerous county newspapers once published across the state. A common practice of the time was to share the local soldiers' war experiences by printing their letters for public consumption. As a result, historically valuable firsthand accounts of the war have been preserved.

What follows is a sampling of excerpts from this correspondence, written by Arkansas soldiers from 1917 to 1919, dealing with various topics that concerned soldiers both stateside and abroad.

We're from Arkansas

"I feel proud to be with the first bunch of Arkansas boys to get over. I am going to do my best to show them Arkansas can raise good soldiers." (Lonoke County: Joe Bond, *Lonoke Democrat*, May 30, 1918, p. 1.)

"The boys often kid me about the slow train in old Arkansas, but I was the first to receive a Christmas package....I told them it was the mail service and fast trains down in good old Arkansas." (Drew County: Hobart Hunt, *Drew County Advance*, February 18, 1919, p. 7.)

"The Arkansas boys are doing finely. There are only seven of them in the guard house, while there are seventy-eight of the Louisiana boys confined therein." (Randolph County: Henry Bode, *Pocahontas Herald*, November 9, 1917, p. 10.)

"I am in a company by myself...no boys from Arkansas. Please send me some of the boys addresses that are over here from home....I wouldn't give one township in Cleveland for all of France....This country does not agree with my mind for the more I see of this country the better I like old Cleveland County." (Cleveland County: Hugh Mosley, *Cleveland County Herald*, March 6, 1919, p. 1.)

"Company A in my warped opinion has more good timber for better soldiers than any company in the state of Arkansas....Woodruff County boys are coming clean with good soldier conduct." (Woodruff County: Joe Arnof, *The Home News*, April 13, 1917, p. 1.)

Fighting for the Old Red, White, and Blue

"Germany will have to face one brave soldier of America, and if they kill me I think I will die for a good cause." (Hempstead County: William E. Thomas, *The Star of Hope*, December 7, 1917, p. 1.)

"It sure makes a man feel like fighting when he sees the bright colors of Old Glory." (Benton County: Clarence Smith, *Springdale News*, September 28, 1917, p. 1.)

"We know we are not fighting simply because we can win, but we are fighting for humanity....It is an honor to be a solider and the experience is worth a barrel of money to him. So with the Stars and Stripes over him why should the soldier not be happy." (Sharp County: Montie Smith, *Sharp County Record*, March 29, 1918, p. 4.)

"It seems hard to leave home and loved ones and bound over to face the unknown dangers of the world, but we must keep in mind that we are fighting for the freedom of our country....It may cost many of our lives but why should we worry? As Christ died to make men holy, let us die to make men free." (Izard County: E. A. Roody, *Melbourne Times*, July 11, 1918, p. 2.)

"I don't know how long it will take to lick the brutal devils but they are most assuredly going to be licked." (Lonoke County: Heber McLaughlin, *Lonoke Democrat*, April 26, 1918, p. 1.)

Contact with Home

"Letters from home are the making or the breaking of the boys over here." (Baxter County: Frank Brigman, *Baxter Bulletin*, August 23, 1918, p. 2.)

"I am awfully glad you wrote." (Hempstead County: R. W. Pollard, *The Star of Hope*, July 31, 1918, p. 1.)

"Well, what is the matter? Why haven't you wrote me? I wish you would write once a week anyway whether you get a letter from me or not. I do not have time to write and you do." (Izard County: Willie Richardson, *Melbourne Times*, August 19, 1918, p. 2.)

"There is nothing that seems to dishearten the boys at the front so much as failure to receive any news from home." (Greene County: H. D. Reeves, *Paragould Soliphone*, August 15, 1918, p. 7.)

"Was glad to have a letter from anyone in the States." (Drew County: Rube Yelvington, *Drew County Advance*, February 11, 1919, p. 3.)

"I would like to know what is the matter with the people down about Saline Siding. I can't get a letter from anyone there. I wrote all the young people and when I didn't get a reply I wrote the old folks a letter and by George they won't write me either." (Cleveland County: Ide Ashcraft, *Cleveland County Herald*, June 7, 1917, p. 8.)

"A letter from home is worth a million dollars to me." (Chicot County: Clifton Barnett, *Dermott News*, August 29, 1918, p. 5.)

Camp Life

"I like the army fine so far. We have plenty of interesting duties....I really did not expect to have much fun." (Randolph County: Luther Brown, stationed at Fort Douglas, Utah, *Pocahontas Star Herald*, October 12, 1917, p. 12.)

"We arise at 5 o'clock in the morning. At 6:15 we stand reveille, then mess or breakfast. At 7:30 we are ready for drill or fatigue duty. It is drill until 11:30, then mail call. At 12 it is mess again. We drill again from 1 until 5, then it is retreat until mess time again....At 9:30 the lights are out and every one is in bed for the night's rest." (Sharp County: Floyd Nichols, stationed at Camp Pike, Arkansas, *Sharp County Record*, February 15, 1918, p. 4.)

"I have been having a real good time since I came to Camp Mills....Women with overalls on, working, some of them were breaking on trains, some driving wagons and doing different things. Women up here drive jitneys. A woman will take a bunch of soldiers out 25 or 30 miles and never think any more about it than a man would." (Drew County: Frank Trantham, stationed at Camp Mills, New Jersey, *Drew County Advance*, September 10, 1918, p. 3.)

"We are doing fine now but say, when we first came down...you would have thought they had been to their own funeral....We had picked up the drill better than any in the second drawn men in Camp Pike." (Baxter County: Allen Skiver, stationed at Camp Pike, Arkansas, *Baxter Bulletin*, October 5, 1917, p. 1.)

Going over the Pond

"...had a delightful trip across. Of course some of the boys were a little seasick, but all of us Arkansas boys made it fine, but Arkansas boys you know can stand anything." (Cleveland County: Ocie Towery, *Cleveland County Herald*, April 10, 1919, p. 1.)

"I'm glad I chose the army as my service to the government, because I can't fancy the sea for mine. Tom Saxton and I are the only two of the band that haven't gotten sea sick. Ha! Ha! Ha! The rest just heaved Jonah." (Jackson County: Walter Stallings, *Newport Daily Independent*, September 5, 1918, p. 2.)

"I had almost decided that the boat must be going round and round as there wasn't anything to be seen but water and other ships." (Ashley County: Zemry Sawyer, *Ashley County Eagle*, September 12, 1918, p. 1.)

"My trip across the great blue sea sure was an unusual experience... could neither sleep or eat nor find a place on the boat where I could rest." (Baxter County: James E. McGuire, *Baxter Bulletin*, May 3, 1918, p. 1.)

"We had a nice trip across. I wasn't sea sick at all, but I guarded against it by sucking lemons and eating lemon drop candy." (Benton County: A. B. Sammon, *Springdale News*, May 17, 1918, p. 3.)

"It sure was some trip over here and I sure was glad when we arrived." (Arkansas County: Joe Oliver, *DeWitt Enterprise*, August 2, 1918, p. 2.)

"The ship was rocking to and fro and a fellow had just filled his mess kit with beans and as the ship made one of those tango dips he stumbled, slapping another rookie in the face with his beans." (Sevier County: Gus Lewis, *De Queen Bee*, May 3, 1918, p. 9.)

Over the Top and into Battle

"When I wrote you last I was only an American soldier abroad, but now I am an old veteran, a seasoned soldier made such by considerable work on the front....I've been right in the midst of the artillery, watched air fights and barrages put on. Taken all together it is about the most wonderful sight that I have ever witnessed....I never heard such a racket in my life and my the destruction those big guns do." (Independence County: Ben Arnold, *Newark Journal*, April 8, 1918, p. 5.)

"The dead have not been buried for we have not had time....There is very very foul air here, caused by the dead Boche and horses....The Germans are shelling the road about a block from where I am writing now. You should see the dirt fly." (Ashley County: Jewell Vick, *Ashley County Eagle*, September 12, 1918, p. 2.)

"...just back from the front line waiting for orders...sent us out to undergo our baptism of fire...we were all more or less nervous for we knew not what the coming battle would bring to us....It seemed as though all the cannon in the world were concentrated on that one spot and the flashes from the guns lighted up the sky as far as we could see." (Chicot County: Paul Johnson, *Dermott News*, November 14, 1918, p. 8.)

"The shell exploded so close to him that he was killed by the concussion as the skin was not even broken....His getting killed broke me all up as he was a good comrade." (Clay County: Charlie Pace, *Clay County Courier*, February 21, 1919, p. 2.)

"The last few days we have been on the front line picking up junk. We see many sights to look at. Have covered up several human skeletons... shells holes 1 ft to 10 ft deep, timber and wire entanglement shot all to pieces....I don't think that anyone after he has visited the western front lines would do anything to bring about another war." (Baxter County: Ernest Cantwell, *Baxter Bulletin*, January 17, 1919, p. 1.)

"After a man has gone through with it, has seen his comrades fall, wounded and dead, and witnessed the sight which mangled and torn bodies present, he doesn't like to think about it." (Jackson County: Eugene Wallace, *Newport Daily Independent*, December 5, 1918, p. 1.)

"I have lost two of my fingers....I was up at the Big Front helping run the Hun and they sent me a shell I could not dodge but I got plenty of them to pay for my fingers." (White County: Homer Grissom, *Judsonia Weekly Advance*, September 18, 1918, p. 1.)

"Well I will tell you something of the war. I went over the top three times, and that was enough war for me. I lay on hills and got my eyes filled with dust from bullets falling in front of me. The big shells were bursting all around me....I was hit three times by pieces falling from bursting shells but was lucky not to be hurt either time. I cannot hardly see how I am living today for I know I went through awful things...sometime so wearied that I could sleep while the shells were bursting all about me." (Sharp County: Tom Kinney, *Sharp County Record*, February 21, 1919, p. 2.)

"I guess I had as narrow escape as one ever had last night. I was on guard at the picket line...shells began to fall at first I did not pay very much attention...in a few minutes they began to fall closer....I couldn't leave my post so I had to stay....I heard something coming like a buzz wagon I couldn't tell...it was coming right toward me...it hit the ground about ten feet from me....I fell on my face just as it went off....It cut down trees and bushes all over me and killed five horses...so you can imagine what a close call I had." (Drew County: Hobart Hunt, *Drew County Advance*, July 16, 1918, p. 4.)

"I had a pretty good taste of war this time....The Germans would shoot gas shells over on us at night and we would have to keep our masks on so we could not get much sleep. Mustard gas has burnt a big blister on my knee but luckily I didn't get any in my eyes or lungs. The blister doesn't amount to anything." (Chicot County: James Morris, *Dermott News*, September 12, 1918, p. 4.)

"...the trenches were about three or four feet deep, and the Germans had a trench about a hundred yards from ours, and to cap the climax 'old Fritz' had a machine gun directly in front of us and when he couldn't think of anything else to do he would turn that loose. The bullets pat pat pat around pretty close." (Ashley County: Clifton Jordan, *Ashley County Eagle*, June 20, 1918, p. 1.)

Longing for Home
"I would like much better to leave this side....I often think of praying a little once in a while to see if that would help me to get out of this place." (Cross County: Willie Harrell, *Wynne Progress*, February 7, 1919, p. 1.)

"...wishing for the day to come when I will start home." (Sevier County: Benjamin Zachry, *De Queen Bee*, January 24, 1919, p. 2.)

"Do hope I won't be in France this winter, anyway, for it's cool here now and gee, what will it be this winter. Too cold for any of us." (Woodruff County: Oscar Bishop, *The Home News*, September 6, 1918, p. 7.)

"All the men are wild to get home, for they are 'well fed up' on this country." (Sharp County: W. C. Yeager, *Sharp County Record*, January 31, 1919, p. 3.)

"...am looking forward to the time when I will be back again in the good Old State of Arkansas." (Ashley County: Claude Everett, *Ashley County Eagle*, January 23, 1919, p. 1.)

Chapter 10

The Armistice: Celebrating the End of the War

By Michael D. Polston

"There sure were a bunch of happy Yanks."
—Edgar Blankinship of Drew County

By the fall of 1918, allied forces launched the war's last major offensive on the Western Front, one which many Arkansas soldiers witnessed and folks back home eagerly monitored. With the German army soon in retreat, chances for a German victory quickly faded. Riots in the city streets and the announcement of the abdication of Germany's ruler, Kaiser Wilhelm, on November 9, 1918, sealed the nation's fate.[1] Though terms for a ceasefire were already being negotiated, a final agreement was not reached until the morning of November 11. The armistice, which was signed at 5:00 a.m. but not effective for another six hours, established a renewable thirty-day ceasefire between the warring nations. At 11:00 a.m., the Western Front grew silent.

Rumors of a ceasefire had been circulating for several weeks, both on the battlefield and on the homefront. On November 9, Lee County soldier Wayne Murdock spoke of a ceasefire "only to find out that...it was premature." Still he believed that "it is only a matter of a few hours before it comes to pass."[2] Even when confirmation was received, Charles Beasley of Scott County reported that many remained skeptical. "There were many doubting Thomasses," he said. He went on to say that the "news came so suddenly they couldn't believe it true."[3]

As Clifton Harris of Randolph County wrote home, "I was waiting for the command Over the Top, when the news came the armistice was signed. You can imagine how we felt."[4] Elgin Moore from the Sharp County town of Evening Shade told the people back home that "we first heard of the signing...from a German lieutenant, but did not believe it and continued to fight until word came from the rear."[5] "Five minutes before eleven o'clock the battle was still raging," stated Conrad Glover of Grant County. "I counted four minutes, three minutes, two minutes; even to one minute...there was constant bombardment...at eleven o'clock the bombardment ceased, and there was calm...the last one of us cried like a baby."[6] Charlie Killian of Drew County added that "up until 11 o'clock there was a living hell on earth and then a dead silence followed."[7] It was finally over. Though the war would not officially end by treaty for months to come, the armistice stopped the mass bloodshed.

Once convinced it was true and not another "false armistice," celebrations began all along the front. Soldiers cautiously came out of their secure positions, greeting both friend and former enemy in "no-man's land." Handshakes, hugs, cheering, and laughter were commonplace.

Louis Johns from Izard County, serving in the 130th Infantry, noted how the Germans in his sector came over and smoked cigarettes.[8] Everyone was overcome with joy. Charles Taft of Scott County, who was at the front positioned next to an artillery piece when the firing ceased, said, "It seemed that a deep sleep had come over everything. I had to throw my cap in the air and yell."[9] "We let em have it to the last minute," wrote John Smith of Lincoln County. Then "everything became quiet, as if the Lord got tired of us and pulled a curtain down on the scene."[10] Dr. S. A. Drennen of Independence County may have described it best: "We had just reached a stretch of the road operated by the Americans when one hears the clang of bells, and deep throated whistle of the engine...such a noise broke loose...the firing of guns and the shouting of soldiers. A combination of Christmas, New Years and the Fourth of July."[11]

For the first time since 1914, on the night of November 11, soldiers could gather in the open, sit around a fire, speak in a normal tone of voice without fear of being detected, or simply light a match. The celebration thus continued well into the night. Charlie Killian recalled that the soldiers "at night we rounded up every flare possible," and that once these were lit, "the night was as light as day. A grander sight was never seen."[12] Within time, the excitement began to calm down, with Ashley County soldier Clarence Gardner, serving in the Eighty-First Division, telling his parents that he "would never forget how quiet everything seemed that night."[13] Robert Jacks of Sevier County observed that "we had been under shell fire so long that when hostilities ceased we could hardly sleep. We almost had to beat on cans, pans and the like to make racket so the boys could sleep."[14]

Many Arkansas soldiers stationed near villages and towns were caught up in the celebration with the jubilant French. "We were heard from over here," said Ross Morgan of Arkansas County, "for the whole camp went wild and we proceeded to town where we joined the French in parades, singing, shouting and shooting of fireworks far into the night."[15] Ernest Edwards of Scott County, then in Paris, recalled for his sister: "Talk about celebration...there was not so much shooting of guns...but the streets were thronged so immensely with people that it was almost impossible to drive a car through them."[16] Dolan Burris of Pope County simply stated that "all of France went crazy."[17] The celebration continued for days to come.

The news of the armistice declaration quickly reached the United States, arriving in Little Rock within hours of the signing. The *Arkansas Democrat*'s newsboys hit the capital city streets by 2:17 a.m. on November 11 with a hot-off-the-presses extra.[18] (The timing in the United States, was affected, of course, by the time difference; the armistice had been signed at 5:00 a.m. in France, to become effective at 11:00 a.m., Paris time.)

As the news spread in Little Rock, people hastily dressed and made their way out onto the streets, where the celebration began in earnest. Cars were loaded to the running boards, dragging strings of tin cans, with yelling occupants driving up and down the streets. "The city went peace mad." People turned out en masse with the streets described as a "bedlam of noise."[19] "Every conceivable method of noise maker" was being used and sold on the city streets. The *Arkansas Gazette* reported that it was a "brutally hard day for tin cans."[20] Firecrackers, cowbells, dinner bells, horns, factory whistles, church bells, and noise makers of all kinds could be heard throughout the city. Cars were modified to backfire so as to sound like a machine gun. American flags and flags of all the victorious nations, balloons, banners, and confetti were everywhere. An estimated 200 factory workers were marching back and forth on Markham Street waving the colors of red, white, and blue. Many celebrants went from house to house, shaking hands and congratulating each other on the victory.[21]

An impromptu parade of thousands formed at 3rd and Main, stretching almost the length of the business district. Workers from the acid plant, high school students, and women from the Food Administration, among others, marched down Markham Street. Carried at the head of the parade was the Blass Department Store service flag. By noon, most businesses in the city had closed, including state and federal offices. Many closed earlier. At 10:00 a.m., church bells began to ring for a five-minute time span, during which men bared their heads and people prayed in silence. There were so many celebrants that parade passed parade.

At the intersection of Capitol and Main, employees of the Missouri Pacific Shop produced a coffin with a straw effigy of the Kaiser marked with the words "The Kaiser has gone to Hell," doused it with kerosene, and set it ablaze. The crowd went wild, becoming so loud as to be described as "almost deafening." The ashes were then piled in the street and labeled with a new sign, "The ashes of the Kaiser, Satan's chief dictator." One group, believed to be from the medical profession, carried a human skeleton labeled with the words "was the kaiser." A number of effigies of the Kaiser were dragged behind automobiles. During the celebration, planes from Eberts Field in Lonoke County flew overhead, performing "most startling feats."[22]

At 10:00 a.m., many in the crowd gathered at Capitol and Main to hear the playing of "The Star-Spangled Banner." The song was followed by brief remarks by Governor Charles Brough, Mayor Charles Taylor, and Colonel Charles Miller from Camp Pike.[23]

Similar events were taking place just across the river in North Little Rock. The celebration began early in the morning, with one parade led by the military band from Camp Pike. One group of happy citizens was carrying a Kaiser effigy and a coffin, followed by two dozen Liberty Bells and a huge American flag. A parade of several thousand marched down Main Street to the City Park. Promptly at 11:00 a.m., members of the United War Work Committee met at City Hall for a large demonstration and then marched to City Park. Included in the several thousand revelers were students from the local public schools led by their superintendent, principals, and teachers. At City Park, Governor Brough delivered a second address, followed by the head of the United War Work Drive for

Pulaski County, L. B. Leighs. With speeches completed, the celebration continued through the day and well into the night.[24]

It did not take long for the excitement to spread to Camp Pike, the infantry training installation on the northern side of the Arkansas River. Most likely, few were happier than the recruits awaiting orders to go overseas. Men, women, and children packed themselves into automobiles and waved flags, honked horns, rang bells, and shouted to the top of their lungs as they drove up and down the camp streets. People continued to carry the celebration through the night and into the next day.

In Malvern, parade marchers stretching some two miles witnessed the dragging of uncounted numbers of effigies of the Kaiser through the streets. A cannon recently presented to the city by Congressman Thaddeus Caraway was fired for the first time. The cannon's discharge broke many of the city's windows.[25] In Morrilton, windows were also broken when revelers began anvil firing. This was a practice of placing one anvil upside down on another with black powder and a fuse placed in between. When the powder is lit, an enormous explosion ensues, and the top anvil is launched into the air. In this instance, not only were there shattered windows, but a flock of geese was knocked out of the sky by the boom.[26] Huntsville citizens were also firing anvils in a celebration that was called the "greatest in the history of the town."[27] More than 20,000 paraded in the streets of Fort Smith. When a train of 250 recently inducted draftees from Greenwood reached the Fort Smith depot and discovered the war had ended, many of them joined in the celebration.[28]

Recruits in Searcy preparing for transport to Camp Pike in North Little Rock knew something was up when they were instructed to wait for further orders. Instead of orders, news of the armistice arrived, and "general pandemonium broke loose" in the city. Young women from Galloway College, carrying signs emblazoned with "Peace," marched to the city square, where they were joined by public school students and local citizens. At the same time, an African American woman began to bang on a large dishpan, exclaiming, "The war's over and my boy's coming home! Glory! Hallelujah."[29]

In nearby Judsonia, every church bell began ringing within fifteen minutes of the announcement of the peace. Blacksmith Frank Rudd joined the celebration with anvil firing. At 2:00 p.m., the town's businesses and school closed to participate in a parade that included floats, one of which was decorated with four devils and a coffin designated to be the Kaiser's. In a short time, the parade stretched all the way to Bald Knob. The celebration ended at 7:00 p.m. with the burning of an effigy of the Kaiser and more anvil firing.[30]

At Mountain Home in Baxter County, charges of dynamite were set off that were so powerful that the explosion could be heard over ten miles away at Norfork. Many of the children gathered in their yards and banged on kettles and buckets.[31] Many years after the war, William A. Davis, who lived near Williford in Sharp County, recalled as a fifteen-year-old doing much the same thing in his front yard, making "just lots of noise."[32]

In the western Arkansas city of De Queen, the message of peace was delivered by Congressman Otis T. Wingo. The announcement quickly turned the town into a den of excitement. Sounds of gunfire, whistles, and bells could be heard in rapid succession. This spontaneous outburst was followed by the closing of the town business district to accommodate a two-hour parade.[33]

Such parades and celebrations took place in communities across the state, and in many cases continued throughout the week. Unofficially, the peace celebrations came to an end on November 17. On the first Sunday following the armistice agreement, thousands gathered at their local churches to observe a proclamation issued by Governor Brough declaring a special day of thanksgiving.[34] Within a few days, life settled back into a regular routine, and all that remained was the return of sons, fathers, brothers, husbands, and uncles to their Arkansas homes.

Americans did not forget the armistice quickly. The next year, President Woodrow Wilson proclaimed November 11 as Armistice Day, a day to be "filled with solemn pride in the heroism of those who died in the country's service and with gratitude for the victory." At precisely 11:00 a.m., businesses across the nation were expected to observe a two-minute suspension of commerce in honor of those who made sacrifices. Additionally, the observance consisted of patriotic parades and gatherings that soon became a tradition across Arkansas and the nation, with many states declaring November 11 a holiday. A federal holiday for federal employees was declared in 1938. After World War II, there was a push to rededicate the day to honor all veterans. Thus, in 1954, President Dwight D. Eisenhower signed legislation to rename the holiday Veterans Day.[35] As a result, Armistice Day remains a part of the fabric of U.S. history and continues to be observed, just under another name.

1. Joseph E. Persico, *Eleventh Month, Eleventh Day, Eleventh Hour: Armistice Day, 1918 World War I and Its Violent Climax* (New York: Random House, 2004), 318.

2. Letter of Wayne Murdock, *Courier Index*, December 13, 1918, p. 1.

3. Letter of Charles Beasley, *Advance Reporter*, February 6, 1919, p. 4.

4. Letter of Clifton Harris, *Pocahontas Star Herald*, January 17, 1919, p. 4.

5. Letter of Elgin Moor, *Sharp County Record*, January 24, 1919, p. 3

6. Michael David Polston, "The Armistice: An Arkansas Perspective," *Over There: A Journal of the First World War*, Special Armistice Issue (November 1988): 13.

7. Letter of Charles Killian, *Advance*, January 14, 1919, p. 7.

8. Letter of Louis Johns, *Melbourne Times*, April 4, 1919, p. 4.

9. Letter of Charles Taft, *Advance Record*, January 9, 1919, p. 6.

10. John I. Smith, *True Stories of Needed Justice: A Biography of Judge Henry Smith* (Little Rock: Rose Publishing, 1979), 113.

11. Letter of S. A. Drennen, *Newark Journal*, December 5, 1918, p. 1.

12. Letter of Charles Killian, *Advance*, January 14, 1919, p. 7.

13. Letter of Clarence Gardner, *Ashley County Eagle*, March 27, 1919, p. 1.

14. Letter of Robert Jacks, *De Queen Bee*, January 3, 1919, p. 2.

15. Letter of Ross Morgan, *DeWitt Enterprise*, January 16, 1919, p. 2.

16. Letter of Ernest Edwards, *Advance Reporter*, February 13, 1919, p. 3.

17. Personal interview with Dolan Burris, 1988.

18. "Democrat Extra Is First to Announce Armistice Signed," *Arkansas Democrat*, November 11, 1918, p. 1.

19. "Little Rock Holds Wild Celebration of Defeat of Hun," *Arkansas Democrat*, November 11, 1918, p. 1.

20. "Carnival Crowds Write Peace Day in City Annals," *Arkansas Gazette*, November 12, 1918, p. 6.

21. "Blass Dry Goods Declared a Holiday for Employees," *Arkansas Democrat*, November 11, 1918, p. 11.

22. Ibid.

23. "Governor, Mayor and Colonel Miller Make Talks," *Arkansas Democrat*, November 11, 1918, p. 11.

24. "North Little Rock Has Big Celebration," *Arkansas Democrat*, November 11, 1918, p. 3.

25. "Whole State in Big Celebration," *Arkansas Gazette*, November 12, 1918, p. 12.

26. Ibid.

27. Kevin Hatfield, *A Chronological History of Huntsville, Arkansas* (Huntsville, AR: Madison County Genealogical and Historical Society, 2013), 169.

28. "Whole State in Big Celebration," *Arkansas Gazette*, November 12, 1918, p. 12.

29. Raymond Lee Muncy, *Searcy, Arkansas: A Frontier Town Grows Up in America* (Searcy: Harding Press, 1976), 205.

30. W. E. Orr, *That's Judsonia* (Judsonia, AR: White County Printing Company, 1957), 119–20.

31. Mary Messick, *History of Baxter County 1873–1973* (Mountain Home Chamber of Commerce, 1973), 213.

32. Personal interview with William A. Davis, 1988.

33. "Collapse and Fall of German Autocracy Is Joyfully Celebrated in De Queen." *De Queen Bee*, November 15, 1918, p. 1.

34. "Sunday Nov. 17 Proclaimed Special Thanksgiving Day," *Arkansas Gazette*, November 12, 1918, p. 2.

35. U.S. Department of Veterans Affairs: History of Veterans Day. http://www.va.gov/opa/vetsday/vetdayhistory.asp (accessed January 27, 2015).

Chapter 11

PLAGUE!: The 1918 Influenza Epidemic in Arkansas

By Nancy Hendricks

Soon after public schools in Hot Springs, Arkansas, started the 1918 fall term, they were closed. The schools later re-opened but closed again. On December 3, 1918, the *Hot Springs Sentinel-Record* ran an article headlined, "ALL PHYSICIANS TO MEET HERE TONIGHT." The article went on to say, "The matter of determining whether the city's schools shall again be closed, or whether they shall not, will be answered tonight by the board of health after a meeting at the Business Men's League quarters at 7:30 o'clock, to which every physician in the city is urged to attend."[1] The issue was influenza.

The group's president, Dr. Leonard Ellis, was quoted in that article as saying, "There are some influenza cases, but not enough to interfere with the schools, as I view the situation, and I believe that the children are as safe in the schools as elsewhere."[2] His last statement was probably true, but not in the way he hoped. No one—children, parents, young people, old people, soldiers or civilians—was safe anywhere.

Worse than Black Death

A deadly influenza outbreak had begun in March 1918 and spread around the world, killing more people within a shorter span of time than any other outbreak of disease in human history. At first it was considered an *epidemic*, meaning that new cases of an infectious disease far exceed what might normally be expected based on past experience. A *pandemic* is an epidemic that spreads across a large region, multiple continents, or around the world. Therefore, a pandemic is an epidemic of worldwide proportions.

The influenza outbreak of 1918 was most definitely a pandemic. It has been said by modern researchers that the 1918 flu killed more people in a year than the dreaded medieval Black Death killed in a century. The pandemic's history remains significant today as world health officials seek to prevent outbreaks of mutated influenza strains as well as viruses such as measles and Ebola.

Influence of the Stars

In the fourteenth century, Italian doctors had noted a mysterious illness that often turned into an epidemic. They called it the *influentia* in medieval Latin, believing it was caused by an adverse influence of the stars or alignment of the planets. By the eighteenth century, it was called *influenza di freddo*, or "influence of the cold," as Italian doctors thought it might be caused by a chill. French doctors called it *la grippe* (from the word "seize" or "grasp," as the illness tenaciously gripped its victims). The disease was very quick, very contagious, and had the ability to mutate into different strains. Treatment for one strain might not work for another.

Influenza—or "the flu"—is characterized by an inflammation of the upper respiratory tract, with accompanying fever and pain throughout the body, especially in joints and muscles. The virus that causes it is particularly contagious, robust, and easily adaptable. The influenza virus can survive outside the body and be transmitted through the air. It can move from animals to humans and vice versa. Unlike with some diseases, immunity is not built up from one case of the flu to the next. Each adaptation or mutation of the influenza virus causes the immune system to battle it as a completely new threat. Often, it weakens the body's defenses to the point that the victim is easily susceptible to deadly complications such as pneumonia. In 1918, the virus proved more lethal than the deadliest war known to man up to that time.

World War I claimed the lives of about nine million people worldwide. With the entry of the United States into the war in April 1917, fresh troops were brought to the battlefield. Almost 350,000 Americans ultimately died during what was called "The Great War" or "The War to End All Wars." (The fact that it later had to be re-labeled as "World War I" is evidence of how wrong that assessment was.)

As catastrophic as the war's casualty rates were, fifty million people around the world died in the influenza pandemic, often called the Spanish Flu. In Arkansas, as in many other states, influenza killed about 7,000 people, several times more than the state lost as casualties during World War I. This is all the more remarkable when one considers that in Arkansas, the vast majority of the state's residents lived in rural areas. There were no major metropolitan areas with large concentrated populations, such as those on the East Coast.

Compared to Bubonic Plague

With the entry of the United States into World War I, men were sent to large training camps across the country before being transported to the battlefields of Europe. One of these training centers was Camp Funston, part of the huge Fort Riley complex in eastern Kansas. The camp was about 300 miles away from rural Haskell County, Kansas. Some scientists theorize that the 1918 strain may have begun in Haskell County, where people lived in close proximity to their poultry and pigs, animals that were succumbing to a mysterious illness at the time.

Other theories as to the 1918 flu's origins have also gained supporters. Some point to a major troop staging area and hospital camp in France where great numbers of pigs and poultry were kept nearby for food. It is theorized that when sailors returned from the French staging area aboard troop ships to the naval facility at Boston, Massachusetts, and the nearby Camp Devens, they brought back an especially deadly strain.

In 2014, one researcher suggested that the virus evolved in China and later mutated after being carried to the United States. Historian Mark

Humphries discovered that, during World War I, thousands of Chinese workers were transported to Europe through North America in order to do manual labor behind allied lines. He found evidence that in November 1917, a severe respiratory illness struck villages in northern China, where people lived close to their animals. Even after the illness was called a "plague" there, laborers from that area continued to be transported to Europe. A year later, the illness was identified by Chinese health officials as identical to what became known as the Spanish Flu.[3]

In any case, by early 1918, there were reports of rural residents in Haskell County, Kansas, dying from a severe strain of flu. In February 1918, several recruits from Camp Funston visited their families in Haskell. When the soldiers returned from leave, they reported back to camp. Researchers note that in early March 1918, a soldier said to be a cook at Camp Funston went on morning sick call. He complained of headache, sore throat, muscle aches, chills, and fever. By noon, more than 100 men joined him. Within a month, 1,000 were sick, and almost fifty soldiers were dead. They were strong, healthy young men whose lungs filled with fluid so quickly that they drowned, sometimes within twelve hours of beginning to feel sick.[4]

Because the lack of oxygen in the blood seemed to turn the victims dark blue, purple, or black, comparisons were drawn to the terrifying "Black Death" (most likely bubonic plague) of the Middle Ages. The 1918 flu would go on to kill more people in one year than the Black Death did in 100.

Floating Caskets

Conditions in 1918 were ideal for spreading the disease. Civilian war workers moved around the country, military recruits were sent to crowded training camps, and soldiers were packed into railroad cars as well as the cramped, stuffy holds of troop ships, which became known as "floating caskets." Influenza spread to cities, rural areas, and army camps before sweeping through Europe and the world.

Combatant countries rarely allowed reports of the illness to be printed for fear of lowering morale during wartime. However, Spain was a neutral country, and the Spanish press was not censored. Newspapers in that country reported on the disease that killed eight million Spaniards with terrible speed. Even King Alfonso XIII of Spain was gravely ill. Because this was the first that most people had heard of the epidemic's specter of death, the illness became known as the Spanish Flu.[5]

From Arkansas to the World

By 1920, the population of Arkansas was slightly over 1.5 million; the flu ultimately killed more than 7,000 Arkansans. The state may also have produced far-reaching consequences around the world. In the port city of Brest in France, where almost half of all U.S. soldiers disembarked, influenza patients had survived an epidemic of a milder flu strain earlier in 1918. But as historian John M. Barry stated, "The first outbreak with high mortality occurred in July, in a replacement detachment of American troops from Camp Pike, Arkansas."[6]

Camp Pike in North Little Rock had been established in 1917 for army basic training (see chapter 2 for more on the facility). With around 50,000 men at Camp Pike during the summer of 1918, its infirmary began admitting up to 1,000 sick men a day. The camp was sealed and quarantined. The infirmary was overwhelmed. Its young patients died in droves, gasping for breath. Fearing panic as well as not wanting to appear unpatriotic during wartime, the commandant ordered that neither the extent of the epidemic nor the names of the dead be released to the press.

Flu had traditionally targeted the very young and very old as its victims. Now, young adults were shockingly vulnerable. The soldiers who died had been healthy young men who in the past would have been considered most likely to survive. Many scientists now believe that healthy young people were killed by the very immune systems that should have saved them. The lethal flu virus may have provoked a violent immune response that inflamed their lungs, leaving their respiratory systems vulnerable to infection. The patients' lungs became flooded with blood and fluids, which essentially drowned them.

A similar situation to that at Camp Pike was occurring at Eberts Field in Lonoke County. Eberts Field opened in March 1918 as a basic aviation school for World War I pilots. With about 2,500 enlisted men and officers stationed there in 1918, it held fewer men than Camp Pike, but the influenza was just as widespread. Eberts Field also played a significant role in transferring the disease, given its role as one of the leading training centers for aviators during the war. The *Arkansas Gazette* reported that it was not uncommon to see several hundred planes flying in formation over the field.[7] After completing primary instruction at Eberts, cadets went on to other air bases around the country for advanced training before traveling to the battlefields of Europe.

Military bases in Arkansas such as Camp Pike and Eberts Field were quarantined and shut off from visitors. When space in base hospitals ran out, which it quickly did, soldiers suffering from the flu were confined to their barracks, a sure way of spreading the disease to any comrades who had somehow remained healthy.

More Interested in War

Despite the quarantine at Camp Pike, the deadly influenza virus could not be contained. It emerged among Arkansas civilians in mid-to-late September 1918. It is, however, difficult to gauge since the national public health service did not require states to report influenza before September 27. Statistics from the central part of the state then began pouring in, but deaths were often attributed to pneumonia rather than influenza.

In early October, Arkansas's state health officials stated that "serious epidemics have been reported from several points." More than 500 civilian cases of influenza appeared in the Little Rock area at this time. Even then, Dr. James Geiger, U.S. Public Health Service officer for Arkansas, downplayed the threat to the state with reassuring statements. Geiger may have been following directives from the national office to maintain a morale-boosting strategy. This was possibly to avert a panic—a real threat, with rumors across America that the disease was caused by germ warfare or chemical agents planted by German infiltrators. Geiger continued issuing reassurances even after he himself caught the flu and his wife died of it.

Newspapers may have been reluctant to print discouraging words about the flu for reasons beyond morale and panic. Like all news media before and since, newspapers of the day found that what sold was the excitement of war—battles won, victories predicted, medals earned, heroics displayed. Arkansas was no different from the rest of the country. The Great War was the most cataclysmic military action the world had ever known up to that point. When Arkansas journalist Erwin Funk of Rogers traveled to Chicago, Illinois, in October 1918, he was curious about the impact of the now-burgeoning epidemic on the big city. The reporter wrote, "Chicago isn't doing any statistical gathering on the subject just now, at least for publication. Chicago isn't interested in the flu anyhow. Chicago is interested in the war."[8]

With state public health officials disinclined to declare the disease a threat, plus the absence of press coverage in wartime, Arkansas had little time to prepare for the epidemic and therefore could not do much to avert the tidal wave. The Arkansas State Board of Health did a commendable job with few resources. In fact, it was simply adhering to its official 1918 guidelines, which did not include influenza among health threats that required reporting and/or quarantine. The influenza epidemic took hold before Arkansas health officials could seek remedial action.

Geiger continued to be reassuring with updates, such as one on October 4, 1918, calling the fatal illness "simple, plain, old-fashioned la grippe." He downplayed the need for a quarantine and stated, "Situation still well in hand."[9] Two days later, on October 6, a quarantine was imposed.

In Pulaski County, where the state's population center of Little Rock was located, the quarantine was not lifted until November 4, 1918. County health boards were given the responsibly for lifting restrictions in rural areas. However, in Little Rock and across rural areas of the state, public schools remained closed even after the quarantine was lifted. Children under the age of eighteen were confined to their homes until December.

Arkansas Women Step Forward

Some soldiers were training on Arkansas college campuses, which were quickly overwhelmed by the disease. Valiant school nurses such as "Ma" Hardin and Belle Blanchard at the University of Arkansas in Fayetteville begged the public for the most basic items such as pillows and bed linens. Soon, the nurses were so inundated by continuing waves of patients that they requested something which, to many, was unthinkable: women, trained or untrained, were asked to face the threat of death by helping nurse the sick young men. Many Arkansas women bravely stepped forward, feeling they were simply "doing their part."[10]

Bringing Death Home

The state's population centers at that time were Little Rock and Fort Smith, but in 1918 about eighty percent of Arkansans lived on farms. Rural areas were especially hard hit by the pandemic. This was due to several factors. First, of course, was the war. Beginning in May 1917, America's young men between ages twenty-one and thirty-one were required to register through the Selective Service for military conscription, or the draft. In August 1918, when it was obvious that more would be needed, the age limit was raised to forty-five. With so many Arkansas families living on farms, soldiers from rural areas were well represented. New recruits were often allowed to go home on leave. Even if they were not manifesting signs of the illness yet, those infected with the flu brought the contagion home to their farm family members, who had no immunity.

Advancing technology also played a part in the flu's devastation among the state's overwhelmingly rural population. Railroad trains were the primary form of transportation for Americans in 1918, with almost a billion passengers traveling by rail each year. These included farmers going to market towns, with germs infesting the enclosed passenger cars.

Additionally, by 1918, affordable automobiles and trucks were increasingly available to average Americans. A network of farm-to-market roads allowed rural people to travel outside their immediate area, becoming exposed to new strains of disease to which they were not immune.

Courting Disaster

Improved transportation also allowed farm people to enjoy the new forms of entertainment that pervaded American culture by 1918. Even the most isolated farm folk could generally find a nearby source of amusement as well as a ride to get there. Dance halls, skating rinks, lodges, pool halls, and saloons attracted people from outlying areas. As a result, new courting rituals exploded onto the scene for young people. In the past, courting in Arkansas generally had been limited to church socials among neighbors, conducted under the watchful eye of parents. Now, young people were exposed to a whole new world of potential mates to be wooed, and they had a new kind of entertainment—motion pictures—to show them exactly how to do it.

Movie theaters were springing up all across America. The new film stars of silent movies became exceedingly popular. Even illiterate rural folk were able to look at pictures of celebrities in fan magazines and follow their latest films. When work on the farm was done, they swarmed to tiny local movie theatres. In 1918 alone, almost 800 movies were made.

Moviegoers had a wide range of choices that changed on a regular basis, including shocking "pre-code" romances such as 1918's *Men Who Have Made Love to Me*. Onscreen embraces became instructional guides. Most popular in 1918 were *Bound in Morocco*, starring the dashing Douglas Fairbanks, *Carmen* with vamp Pola Negri, and *Salomé* with seductive Theda Bara. Young people turned out in droves to be shocked, titillated, and delighted to find other like-minded individuals in the dark.

With people packed into tiny movie houses, germs bred and spread. Shared kisses as seen on the movie screen could be lethal. When the influenza pandemic became more widely known, public health officials ordered movie houses closed, though it was often too late.

Rural Calamity

The flu tore through rural areas of Arkansas, where most of its residents lived. When farm folk became ill, it was a new breed of disease they had not seen before. Not only were people dying in droves, but many deaths likely went unreported to the point that it cannot be determined how many rural residents died. Although telephones existed in 1918, they were expensive and generally not available in the state's rural areas. With no telephones or other means of communication, rural residents often could not summon help when entire families became bedridden. Nor could they let others know when their loved ones had died.

There was also a lack of medical care in isolated rural areas. Even if they could be summoned, Arkansas country doctors were few, and they were overwhelmed by the number of cases pouring in. In addition, they had to cover vast areas, often via horse and buggy. Though there were more farm-to-market roads in 1918, roadways were still limited. The doctors and nurses who could afford cars often used rocky dirt roads that punctured their tires or stranded them in a sea of mud. In dry, dusty conditions, engines routinely failed. Many doctors depended on horses, but it was slow going. Worn down by the elements, relentless hours of travel, tending to patients, and exposure to the new strain of influenza, country doctors and nurses often themselves became sick.

Unrecorded Death, Lifelong Suffering

Deaths frequently went unrecorded in Arkansas's rural areas; this was often due to the lack of literacy skills needed to record the deaths. Thus, many families left no cemetery records. Many people were hastily buried in unmarked graves at family burial grounds or wherever they could be quickly laid to rest. Sometimes entire families, too weak to draw water or prepare food, died of disease, thirst, or starvation. Country people, known for helping each other in times of trouble, often did not help their neighbors in 1918, either out of fear of the illness or from being too sick themselves. The epidemic swept through small communities, some which became ghost towns.

In addition to immediate deaths from the flu, which especially seemed to prey on the youngest and healthiest country folk, the 1918 influenza pandemic left many survivors in a weakened state. This rendered them vulnerable to complications and a wide range of conditions including bronchitis, ear infections, and pneumonia. The flu also made existing health problems worse for those with asthma and heart problems. Babies of women stricken with the flu during their pregnancies often suffered lifelong impairment. This long-lasting impact led to decades of suffering for thousands of people in Arkansas even after the 1918 pandemic subsided.

Like other rural populations of the South, the people of Arkansas still struggled with health conditions that went back to the Civil War and before, including malnutrition, malaria, hookworm, pellagra, and typhoid. It is little wonder that the 1918 flu epidemic cut a wide swath of devastation among already weakened Arkansans who lived in rural areas. Modern-day genealogists often encounter multiple family members who died in 1918–1919, as well as records for entire families that simply ended there.

"Whites have the whole big show..."

Generally, people with the best chance of surviving the flu were those who had the luxury of lying down soon after the first symptoms appeared, staying in bed for several weeks, and having the best care and nutrition. Few poor people had those luxuries. In Arkansas, as across the nation, the poor died in larger numbers than the rich.

Race was also a factor. African Americans were likely to suffer from poverty, malnutrition, and untreated pre-existing health conditions. They tended to be vulnerable to disease and to die in large numbers from influenza and related illnesses. In Arkansas as well as in much of the country at that time, African Americans suffering from influenza were typically—often by law—able to be treated only by black caregivers. Limited numbers of black physicians meant that many African Americans suffering from influenza were unable to obtain the services of a doctor or nurse.

Among African Americans in rural areas of Arkansas, it is not known how many people went untreated or died unrecorded. According to organizations such as the Little Rock–based Preservation of African American Cemeteries, Inc. (PAAC), "Many African-American cemeteries have never been registered, are rarely documented, infrequently appear on maps, and are almost never shown on historic plats. African-American cemeteries, many of which are considered 'slave burial grounds,' have been used for generations by tradition and are rarely described by deeds or other legal instruments."[11] It is unknown how many African American flu victims were laid to rest in such places.

During the 1918 flu epidemic, the lack of literacy skills among African Americans added to the problem of recording the deaths of Arkansas's black citizens. In addition, the deaths of black citizens were not usually recorded in white newspapers. When they were reported, they were often marginalized. In a flu-related article on December 12, 1918, the *Hot Springs Sentinel-Record* stated, "There has been but one death from the disease locally, and that was a negro boy." Without naming the victim, it went on to say that a local health official felt "there was some doubt about influenza being the sole cause of that death, and that it is likely there were other assignable reasons."[12]

Diseases prevalent in black neighborhoods were generally reported in the white press only to underscore social problems among blacks or to emphasize areas for whites to avoid. When mainstream newspapers finally began covering the 1918 influenza epidemic, they concentrated on their predominantly white readership. This was not the case only in Arkansas. A letter-writer to one East Coast newspaper aimed at a black readership, the *Baltimore Afro-American*, stated, "As far as the 'Flu' is concerned, the whites have the whole big show to themselves."[13]

Virtual Quarantine

When the 1918 influenza epidemic began, African American communities mounted efforts to care for their own citizens. Some sources have stated that the death rate among blacks appeared at first to be lower than that of the white majority. Others point out that many deaths among blacks simply went unrecorded, particularly in areas such as rural Arkansas, where there were generally no black newspapers to report on local deaths. Ironically, if there were truly fewer deaths from the flu among African Americans, it may have been due to an unlikely cause: the nature of the communities themselves under the scourge of Jim Crow.

What became known as the Jim Crow laws were decrees of legalized racial segregation enacted in the United States between 1876 and 1965 at state and local levels. "Jim Crow" began in the nineteenth century as an exaggerated, stereotyped black character performed by a white actor in blackface. The name became associated with racial segregation and the legalized oppression of blacks. African Americans lived, worked, and went to school in segregated environments. It may be that, since they did not generally mix with the white mainstream, they were not as susceptible to the introduction of influenza that was circulating outside their own community. Segregation may have essentially functioned as a virtual quarantine that limited the exposure of African Americans to the deadly influenza.

However, health journals have noted that when African Americans did contract the disease, it was almost always fatal. The actual numbers probably went unrecorded, however, in Arkansas as well as overseas. Historian John Barry quoted an article in the *New York Times* of August 19, 1918, that stated that "a considerable number of American negroes" who went to France on horse transports contracted the flu and died in French hospitals. It is not known how many "a considerable number" of the nameless African American dead might be.

Army-Navy Hospital

Hot Springs, Arkansas, was renowned in the early 1900s as a health spa. Its healing thermal springs attracted a booming medical tourist trade starting in the mid-1800s that lasted into the mid-1900s. It was also home to the Army-Navy Hospital, the first combined general hospital in the nation for both U.S. Army and Navy patients. The institution was founded by two other traditional rivals. In 1882, a former Confederate army surgeon gave a dinner in Hot Springs honoring a former Yankee general who had become a U.S. senator. The senator found that Hot Springs was "an ideal location" for the combined hospital.[14] Under his sponsorship, the Army-Navy Hospital in Hot Springs opened to patients in 1887.

With recruits being among the first to succumb to the influenza of 1918 and with military hospitals overwhelmed, it would seem natural for many of the patients to be sent to Arkansas to recover from the illness in Hot Springs. However, it is difficult to know because hospital records are sealed. Sadly, the fact that many of the flu's victims died within twelve hours of their first symptoms make it doubtful that many would have survived the trip from around the country to the Army-Navy Hospital in Arkansas.

$10,000 a Day

In addition to its human toll, the great flu epidemic devastated the economy of Arkansas. A study was released in 2007 by Thomas A. Garrett, economist for the Federal Reserve Bank of St. Louis, Missouri, the district in which Arkansas is located. His research paper was titled "Economic Effects of the 1918 Influenza Pandemic Implications for a Modern-day Pandemic." In it, Garrett quoted an item from the *Arkansas Gazette* of October 19, 1918, when the epidemic was still in its early stages. Headlined "How Influenza Affects Business," the article stated:

> Merchants in Little Rock say their business has declined 40 percent. Others estimate the decrease at 70 percent. The retail grocery business has been reduced by one-third. One department store, which has a business of $15,000 daily [$200,265 in 2006 dollars], is not doing more than half that. Bed rest is emphasized in the treatment of influenza. As a result, there has been an increase in demand for beds, mattresses and springs. Little Rock businesses are losing $10,000 a day on average [$133,500 in 2006 dollars]. This is actual loss, not a decrease in business that may be covered by an increase in sales when the quarantine order is over. Certain items cannot be sold later. The only business in Little Rock in which there has been an increase in activity is the drug store.[15]

Garrett also cites intangible economic effects of the epidemic. "The fact that males aged 18 to 40 were the hardest hit by the influenza had serious economic consequences for the families that had lost their primary breadwinner," he wrote, adding, "The significant loss of prime working-age employees also had economic consequences for businesses."[16]

A third of Little Rock's grocery stores closed permanently, with the loss of many jobs. In some areas, the telephone company had to limit calls to only emergencies because telephone operators succumbed to the flu. In Arkansas, many voters were too sick or afraid to go out on the rainy election day of November 5, 1918. The proposed state constitution, which contained provisions for women's suffrage and the prohibition of alcohol, was said to have been defeated in part because of low voter turnout. Newspapers around the state also carried items on the great number of church, school, and theater closings. Many businesses, especially those in the service and entertainment industries, suffered devastating losses in revenue.

Long-Term Consequences

Far-reaching socioeconomic data for Arkansas was also cited in the Federal Reserve's research. Using U.S. census information from 1960 through 1980, researchers saw that babies born or in utero during the 1918 pandemic had "reduced educational attainment, higher rates of physical disability and lower income" throughout their lives. Their findings determined that, in the Arkansas district, "men and women show large and discontinuous reductions in educational attainment if they had been in utero during the pandemic. The children of infected mothers were up to 15 percent less likely to graduate from high school. Wages of men were 5–9 percent lower because of infection."[17]

There is also the intangible yet valid fact that the 1918 flu cut down young adults just beginning their careers. It is impossible to say what contributions these young people might have made to Arkansas and to society as a whole if they had survived. Therefore, the 1918 influenza epidemic caused untold social and economic consequences for Arkansas, its effects persisting well over a half century after it cut its deadly swath through the state.

"Cover up each cough and sneeze..."

Like the many terrified people across the country during the epidemic, Arkansans sometimes relied on home remedies or products that were "guaranteed" to ward off the disease. Arkansas country folks sometimes relied on carrying talismans or hanging Asafoetida bags around the neck.

Asafoetida is a plant byproduct characterized by its strong, offensive odor. Its common names of "stinking gum" and "devil's dung" may provide clues to its aroma. It was widely used to fight the 1918 influenza pandemic in rural areas of Arkansas as well as elsewhere. Though it is not held in high regard today, modern researchers have discovered that Asafoetida roots do produce natural antiviral drug compounds. Some scientists have found these to be substances of interest in developing new drugs to treat

Influenza A (H1N1). Others consider quite seriously that the malodorous Asafoetida bags might have been effective in fighting the 1918 flu simply by keeping people from close contact.

During the epidemic, there were some who recommended commercial products such as Listerine to prevent infection. Others who saw a profit in the widespread misery struck while they could, buying advertising space in Arkansas newspapers for dubious products. One in the *Arkansas Gazette* for Dr. Jones Catarrhal Oil promised to "Prevent Spanish influenza."[18] While some may scoff at its simplistic nature, one easy-to-remember adage put forward by Dr. Geiger of the Arkansas Public Health Service in 1918 may have been as good as any: "Cover up each cough and sneeze; if you don't you'll spread disease."[19]

Prediction Off by a Year

After the war ended on November 11, 1918, more press attention was given to the epidemic. Some communities were proud of how they managed the now acknowledged crisis. The *Hot Springs Sentinel-Record* of December 12, 1918, headlined, "INFLUENZA HERE IS HANDLED WELL." The article said that the Spa City had been commended by state health officials who "frankly admit that the influenza situation here has been handled better than any other place in the country." The article credits Hot Springs with "the grasping of the situation early" as well as "the action of the physicians in helping the local board by prompt reports, and by isolation."

That same article also stated that local health officials predicted the disease would soon be stamped out if people would remember "the simple rules that help prevent the spread of the epidemic. They are to take care of yourself, keep the bowels open, keep in the open air, take prompt action when you have colds, do not sneeze or expectorate in public places, and do not mix and mingle in crowds under any conditions. The influenza has been prevalent here for eleven days now, and it usually runs a course of about four weeks."

That prediction was off by about a year. Arkansas remained in the grips of influenza through much of 1919, though the death rate began to drop. The exception was in the rural areas of the state, where more new cases continued to be reported into 1920.

Some See the Bright Side

With cases reported into 1920, the *Hot Springs Sentinel-Record* reported a new development in light of the Eighteenth Amendment, which took effect on January 17, 1920. Commonly known as Prohibition, the new law of the land made the sale of alcohol illegal in the United States. On January 28, 1920, the *Sentinel-Record* noted that, according to John F. Kramer of Washington DC, "who is in charge of the enforcement of prohibition throughout the United States," influenza patients were eligible for whiskey through their local health department. The article went on to state, "The maximum amount which may be prescribed for one patient during a period of ten days is one pint." The "prescriptions" were to be filled by confiscated whiskey held by the local U.S. marshal. "Following the announcement this afternoon that whisky will be issued," the article continued, "reports of cases jumped from thirty-four to 123 within a few hours according to the city health department."

The Crisis Ends

Most sources agree that the 1918 influenza epidemic generally ended in 1919, though some areas were afflicted into 1920. By that time, the flu's death toll included at least 675,000 Americans. About 7,000 Arkansas deaths were recorded, out of the state's population of roughly 1,500,000. However, the exact number of deaths in Arkansas, especially among African Americans and all people in rural areas, may never be known.

The pandemic disappeared almost as suddenly as it struck. When it was all over, the disease had affected every corner of the world. Some Alaskan villages saw every inhabitant die. Tahiti lost more than ten percent of its population in just two months; Samoa lost twenty percent. The president of Brazil died. U.S. president Woodrow Wilson was weakened by flu while negotiating the World War I peace treaty.

Milder types of influenza have followed in the years since the pandemic, such as the Asian and Hong Kong varieties, challenging medical science to treat each new form. Today, science confronts forms of "swine flu" and "avian flu," as there is evidence that the 1918 outbreak began in poultry and/or pigs. In Arkansas, as elsewhere, with better communication and a lack of the media censorship present during World War I, life-saving information might be conveyed more effectively and such a disaster averted.

1. "All Physicians to Meet Here Tonight," *Hot Springs Sentinel-Record*, September 3, 1918.
2. Ibid.
3. Dan Vergano, "1918 Flu Pandemic That Killed 50 Million Originated in China, Historians Say," *National Geographic* (January 23, 2014). Online at http://news.nationalgeographic.com/news/2014/01/140123-spanish-flu-1918-china-origins-pandemic-science-health (accessed November 30, 2014).
4. John M. Barry, *The Great Influenza: The Epic Story of the Deadliest Plague in History* (New York: Viking, 2004), 170.
5. Gina Kolata, *Flu: The Story of the Great Influenza Pandemic of 1918 and the Search for the Virus That Caused It* (New York: Touchstone, 2001), 9.
6. Barry, 181.
7. Johnnie Carolyn Bransford, "Eberts Training Field," *Encyclopedia of Arkansas History & Culture*, http://www.encyclopediaofarkansas.net/encyclopedia/entry-detail.aspx?entryID=1184 (accessed November 30, 2014).
8. Kim Allen Scott, "Plague on the Homefront: Arkansas and the Great Influenza Epidemic of 1918," *Arkansas Historical Quarterly* 47 (Winter 1988): 320.
9. C. Fred Williams, *Historic Little Rock: An Illustrated History* (San Antonio, TX: Historical Publishing Network, 2008), 59.
10. Ibid., 325.
11. Tamela Tenpenny-Lewis, Preservation of African American Cemeteries, http://

paacarcemeteries.com (accessed December 4, 2014).

    12. "Influenza Here is Handled Well," *Hot Springs Sentinel-Record*, December 12, 1918.

    13. J. F. Johnson, "The Forum," *Baltimore Afro-American*, November 1, 1918, p. 4.

    14. "Army and Navy General Hospital Historic District," National Register of Historic Places nomination form, on file at Arkansas Historic Preservation Program, Little Rock, Arkansas. Online at http://www.arkansaspreservation.com/!userfiles/GA0218.nr.pdf (accessed January 13, 2015).

    15. Thomas A. Garrett, "Economic Effects of the 1918 Influenza Pandemic: Implications for a Modern-Day Pandemic," Federal Reserve Bank of St. Louis (November 2007): 19.

    16. Ibid.

    17. Ibid., 20–21.

    18. *Arkansas Gazette*, October 22, 1918.

    19. Williams, 59.

Chapter 12

Memorializing the Great War

By Mark K. Christ

"Monuments are history made visible. They are shrines that celebrate the ideals, achievements, and heroes that existed in one moment in time. They commemorate singular individuals, heroic accomplishments, or the millions of lives swept away by war or disaster."
—Judith Dupre, *Monuments: America's History in Art and Memory*

The "butcher's bill" for World War I was appalling. Of the 65,038,810 soldiers who fought in the war, 8,528,831 died, 21,189,154 were wounded, and 7,750,919 were missing or taken prisoner—an overall casualty rate of 57.5 percent. Of the 4,355,000 Americans who served, 116,516 died, 204,002 suffered wounds, and 4,500 were missing or imprisoned—a 7.1 percent casualty rate. This rate was dwarfed by Russia's 76.3 percent and France's 73.3 percent, but it was still keenly felt by the folks at home.[1] And as was the case with the United States' allies in Europe, the call to memorialize the valor and suffering of its soldiers was not long in following the armistice.

Arkansas sent 71,862 soldiers to serve in World War I, of which 2,183 died of disease or wounds and 1,751 were injured.[2] In Arkansas, too, efforts to raise monuments to newly returning doughboys began soon after they returned from overseas. The first known Arkansas monument to America's World War I soldiers was placed at the Crawford County Courthouse in Van Buren by Colonel Sam Chew, a local attorney, on November 3, 1917. It was dedicated to the first three U.S. soldiers to die in the war and was inscribed:

In memory of
Merle D. Hay
Thomas Enwright
James B. Gresham
They were the first members of the Expeditionary Army of the United States in France to die that we might live, stricken on the field of glory,
November 3, 1917.
Dulse et decorium est pro patria mori.[3]

The efforts to memorialize the American doughboys were not without controversy. American progressives were often opposed to the creation of traditional monuments, such as those commemorating the soldiers of the Civil War, and preferred "living memorials." As G. Kurt Piehler observed:

Many progressive reformers insisted that efforts to remember the

Civil War had left a dubious legacy in the form of useless and horrendous statues. Urging Americans not to repeat this mistake in commemorating the First World War, they recommended living memorials, instead, including bridges, parks, libraries, playgrounds, and community centers. War memorials, they maintained, should contribute to the reconstruction of American society and meet the needs of communities.[4]

This advice was followed with at least two examples in Little Rock: the Broadway and Main Street bridges. On June 12, 1917, engineers had determined that the "Free Bridge" over the Arkansas River was no longer adequate for the volume and weight of the traffic it bore, leading the Pulaski County Board of Commissioners to set its sights on a new structure, this time made of concrete. It was determined that one new bridge should be installed at the foot of Broadway and another near the existing bridge on Main Street. On March 3, 1920, the Missouri Valley Bridge and Iron Company of Kansas City, Missouri, was selected to build both bridges.[5]

On March 14, 1923, the opening of the Broadway Bridge began with a parade that started at Main and Markham, crossed over and marched through North Little Rock, and then returned to the capital city. U.S. senator Joseph T. Robinson gave a speech dedicating the new structure to the Arkansans who served in World War I. He stated:

To do honor to the memory of the gallant men who served in the World War, our citizens by common consent have suspended their toll....It is fitting that we dedicate this triumph of engineering skill to the memory of our gallant soldiers, sailors, and marines who fell maintaining the cause of our country on foreign battlefields.... Arkansas gave the flower and pride of her citizenship to the service of the country and mankind.

O. L. Bodenhamer, state commander of the Arkansas Division of the American Legion, followed with an homage to the soldiers who died in World War I and to the veterans of the conflict. The celebration ended when Ruby Gibson of El Dorado, the "Princess of Union County," broke a vial of crude oil on the center span "and christened the bridge to all the fighting men of Arkansas who died in the World War."[6]

It would be more than a year before the Main Street Bridge was dedicated. On May 22, 1924, another parade crossed the Arkansas River and snaked through North Little Rock before crossing the new bridge to return to Little Rock. A rear admiral, Sumner E. W. Kittelle, accepted the bridge on behalf of the U.S. Navy, saying: "My fellow countrymen and countrywomen, as representatives of the Navy Department and in behalf of all navy and marine forces and the women nurses who give us spirit and comfort in all campaigns, and in behalf of those who have gone beyond,

I accept this beautiful and lasting monument."[7] However, only several months later, on Armistice Day 1924, did the bridge became an official World War I monument. The Nicholas Headington Chapter of the United Daughters of 1812 had installed a memorial on the Main Street Bridge that read: "In memory of the men and women who served with the naval and marine forces of the United States of America during the World War." Some 12,000 people paraded over the bridge to celebrate its dedication.[8] The bridge itself was replaced in 1998, and the Headington Chapter's memorial was moved to a new location, behind the MacArthur Museum of Arkansas Military History in MacArthur Park in Little Rock.[9]

Other "living memorials" included such buildings as the National Guard Armory built on the grounds of Arkansas Agricultural and Mechanical College—now the University of Arkansas at Monticello (UAM). The college shared the armory with the National Guard, using it for classroom space, basketball games, and dances. The armory included a concrete monument, approximately three feet tall and two feet wide, that listed students from the college who died during the war. The building was demolished in 1979, and the monument is now held by the special collections division at the Taylor Library at UAM.[10]

An Arkansas landmark was repurposed as a World War I memorial in 1921 when Little Rock's Old State House, the original state capitol, was designated the "State War Memorial." A number of patriotic and descendant organizations had sought to preserve the Old State House since the capitol moved west in 1911, but it took the political muscle of the American Legion, a group formed by and for World War I veterans, to gain official preservation status for the venerable structure. Act 385 of 1921 "declared the old state house to be the Arkansas State War Memorial." Despite this official declaration and its requirement that the building be used by the American Legion and other patriotic organizations, the University of Arkansas's medical school continued to be the primary tenant in the building until it left in 1935.[11]

The Marion Chapter of the Daughters of the American Revolution sponsored a rather unusual memorial to the war dead—an allegorical painting by New York artist William Steene. The people of Washington County raised around $1,400 for the painting, and the Marion Chapter commissioned Steene, who had recently created a similar painting in Tulsa, Oklahoma. The resulting piece is eight feet tall and thirty-six feet wide. It was unveiled on July 5, 1920, at the Ozark Theater next door to the Washington County Courthouse and moved to the courthouse shortly afterward. The mural depicts figures from antiquity through all of the United States' wars up to World War I and features an angel in the center flanked by tablets with the names of Washington County's Great War servicemen. It was restored and cleaned in 1976 and again in 2010 and can still be seen on the second floor of the courthouse.[12]

The majority of the memorials to World War I servicemen erected in the aftermath of the conflict, however, came in the form of statuary, which

is not surprising in a state that had seen some twenty-five sculptures—
the last erected in 1934—dedicated to the soldiers who fought in the
Civil War.[13] And while the newly formed American Legion was often the
driving force behind the sculptures honoring the dead of the Great War,
such groups as the United Daughters of the Confederacy (UDC), Southern
Memorial Association, Daughters of the American Revolution, and other
patriotic organizations were often involved. The Fannie Scott Chapter of
the UDC, for instance, in 1921 sponsored a memorial stone bench on the
grounds of the Boone County Courthouse in Harrison. It was inscribed as
follows:

In honor of the Boone County Boys who served in the World War
In Memoriam
Roy Allen
Otto G. Robinson
Ernest House
Douglas Jones
Troy Matlock
Ezra Pottenger
R. L. Lafferty
Doc Fenix
James Wilburn

One of the first World War I memorials in Arkansas was erected through
the efforts of the students and faculty of Hendrix College in Conway to
remember Hendrix students who died in the conflict. Six Hendrix students
lost their lives in World War I. Five of these men—Tabor Blevins, James
Craddock, James Dowdy Jr., Arthur McGuire, and J. Watson Reynolds—
died of diseases, while the sixth, Robert W. Young, died in combat.[14]

Two accounts exist on the events leading to Young's death. *The Stadium
Book*, published in 1923 in conjunction with the dedication of Young Stadium
at Hendrix, states that Young and fellow lieutenant A. F. Ruff of Rock Hill,
South Carolina, were ordered to take their company and capture the town of
Aincreville, France. Ruff is quoted as saying, "When we received our orders
I, knowing it was a sacrifice detail, said very little, but I will never forget the
remark made by Young: 'I thank you, sir; I appreciate very much the honor
you are conferring on me. I will carry this through or not come back.'"[15]
Sergeant Olsen Thornton of Chicago, Illinois, is then quoted: "We took the
town under a heavy machine gun and artillery fire, Lieut. Young being
in the lead and always doing or saying something to encourage his men...
the lieutenant and I started out to explore the town when we saw some
Germans enter one of the buildings. We started out to get them and were
close to the entrance of said building when another Hun on the opposite side
of the street opened fire, wounding the lieutenant who, although mortally
wounded, showed what he was made of by lifting his pistol and firing, killing
two of the five Germans who rushed from the building."[16]

State American Legion commander James J. Harrison gave a different account at the dedication of the Young Memorial at Hendrix. Harrison claimed that Young was leading his platoon toward an enemy position in the Argonne Forest when he left his cover to shoot a German who was stabbing wounded Americans with a bayonet. Although Young managed to hit the German, his exposed position left him vulnerable to enemy fire, and he was fatally shot in the head by a sniper's bullet.[17]

The idea for a war memorial on the Hendrix campus was conceived by the student-run Hendrix Memorial Association in 1919. With the help of faculty advisor Professor W. O. Wilson, they quickly raised $800 of the expected $1,200 to $1,500 cost through student and alumni donations. By the spring of 1920, plans for the monument were taking shape, and construction began on April 16 of that year. The design for the monument came from George Currie, a substitute Latin teacher at Hendrix whose father was a well-known marble dealer in Kirkland, Indiana.[18]

The monument was originally scheduled to be finished in time for commencement in early June, but construction delays forced the completion date back to November. Finally, on November 21, 1920, the War Memorial was unveiled before a large crowd on the west lawn of Hendrix's Tabor Hall. The featured address was given by Commander Harrison of the American Legion, who stated that "it is befitting indeed that we raise here this material memorial, but the spiritual memorial which these men have left will far outlast any crumbling marble or corroding bronze." The ceremony, which was presided over by Professor Wilson, also included vocal and instrumental music, other speeches, and a twenty-four-gun salute in honor of the dead. At the end of the service, a large American flag draped across the monument—which had been an actual World War I battle flag—was removed to reveal the completed work.[19]

The memorial was moved from its original position to the newly constructed Young Stadium and athletic field at Hendrix in 1923 and subsequently became known as the "Young Memorial." In 1973, Young Stadium was demolished to make room for the new Mills Center, and the memorial was moved to a temporary location, where it was restored by Hendrix art professor Bill Hawes. It was returned to near the spot of its original 1920 site in 1974, and on December 8 of that year, it was rededicated by the Faulkner County Historical Society, which added a second plaque.[20]

The Young Memorial was moved again in 2013 and expanded to honor two other Hendrix alumni, Benjamin Wise (a U.S. Navy Seal) and Jeremy Wise (an Army Special Forces soldier), brothers who lost their lives fighting in Afghanistan. Designed by sculptor Ken Hruby of Boston, the Young-Wise Memorial Stadium and Plaza includes large bronze negative silhouettes of military helmets. The revamped memorial was dedicated on November 9, 2013.[21]

The first Great War memorial to grace the grounds of a county courthouse in Arkansas was erected at the Craighead County Courthouse in Jonesboro. The people of the county selected the *Over the Top* sculpture by Chicago artist John Paulding, which depicts a charging doughboy with his right arm raised in challenge and a rifle gripped in his left hand. The monument reportedly cost several thousand dollars. The marble base was purchased from the Robert Morris firm in Memphis, Tennessee, a well-known company that specialized in grave markers, and it was inscribed: "To the 1,385 sons of Craighead County, who, during the World War served their country on land and sea, and well maintained the highest ideals and traditions, this monument is erected by their fellow citizens as a testimonial of gratitude and affection." The shaft also is inscribed with a list of Craighead County residents who lost their lives during the war.[22]

The monument was dedicated on May 30, 1920, Memorial Day, and the people of Craighead County claimed that it was the first of its kind to be raised in the southern United States. As part of the dedication, a parade with bands and veterans was held.[23]

Another Paulding sculpture was selected to honor the men of Greene County who lost their lives in World War I. American Legion records show that 476 men from Greene County served in World War I. Of those, forty did not survive the war. It was decided that a tribute should be made in honor of those who died, so $2,000 was raised by public subscription for a memorial in Paragould. Paulding's 1920 Statue of Liberty replica design was selected for the monument.[24]

The Paragould War Memorial was unveiled on Armistice Day, November 11, 1924, before 5,000 onlookers. The ceremony began with an elaborate parade through town that featured the mayor, mounted police, the senior band, and, in the words of the *Paragould Soliphone*, "veterans of the World War, labor organizations, gold star mothers and fathers, DeMolays, Rainbow girls, Boy Scouts, junior band, school children, and several floats." Many businesses, which were closed for the occasion, and homes were patriotically decorated. The featured speaker of the day was the Honorable Harry L. Ponder of Walnut Ridge, who reviewed past wars, praised the spirit of the soldiers, and explained that "this memorial is an outstanding page in the history of Greene County and an honor to those who gave their lives on foreign soil and a reminder to the gold star mothers and fathers that their sons died for a worthy cause." Afterward, the ladies of the United Daughters of the Confederacy and the American Legion Auxiliary served lunch.[25]

Another monument erected in the 1920s honored a specific doughboy: Herman Davis of Manila in Mississippi County, Arkansas's most-recognized World War I fighter. Davis was born on January 2, 1888, near Big Lake Island (now Manila). After his father died when Davis was in the fourth grade, Davis became a guide for sportsmen from nearby Blytheville. He also became an expert hunter, reportedly killing as many as 400 ducks a day on Big Lake for shipment to northern markets. His expertise as a marksman, gleaned from a lifetime on Big Lake, would serve him well when he was called to duty in World War I.[26]

Davis was inducted into the army on March 4, 1918, and sent to Camp

Pike near Little Rock for his ninety-day military training. He was assigned to Company I, 113th Infantry, Twenty-Ninth Division, and sailed to France on June 15, 1918. Davis served in the center sector of Haute-Alsace from July 25 to September 22, 1918, and in the Meuse-Argonne offensive of October 1918. On October 10, 1918, Davis, serving as a runner, was advancing through some woods around Molleville Farm near Verdun with his company's assault platoon when the Americans came under machinegun fire. As the rest of the company moved into position to flank the gun, Davis crawled forward on his own to a position about fifty yards from the machinegun nest, which was located atop a strategic hilltop. According to reports: "One at a time, he picked off the four Germans as casually and as accurately as he had picked off ducks on Big Lake." An officer from another company observed Davis's attack on the machinegun and its crew and sent word of the private's one-man assault to Paris, France, and to Washington, recommending him for recognition of his valor.[27] That recognition came in 1919 when Davis was awarded the Distinguished Service Cross from the United States. and the Croix de Guerre with Palm and the Medaille Militaire from the government of France. He was later awarded a gilt star for his Croix de Guerre for his actions near Molleville Farm.[28]

Honorably discharged from the army on May 29, 1919, Davis returned to farming, fishing, and hunting at Big Lake. The reticent hero made no mention of his activities in the Great War, and his neighbors knew nothing of his many awards. This changed when General John J. "Black Jack" Pershing issued his list of the "100 Greatest Heroes of the World War." Fourth on the list was Private Herman J. Davis of Manila. Friends and neighbors, who knew nothing of Davis's exploits, urged him to show them his medals. When he reluctantly complied, he removed them from his old fishing tackle box, where they rested amid his fishing lures. Davis was embarrassed by his celebrity and wore his medals in public only once, when his mother urged him to do so at Christmas. His wife would occasionally wear them at public functions.[29]

Despite his fame, Davis's health had suffered because of the war. The former private had inhaled poison gas during his time in the trenches, and it swiftly took a toll on his health. By autumn of 1922, he was suffering from an advanced case of pulmonary tuberculosis. The proud and independent woodsman was soon incapable of working, and, on December 9, he was admitted to United States Hospital No. 88 in Memphis. He died there on January 5, 1923, two days after his thirty-fifth birthday. He was buried on January 8 in a small church cemetery in Manila.[30]

Following Davis's death, he was the subject of a speech to the U.S. Senate by Senator Thaddeus H. Caraway of Arkansas, who complained that the late hero had never received compensation from the government and had been denied a caretaker's position at the Big Lake federal wildlife refuge because he could not meet Civil Service requirements. The Arkansas General Assembly also marked the former private's death, unanimously passing House Concurrent Resolution No. 3, proclaiming Davis to be

"Arkansas's most distinguished son in action in World War I."[31]

In early 1923, veterans in eastern Arkansas decided that it was time Davis's wartime heroics were appropriately noted. The Julius Benham Jr. Post No. 5 of the American Legion, based in Marianna, sponsored the Herman Davis Memorial Association. This initial group was assisted by the state American Legion organization, other legion posts, and the Lions, Rotary, Kiwanis, and Elks Clubs of Arkansas. As a May 1923 article in *The Arkansas Legionnaire* explained, "The object of the association is to suitably mark and maintain the grave of Herman Davis near Manila, Mississippi County, Arkansas, and for the purpose of commemorating the distinguished service of this hero by the erection of memorials within the state of Arkansas, and for the further purpose of establishing one or more scholarships in the University of Arkansas, thereby doing something that will be of untold advantage to the young people of our state."[32]

The Herman Davis memorial movement received two major boosts in the fall of 1923. General Pershing wrote to the association, saying, "I sincerely hope that the Herman Davis Memorial Association is meeting with the complete success it deserves in its efforts to perpetuate the memory of this gallant soldier of Arkansas." Perhaps coincidentally, Governor Thomas McRae declared September 24–29 "Herman Davis Week." By November 1923, more than 1,000 Arkansans from across the state were participating "in the distribution of educational publicity and solicitation of funds," the *Legionnaire* reported. By late October in 1924, the granite shaft for the memorial was on its way to Mississippi County from the quarries of Milne, Gray and Varnum in Rutland, Vermont. John C. McHaney Jr. received the contract to erect the shaft alongside the highway that had been designated the Herman Davis Memorial Highway.[33]

A marble likeness of Davis was ordered from carvers in Cararra, Italy, but it was never delivered. The unveiling of the twenty-five-foot-tall granite shaft from Vermont was set for May 31, 1925, and a newspaper article noted, somewhat peevishly, that "tentative plans for the unveiling are being held somewhat in abeyance by the possibility that the Carrara marble statue of the hero may yet arrive from Italy after nearly a year's delay. The importer has several times assured Contractor John C. McHaney, Jr., that the statue had been shipped, naming the vessel, but the statue did not arrive." The memorial was dedicated that Memorial Day, though it is not known whether the marble statue was attached at that point. Davis's remains were also moved from the small Manila graveyard where they were marked only by a small wooden cross and a pair of "faded, torn American flags" to be reinterred in a plot at the rear of the imposing new monument.[34]

The initial enthusiasm for the project apparently waned, and, by mid-1925, plans for a scholarship and a second memorial at the state War Memorial Building in Little Rock were abandoned. A May 1925 article in the *Legionnaire* reported that "the statewide campaign has largely been a failure, except in this [Mississippi] county, where the bulk of the money was raised. It was decided to go ahead with erecting the monument at the home of the hero, and to take up the other work of the association when conditions are more propitious."[35]

In 1953, the Herman Davis Memorial Park was designated as a state park by the Arkansas General Assembly; the Department of Parks and Tourism has been responsible for its upkeep since that time. It remains a picturesque monument to a war hero who has largely been forgotten by most Arkansans. In 1967, the original marble statue was destroyed by vandals during the turbulent period of the Vietnam War; it has since been replaced with an exact duplicate executed in Barre granite.[36]

The next two World War I monuments raised in Arkansas were the creation of an artist described by one critic as "more P. T. Barnum than Michelangelo." Ernest Moore "Dick" Viquesney of Spencer, Indiana, was living in Americus, Georgia, when World War I ended, and, the critic said, "sensing that the market for war memorials would soon explode, he focused his energy on the creation of a statue that would honor the American soldiers who had proved victorious on the Western Front." The result was the *Spirit of the American Doughboy*, a work that appears in all its seven-foot-tall glory in some 140 towns in thirty-five states from coast to coast. The industrious Viquesney also offered the statue in a twelve-inch version for display in homes and offices and even created a variety supporting a light bulb and shade.[37]

The sculpture was not without controversy. The *Spirit of the American Doughboy*, which Viquesney patented in December 1920, depicted a charging doughboy with right arm raised high and a rifle gripped in his left hand. The American Art Bronze Foundry, which produced John Paulding's *Over the Top* sculpture, sued Viquesney in 1922, claiming copyright infringement since Paulding had patented his work several months earlier. Viquesney either lost the case or paid a settlement, and he sold the rights to the statue. The artist did reportedly "continue to cook up marketing strategies for the statue and remained a source for its often ingenious advertising."[38]

The first *Spirit of the American Doughboy* erected in Arkansas was a project of a group more associated with memorializing the dead of the Civil War: the Phillips County Memorial Association. In 1869, that organization had created the Helena Confederate Cemetery to hold the graves of many of the casualties of the July 4, 1863, Battle of Helena, as well as the remains of Confederate veterans. It also erected two large monuments in the Confederate Cemetery.[39]

After the Great War ended, the Phillips County Memorial Association decided to raise funds for a monument honoring the local men who had fought in World War I, and it chose Viquesney's design, which the *Helena World* described as "the only true representation of the real Doughboy and his indomitable spirit." The Helena monument would be the culmination of nine years of work by the Phillips County Memorial Association, aided by the Seven Generals Chapter of the United Daughters of the Confederacy. It was financed through donations from Phillips County residents, but progress was repeatedly slowed by factors beyond the association's control. The *Helena World* explained that "there have been droughts and floods and boll weevils and cotton worms and financial deflations during the nine years in which the Memorial Association has sought its goal, and all these have helped to retard the movement." In 1927, the monument was finally completed after nearly a decade of effort.[40]

On July 10, 1927, the *Spirit of the American Doughboy* monument was dedicated before a crowd of 2,500. The program began with the Marianna military band marching down Cherry Street, which was lined with American flags. The featured speaker for the afternoon was Senator Joseph T. Robinson, who recalled his 1917 Senate vote in favor of war and praised the men and women who responded to the call to arms. The ceremony also included music, as the crowd sang along with the band on "America" and "Arkansas." Finally, seven young girls, representing the towns of the county, removed the curtain to reveal the completed statue. After the festivities had concluded, the monument was lit with a special floodlight that illuminated the doughboy figure. The monument still stands today in the center of Cherry Street adjacent to the Phillips County Courthouse.[41]

The other *Spirit of the American Doughboy* monument in Arkansas is directly related to an organization born at the end of World War I: the American Legion. The Fort Smith American Legion post was named after Victor Ellig, the first Fort Smith soldier to die in the war. He was shot through the heart by a German sniper while advancing on an enemy position on July 22, 1918. The *Arkansas Legionnaire* said that the Ellig Post was enthusiastic and "a model organization." For several years, it was always among the leaders in the American Legion's perennial state membership drives, being ranked as the state's largest at least twice, in 1923 and 1926. The Ellig Post was always heavily involved with creating and promoting parks and playgrounds in Fort Smith. In 1928, Post No. 31 commander Henry Armstrong was named permanent chairman of the city's parks and playgrounds commission. A committee was formed then, tasked with "investigating the immediate needs of Lewis Tilles children's park."[42]

It was at about this same time that the post began a drive to install a World War I memorial at Tilles Park. That effort came near fruition in April 1930, when the *Arkansas Legionnaire* stated that an "announcement has been made that with the city park board paying $500 of the $1,000 necessary, a lifesize bronze statue of a Doughboy will be erected at the entrance to the Lewis Tilles Children's park, Grand avenue, as a memorial to the men who served in the World War."[43] The statue had already been ordered, and a dedication was planned that summer.

Appropriately, the dedication was scheduled for July 4, 1930. More than 2,000 people gathered at Tilles Park that evening for a ceremony "including the unveiling and dedication of 'The Spirit of the American Doughboy,' the first night tennis match ever held in the city, and a band concert." Victor

Ellig's parents and several Gold Star mothers were in attendance. Dr. W. R. Brooksher, who led the committee that since 1928 had worked to acquire a World War I memorial, presented the statue to Victor Ellig Post No. 31 commander John Coley, who in turn presented it to Henry Armstrong of the parks and playgrounds commission. Armstrong then formally presented the monument to Mayor Fagan Bourland. The statue was unveiled by "two little misses," Jo Ann Carroll and Nancy Mae Connor, and the ceremony ended with the singing of "America." [44]

The Fort Smith monument remained in Tilles Park for half a century but was warehoused by the city after frequent vandalism, including the destruction of the figure's rifle. It was restored and placed in front of the American Legion building at 4901 Midland Avenue around 1989.[45]

The last two historic World War I memorial sculptures in Arkansas were not bronzes depicting charging doughboys but instead marble statues of doughboys standing at attention and gazing into the distance. The first of these was placed at Basin Park in Eureka Springs and was the result of a project by Annie Ross House, a local newspaper reporter who began a campaign to raise money for a memorial to Carroll County's war dead in December 1919.[46]

It apparently took some time for the funds to be raised, and there was local turmoil over what names should be included on a marker on the statue's base, with some supporters wanting to include the names of all Carroll County residents who had served in World War I, others wanting only the names of those who had seen combat, and another faction advocating only for the names of the war dead. Finally, a contract was awarded on December 7, 1928, to erect the statue, which the *North Arkansas Star* reported "will be approximately 11 feet high and carved from marble. Four drinking fountains will be at the base, fed from the Basin spring. Funds for the statue were raised several years ago by subscription."[47]

The statue was apparently erected sometime in 1929, and while the sculptor is unknown, the base was the product of the Eureka Springs Monumental Works. The front of the base is inscribed: "In memory of our deceased World War veterans, Western District of Carroll County." Oddly, another plaque honoring Spanish-American War veterans was affixed to the rear of the base in 1939.[48]

Less is known about the marble doughboy that stands before the Izard County Courthouse at Melbourne. A 1980 article in the *Izard County Historian* stated that "this monument was originally constructed about 1930 as a memorial to the twenty men who died in the service of their country during the first world war." The monument's base is inscribed: "They gave their lives to make the world safe for democracy that we might be free" and includes the names of twenty Izard County men who died during the Great War. The monument was rededicated on July 13, 1980, when the names of Izard County's World War II dead were added to the memorial.[49]

At least thirty-nine Arkansas counties have stone monuments dedicated to local war dead, and the majority of them include the names of World War

I casualties along with others who died in World War II, Korea, Vietnam, and the various conflicts that the United States has been involved in, up to and including Iraq and Afghanistan.[50] While most are simple stone markers of varying designs, one modern memorial includes a doughboy sculpture. The Randolph County Veterans Memorial, dedicated on October 8, 2006, includes sculptures by Fred Hoppe of Lincoln, Nebraska, depicting combat soldiers from World War I, World War II, and Vietnam.[51] In the twenty-first century, Arkansas continues to remember the men and women who serve their country in foreign wars.

1. "WWI Casualty and Death Tables," Public Broadcasting Service, http://www.pbs.org/greatwar/resources/casdeath_pop.html (accessed October 14, 2014).

2. Steven Teske, "World War I," *Encyclopedia of Arkansas History & Culture*, http://www.encyclopediaofarkansas.net/encyclopedia/entry-detail.aspx?entryID=2401 (accessed October 14, 2014).

3. Information found at http://www.arkansasties.com/WhatsNew/2007/10/crawford-county-war-memorials/ (accessed November 5, 2014). The original monument was broken in 1970 by an Arkansas Highway Department crew widening the road in front of the courthouse. A new marker was placed in 1971 and destroyed by vandals in 1975. This marker, in turn, was replaced with a marker donated by the Cotner Monument Company, which stands on the courthouse grounds to this day. E-mail to author from Tom Wing, October 28, 2014.

4. G. Kurt Piehler, *Remembering War the American Way* (Washington DC: Smithsonian Institution Press, 1995), 108–9.

5. Bryan McDade, "The Six Bridges at Little Rock: Understanding the Historical Significance and Relevance of the Six Bridges that Span the Arkansas River at Little Rock" (MA thesis, University of Arkansas at Little Rock, 2004), 80–84.

6. Ibid., 88–91.

7. Ibid., 93–94.

8. Ibid., 95–97.

9. Ibid., 109.

10. Mary Heady, Special Collections and Reference Library, University of Arkansas at Monticello, e-mail to author, October 17, 2014.

11. Donald Richard Brown, Marvin Ray Franklin, and Michele Roussel Wasson, *The Old State House: Its Survival and Contributions, 1911–1947* (Little Rock: Arkansas Commemorative Commission, 1978), 83–87, 140.

12. Information found at https://www.co.washington.ar.us/index.aspx?page=499 (accessed October 25, 2014) and at https://www.co.washington.ar.us/index.aspx?page=438 (accessed April 29, 2014).

13. For a good account of the efforts to memorialize Civil War soldiers, see Charles Russell Logan, *"Something so dim it must be holy": Civil War Commemorative Sculpture in Arkansas, 1886–1934* (Little Rock: Arkansas Historic Preservation Program, 1994); online at http://www.arkansaspreservation.com/pdf/publications/Civil_War_Sculpture.pdf (accessed November 11, 2014). In addition to the commemorative sculptures, dozens of obelisks and memorial boulders also were dedicated to the state's Civil War dead.

14. According to the November 22, 1920, edition of the Conway *Log Cabin Democrat*, Reynolds, of Ashdown, died of blood poisoning at Camp Perry; McGuire, of Mountain Home, died of disease at a French disembarkation point; Dowdy, of Clarksville, died the day before he was to ship out for France; and Craddock, of England, and Blevins, of Booneville, died of influenza.

15. Elmer T. Clark, *The Stadium Book* (Conway, AR: Hendrix College, 1923), 14.

16. Ibid.

17. Mark Christ, "Young Memorial," National Register of Historic Places nomination form, on file at Arkansas Historic Preservation Program, Little Rock, Arkansas; online at http://www.arkansaspreservation.com/!userfiles/FA0875S.nr.pdf (accessed October 24, 2014). The Young Memorial was listed on the National Register on July 19, 1996.

18. Ibid.

19. Ibid.

20. Ibid.

21. Information found at https://www.hendrix.edu/news/news.aspx?id=67665 (accessed October 24, 2014).

22. Harry Lee Williams, *History of Craighead County Arkansas* (Little Rock: Parker-Harper Co., 1930), 373; Charles A. Stuck, *The Story of Craighead County* (Jonesboro: The Hurley Company, 1960), 143.

23. Williams, *History of Craighead County Arkansas.*

24. John Slater, "Paragould War Memorial," National Register of Historic Places nomination form, on file at Arkansas Historic Preservation Program, Little Rock, Arkansas; online at http://www.arkansaspreservation.com/!userfiles/GE0052S.nr.pdf (accessed October 24, 2014). The Paragould War Memorial was listed on the National Register on June 20, 1997. Given Paragould's proximity to Jonesboro, one wonders whether the Statue of Liberty motif for the Greene County memorial was selected to keep from duplicating the doughboy sculpture at the nearby Craighead County Courthouse.

25. Ibid.

26. Mark Christ, "Herman Davis Memorial," National Register of Historic Places nomination form, Arkansas Historic Preservation Program, Little Rock, Arkansas; online at http://www.arkansaspreservation.com/!userfiles/MS0218S.nr.pdf (accessed October 24, 2014). The Herman Davis Memorial was listed on the National Register of Historic Places on April 7, 1995.

27. Ibid.

28. Ibid.

29. Ibid.

30. Ibid.

31. Ibid.

32. Ibid.

33. Ibid.

34. Ibid.

35. Ibid. While the second statue was never erected, in 1954, the iron fountain at the Old State House in Little Rock, a relic of the 1876 Centennial Exhibition in Philadelphia, was dubbed the Herman Davis Memorial Fountain and an exhibit panel was later added to the fountain to explain its link to the hero of the Great War. Donna Brewer Jackson, "Herman Davis," *Encyclopedia of Arkansas History & Culture*, http://www.encyclopediaofarkansas.net/encyclopedia/entry-detail.aspx?entryID=48 (accessed October 24, 2014).

36. Christ, "Herman Davis Memorial."

37. Piehler, 110–12.

38. Ibid., 112–13.

39. John Slater, "Spirit of the American Doughboy Monument," National Register of Historic Places nomination form, Arkansas Historic Preservation Program, Little Rock. Arkansas; online at http://www.arkansaspreservation.com/!userfiles/PH0260S.nr.pdf (accessed October 25, 2014). The Spirit of the American Doughboy Monument in Helena was listed on the National Register on May 23, 1997.

40. Ibid.

41. Ibid.

42. Mark Christ, "Spirit of the American Doughboy Monument," National Register of Historic Places nomination form, Arkansas Historic Preservation Program, Little Rock, Arkansas; online at http://www.arkansaspreservation.com/!userfiles/SB0482S.nr.pdf (accessed October 25, 2014). The Spirit of the American Doughboy Monument in Fort Smith was listed on the National Register on May 23, 1997. "Legion Leader is Named Head of Fort Smith Park Board," *Arkansas Legionnaire*, July 14, 1928, p. 2.

43. "Fort Smith Has Big City Program," *Arkansas Legionnaire*, March 1, 1930, p. 1.

44. Christ, "Spirit of the American Doughboy Monument."

45. Ibid.

46. "Unknown (Doughboy)," Arkansas Historic Preservation Program Outdoor Sculpture Survey Form, Arkansas Historic Preservation Program, Little Rock, Arkansas;

Mary Jean Sell, e-mail to author, October 15, 2014.

47. Sell e-mail; "Statue for Eureka Springs Park," *North Arkansas Star*, December 13, 1928, p. 1.

48. "Unknown (Doughboy)" form.

49. Mary Cooper Miller, e-mail to author, October 14, 2014; Helen Lindley, "July, 1980, Meeting of the Izard County Historical Society—Rededication of the War Monument," *Izard County Historian* 11 (October 1980): 12–17. The twenty Izard Countians memorialized on the monument are Lt. Cecil C. Smith, Morrill B. Jackson, Manuel Thomason, Nealey May, Oscar Moore, Herbert S. Rowden, Troy Forrest, Lee Pentecost, Herman Hodges, Luther Clifft, Henry Vannatter, Ernest Tomlinson, Vol Simpson, Herman Weaver, Osco Berry, George Kankey, Conrad Miller, Willie Warren, and Silas Layton.

50. Information found at http://www.arkansasties.com/WhatsNew/arkansas-war-memorials/ (accessed September 5, 2014).

51. E-mails to author from Dorothy McReynolds, administrative assistant to Randolph County Judge David Jansen, October 27 and November 3, 2014.

Contributors

Mark Christ is community outreach director for the Arkansas Historic Preservation Program, an agency of the Department of Arkansas Heritage. He has written, edited, and co-edited several books, including *Rugged and Sublime: The Civil War in Arkansas*; *Sentinels of History: Reflections on Arkansas Properties Listed on the National Register of Historic Places* (which won an Award of Merit from the American Association for State and Local History); *"All Cut to Pieces and Gone to Hell": The Civil War, Race Relations, and the Battle of Poison Spring*; *Civil War Arkansas, 1863: The Battle for a State* (which won the Military Order of the Stars and Bars' 2010 Douglas Southall Freeman Award and the 2013 Booker Worthen Literary Prize); *"This Day We Marched Again": A Union Soldier's Account of War in Arkansas and the Trans-Mississippi;* and *I Do Wish This Cruel War Was Over: First-Person Accounts of Civil War Arkansas from the* Arkansas Historical Quarterly. The Civil War Trust awarded Christ the 2013 State Preservation Leadership Award.

Nancy Hendricks of Hot Springs, Arkansas, and Washington DC holds an EdD and is the author of the books *Senator Hattie Caraway: An Arkansas Legacy* and *Dear Mrs. Caraway, Dear Mr. Kays*. Her other published works include *America's First Ladies: The Remarkable Women of the White House* and *Terrible Swift Sword: The Long Road to the Sultana*, the latter a historical novel about the worst maritime disaster in American history. She presents the program *Hattie to Hillary: Women in Politics* nationwide. Productions of her plays include *Second to None* and *Boy Hero: The Story of David O. Dodd*. Hendricks is a founding member of the National Women's History Museum in Washington DC and has received a Pryor Award for Arkansas Women's History, an Arkansas Governor's Arts Award, and a White House Millennium Award.

Elizabeth Griffin Hill returned to college following her retirement from a federal human resources position, receiving her master's degree from the Department of Rhetoric and Writing of the University of Arkansas at Little Rock in May 2013. Midway through the program, Hill accepted the opportunity to do extensive research at the National Archives at Fort Worth, Texas, going on to write the book *A Splendid Piece of Work— 1912–2012: One Hundred Years of Arkansas's Home Demonstration and Extension Homemakers Clubs*. She continues to research and write on Arkansas women's history.

Guy Lancaster serves as the editor of the online *Encyclopedia of Arkansas History & Culture*, a project of the Butler Center for Arkansas Studies at the Central Arkansas Library System. He holds a PhD in Heritage Studies from Arkansas State University. He is the author of

Racial Cleansing in Arkansas, 1883–1924: Politics, Land, Labor, and Criminality and editor of *Arkansas in Ink: Gunslingers, Ghosts, and Other Graphic Tales*.

J. Blake Perkins is an assistant professor of history at Williams Baptist College in Walnut Ridge, Arkansas. His scholarly articles have appeared in such publications as the *Arkansas Historical Quarterly*, *History of Education Quarterly*, and *Missouri Historical Review*. He is currently working on a book that explores rural resistance to government power in the Arkansas Ozarks during the late nineteenth and twentieth centuries.

Michael D. Polston is a graduate of Arkansas State University and a longtime educator. During his career, he has been active in the preservation of local and state history, including helping to found the Museum of American History in Cabot, Arkansas. Since 2005, he has served as the staff historian of the *Encyclopedia of Arkansas History & Culture*. He has published articles in numerous state journals and newspapers and is the co-author of a book on Cabot history.

William H. Pruden III is the director of civic engagement and a college counselor at Ravenscroft School in Raleigh, North Carolina. A history major at Princeton University, he earned a JD from Case Western Reserve University, as well as master's degrees from Wesleyan University and Indiana University. An educator for over thirty years, he has taught American history and government at both the collegiate and secondary levels and has also published articles on a wide range of historical, political, and academic topics.

Shirley Sticht Schuette is an archival assistant at the Butler Center for Arkansas Studies. She holds a bachelor's in German studies and a master's in public history, both from the University of Arkansas at Little Rock. Her undergraduate capstone project was based on oral history interviews of Germans who had immigrated to Arkansas since World War II. Following on the work of her master's thesis, "Strangers to the Land: The German Presence in Nineteenth-Century Arkansas," she has written related articles for state and local journals. She is also the co-author of the centennial history of the Central Arkansas Library System.

David Sesser is a librarian at Huie Library of Henderson State University, where he manages the special collections and cataloging departments. He holds undergraduate and graduate degrees in history from Henderson, a master's in public history from the University of Arkansas at Little Rock, and a Master of Library and Information Science degree from the University of Southern Mississippi. The author of many articles and one book, *The Little Rock Arsenal Crisis: On the Precipice of the American Civil War*, he is currently completing a work celebrating the 125th anniversary of the founding of Henderson State University.

Phillip Stephens is a writer, student, and haphazard historian of Arkansas's brief and unusual forays into leftist politics. He holds an undergraduate degree in history from Hendrix College and is working on a master's degree in English at the University of Arkansas in Fayetteville, where he is also employed. After processing the Clay Fulks Papers for the Special Collections department, he contributed material to the *Encyclopedia of Arkansas History & Culture* and began exploring the state's odd flirtations with now-anathema socialist politics. He lives in Fayetteville.

Steven Teske is an archival assistant at the Butler Center for Arkansas Studies; before taking that position, he was the fact-checker for the *Encyclopedia of Arkansas History & Culture*, and he has written numerous entries for the encyclopedia. Teske is also an adjunct instructor for Arkansas State University–Beebe's campus on the air force base in Jacksonville, teaching classes in world history, comparative religions, and philosophy. On Sundays, he preaches in a Lutheran church. Teske is co-author of *Homefront Arkansas: Arkansans Face Wartime* and author of *Unvarnished Arkansas: The Naked Truth about Nine Famous Arkansans* and *Natural State Notables: 21 Famous People from Arkansas*. He and his family live in North Little Rock, Arkansas.

Further Reading

Allen, Desmond Walls. *Index to Arkansas's World War I Soldiers.* 7 vols. Conway, AR: Arkansas Research, Inc., 2002.

Arkansas and the Great War. Digital Collection of the Butler Center for Arkansas Studies. http://www.butlercenter.org/arkansas-and-the-great-war/ (accessed February 27, 2015).

Assenmacher, Hugh, OSB. *A Place Called Subiaco: A History of the Benedictine Monks in Arkansas.* Little Rock: Rose Publishing Company, 1977.

Blair, Diane D., and Jay Barth. *Arkansas Politics and Government: Do the People Rule?* 2nd ed. Lincoln: University of Nebraska Press, 2005.

Bransford, Johnnie Singleton. "Lonoke's Vanished Airport." *Newsletter: Lonoke County Historical Society* 2 (Winter 1983): 1–2.

Carruth, Joseph. "World War I Propaganda and Its Effects in Arkansas." *Arkansas Historical Quarterly* 56 (Winter 1997): 385–98.

Dougan, Michael. *Arkansas Odyssey: The Saga of Arkansas from Prehistoric Times to Present.* Little Rock: Rose Publishing Company, 1994.

"The Doughboy Statue at Hendrix (1920)." *Faulkner Facts and Fiddlings* 37 (Fall/Winter 1995): 85–87.

Finley, Randy. "Black Arkansans and World War One." *Arkansas Historical Quarterly* 49 (Autumn 1990): 249–77.

Gordon, Fon Louise. *Caste and Class: The Black Experience in Arkansas, 1880–1920.* Athens: University of Georgia Press, 1995.

Graves, John William. *Town and Country: Race Relations in an Urban-Rural Context, Arkansas, 1865–1905.* Fayetteville: University of Arkansas Press, 1990.

Hanley, Ray. *Camp Robinson and the Military on the North Shore.* Charleston, SC: Arcadia Publishing, 2014.

Herndon, Dallas T. *Centennial History of Arkansas.* Chicago: S. J. Clarke Publishing Company, 1922.

Hill, Elizabeth Griffin. *A Splendid Piece of Work—1912–2012: One Hundred Years of Arkansas's Home Demonstration and Extension Homemakers Clubs.* N.p.: 2012.

Kiser, G. Gregory. "The Socialist Party in Arkansas, 1900–1912." *Arkansas Historical Quarterly* 40 (Summer 1981): 119–53.

Lisenby, Foy. *Charles Hillman Brough: A Biography.* Fayetteville: University of Arkansas Press, 1996.

Moneyhon, Carl. *Arkansas and the New South, 1874–1929.* Fayetteville: University of Arkansas Press, 1997.

Nieser, Tracy. "The History of Camp Pike, Arkansas." *Pulaski County Historical Review* 41 (Fall 1993): 64–71.

Niswonger, Richard L. *Arkansas Democratic Politics, 1896–1920.* Fayetteville: University of Arkansas Press, 1990.

———. "William F. Kirby, Arkansas's Maverick Senator." *Arkansas Historical Quarterly* 37 (Autumn 1978): 252–63.

Polston, Mike. "'Dear Home Folks': The Camp Pike Letters of an Iowa Sammy in the Great War." *Pulaski County Historical Review* 62 (Fall 2014): 70–76.

Schuette, Shirley Sticht. "Strangers to the Land: The German Presence in Nineteenth-Century Arkansas." MA thesis, University of Arkansas at Little Rock, 2005.

Scott, Kim Allen. "Plague on the Homefront: Arkansas and the Great Influenza Epidemic of 1918." *Arkansas Historical Quarterly* 47 (Winter 1988): 311–44.

Smith, Kenneth L. *Sawmill: The Story of Cutting the Last Great Virgin Forest East of the Rockies.* Fayetteville: University of Arkansas Press, 1986.

Stockley, Grif. *Blood in Their Eyes: The Elaine Race Massacres of 1919.* Fayetteville: University of Arkansas Press, 2001.

Weller, Cecil Edward, Jr. *Joe T. Robinson: Always a Loyal Democrat.* Fayetteville: University of Arkansas Press, 1984.

Whayne, Jeannie M. *A New Plantation South: Land, Labor, and Federal Favor in Twentieth-Century Arkansas.* Charlottesville: University Press of Virginia, 1996.

Willis, James F. "The Cleburne County Draft War." *Arkansas Historical Quarterly* 26 (Spring 1967): 24–39.

Index

CPSIA information can be obtained at www.ICGtesting.com
Printed in the USA
LVOW10s0749130415

434196LV00001B/3/P